About the author

George Irvin retired as UHD Professor of Economics at the Institute of Social Studies, The Hague in 2001 and is currently Professorial Research Fellow at the School of Oriental and African Studies of the University of London. He is author of five books and some fifty academic journal articles dealing with economic issues in Africa, Asia and Latin America. He lives in Brighton where he teaches and does research on a part-time basis. In 2005, he benefited from a Fellowship at the International Centre for European Research (ICER) in Turin to write this book.

Table of Contents

Figures

Preface

Neither European integration nor Keynesian economics is much in vogue in the UK these days. Following the defeat in mid-2005 of the EU constitution in France and The Netherlands, Europe – or more precisely, the core of the Eurozone – is economically stagnant and politically in crisis. Keynesian fiscal policies, always more familiar in Britain than in Brussels, have been superseded by monetary adjustments placed in the hands of an independent central bank. Fashionable economists in Europe now debate whether economic policy in the Eurozone and Britain is 'less discretionary' than in the United States; ie, whether US policy-makers still attempt to 'steer' the economy in a manner that combines growth and employment creation without generating damaging inflation. We are told that Britain has done well in contrast to its continental neighbours because we regulate our economy less, encourage greater labour market flexibility and have eschewed the 'tax and spend' policies of old Labour. If our neighbours do less well, it is because their sclerotic economies labour under the burden of bureaucracy and debt. In such a narrative, Britain has little need for Brussels, and certainly none for the euro.

Every parable contains a kernel of truth and the above is no exception. The Eurozone is performing badly, and in countries like Italy (and to a lesser degree France), the state needs to be modernised and streamlined. In other ways, however, the story is at odds with some important facts. Economic growth in the UK is forecast to slow down to the Eurozone average, and UK industrial output has been stagnant for nearly a decade. By contrast, Germany's industrial sector is strong; it has recently overtaken the United States as the world's leading exporter, and its income distribution is far more equal. France's educational system is exemplary; the health service is first-rate, public transport is ultra-modern and its aerospace industry is cutting-edge. Italy is not quite as impressive, but who would deny the quality of life it enjoys? Perhaps Britain can still learn something from its continental neighbours. More to the point, the rhetoric of 'mine is better than yours' seems dated in today's Europe. After all, for all its particularities, Britain is a European country by history, by geography and most of all today because it is deeply integrated economically with the rest of Europe. Its future is quite literally our future. For this reason, we have every reason to be concerned with the Eurozone's economic state of health.

In this book I argue that further European integration is not just desirable, it is vital. If the integration project is in crisis, it is mainly because the Maastricht blueprint for economic and monetary union was insufficiently federal and deeply flawed.

When Maastricht was signed in 1992, the member-states of the Community were still vulnerable to currency shocks and had only just emerged from over a decade of high inflation, which left public finances in a precarious position. The Delors Committee (which laid the basis for the Treaty) was dominated by conservative bankers. In the Committee's view, economic and monetary union (EMU) would only work under the aegis of a European central bank modelled on German lines whose main purpose was to avoid inflation and keep the currency strong. Fiscal policy could be left to member-states as long as they were prudent and reigned in spending. If Brussels could sustain an environment of low inflation, balanced budgets and currency stability, it was assumed that the private sector would deliver growth and employment. Delors was sceptical – his 1993 White Paper would target employment creation though EU-level infrastructure investment – nevertheless, if EMU was to proceed, he had little choice but to accept the bankers' blueprint. The 1980s' vision of a federal Europe with a sizeable budget, of a European Union able to combine and co-ordinate monetary and fiscal policies in the Keynesian tradition, was abandoned at Maastricht.

Ironically, everybody agrees today – from the OECD to the IMF – that the main constraint on Eurozone growth is deficient aggregate demand; ie, that households and governments simply don't spend enough to create a buoyant investment climate for industry. Disagreement is mainly about how important a role is played by 'supply side' constraints such as over-regulation. Most important, now that the euro is in place, Eurozone governments can safely return to promoting Keynesian-style investment. The euro, far from being a liability, is an extraordinary asset, since it shields Europe from speculative attacks by international currency markets that plagued major EU economies in the 1980s and early 1990s – symbolised in Britain by Black Wednesday.

This book argues for the redesign of the EU's economic architecture. But growth is never an end in itself; rather, it is instrumental to resolving underlying problems. The first of these is employment. Unemployment in the core states of the Eurozone has remained too high for far too long. It is glib to attribute unemployment to 'globalisation', a term explaining everything and therefore nothing. Rising unemployment emerged in the unstable and inflationary years of the 1970s and 1980s; it gained impetus in the 1990s as public spending was squeezed to comply with the provisions of Maastricht. Since then it has remained high in the core states, in part because of a failure to modernise employment legislation – often simplistically confused with adopting a neo-liberal agenda

– and in part because of the fiscal corset of the Stability and Growth Pact. Moreover, unemployment in the EU is particularly concentrated amongst youth, while part time employment for the most part suffers from gender bias. Creating part time jobs is a useful palliative only if these lead to full-time jobs in a labour market lubricated by continuing high-quality education. Active labour market policies alone are not enough. The Nordic countries provide particularly useful lessons about what can be done to boost full-time employment, providing member-states are able and willing to invest in future job creation. What is certain is that in the absence of action, the 'promise' of Europe will continue to sound cynically empty to a new generation.

Equally, growth is needed to maintain the EU's unique blend of market economics and social provision. Neo-conservative commentators, particularly in the United States, like to blame Europe's ills on too much 'welfare', echoing Francis Fukuyama's derisive reference to those 'flabby, self-satisfied, inward-looking, weak-willed states whose grandest project was nothing more than the creation of a Common Market.'[1] In truth, the challenge is to increase social investment. As our societies become richer and more multicultural, more public spending is needed on everything from continuing education to universal crèche provision. The pensions crisis – discussed in some detail below – is exemplary in this respect. The next generation can only afford to retire for longer at a decent standard of living if productivity rises substantially, and raising productivity depends on carrying out new investment. In sum, the EU needs to rethink its economic governance if it is to maintain and strengthen its 'social market' economy.

Most important, EU growth is needed to keep the world economy moving, including the highly trade-dependent economies of the developing world. The United States has for more than half a century served as the motor of the world economy. It may not be quite true to claim that as long as the US economy grows, the world prospers; what is certainly the case is that when the US economy is in trouble, the rest of the world slows down. At present the US economy shows every sign of slowing down. Moreover, were it to grind to a halt, it is likely that the rest of the world would stop lending the US money. In consequence, the huge US trade deficit could only be cured by a massive dose of deflation. Such a scenario would be very unpleasant – not just for the US but also for the rest of the world. This need not happen. Today, the EU economy is larger than that of the US, and the median European is nearly as prosperous. Any contraction in America can in principle be offset by an equal expansion in Europe – or at least in principle.

---

[1] See Dinan (2004: 6).

In practice, European expansion is highly problematic. The economic performance of the EU, particularly since the advent of the single currency, should have been strongly positive. Instead it has been barely satisfactory in the three core countries of the Eurozone – France, Germany and Italy – which account for 70% of its output. Economic stagnation is now so serious that Italy is technically in recession and Germany is dangerously close. Since 2002, major international organisations have warned that the Eurozone could face Japanese-style deflation unless new policies are adopted. Economic and Monetary Union (EMU) based on an all-powerful central monetary authority with the fiscal policy of member-states constrained by treaty – in the words of one academic, 'a monetary giant surrounded by fiscal dwarves' – is wholly inadequate. Unless Europe reforms its economic governance, it cannot replace the United States as the economic locomotive of world trade. If the reader retains anything from this book, it should be this one argument.

I have written the book for the general reader rather than the specialist, or at least that was my intention. Writing economics for the non-technical reader is not an easy task at the best of times, particularly today as the language of economics becomes ever more technical and inaccessible. Much of my professional life has been spent as an economist specialising in problems of developing countries; teaching, writing and doing research on various continents. I am not an academic specialist on Europe; some colleagues who are may take exception to my presumption in this respect. But because I have lived and worked so much outside of Britain, Europe has become a major preoccupation. Years of living on 'the Continent' – as people in Britain still say – have made me a convinced European and a strong advocate of further integration. I might add that I declare this interest despite my knowledge of Brussels rather than because of it.

Doubtless another factor shaping my views has been that in the 1990s, my professional interests focussed mainly on South East Asia. Over the past two decades, the growth of countries like China, South Korea and Vietnam has been quite extraordinary. Standing in Shanghai or Seoul at the turn of the 21st century, it is difficult to imagine that within my lifetime these cities have been pulled out of dire misery into the ranks of major industrial centres. Hanoi is a more modest place, but it has survived one of the longest and cruellest wars of the 20th century and even amongst the poorest 10% of the population, the literacy rate is higher than that of the comparable segment of the US population. Asia is quickly becoming an industrial giant, one that will in this century dwarf Europe.

I suspect that many people who know Asia share this feeling. Viewed from Asia, Europe's petty squabbles seem dated and irrelevant. The world is rapidly becoming divided into major trade and currency blocks. The economic, political and cultural hegemony of the United States, which so dominated the second half of the 20th century, is receding, whatever extravagant claims to the contrary are made by neo-conservatives. Within this historical space is a window of opportunity for Europe, a time for the 'old world' to put aside its ancient rivalries and assert its own identity.

To be sure, that new identity cannot be based on Europe's imperial past; hopefully, colonialism is permanently dead. Nor can it be based on a repackaged version of the market fundamentalism preached by the United States and some of the multilateral agencies. What Europe can offer the world is a version of the market economy tempered by its own post-war social agenda, one based on the notion of inclusive citizenship and universal entitlements to common levels of education, health and welfare. Pessimists will claim that the above is idealistic nonsense; that globalisation makes it unlikely that a common project will survive within the European Union, much less become attractive to the rest of the world. I am not naturally sympathetic to this view, one often expressed as a matter of faith rather than fact. At the same time, I must admit that the current political outlook in the core EU states, namely the accession to power of strongly neo-liberal politicians, does not augur well for adopting a more federalist structure of economic governance. But enough said about such issues for the moment.

Writing this book would not have been possible without support from many quarters. I received research facilities and a generous grant from the International Centre for European Research (ICER) in Turin; a debt of gratitude is owed to the Director, Professor Enrico Colombatto, as well as to friends and colleagues at the University of Turin who supported me in this endeavour, most particularly Professors Enrico Luzzati, Astrig Tasgian and Vittorio Valli. In London, particular thanks goes to Brendan Donelly, Director of Federal Trust, as well as to my colleagues on the board of Federal Union. There are many other individuals I should name; inevitably, though, a list of names contains omissions, and such a list is best eschewed. But I do want to thank my family: my adult children Marc and Leonora, and my wife Lindsay Knight. In particular, it is Lindsay – herself a journalist – who has provided not just loving support and encouragement, but long hours of proofing copy and invaluable suggestions about how the text might be improved. The usual caveat about errors applies. It is to Lindsay, Marc and Leonora that this book is dedicated.

Brighton,
September 2005

CHAPTER 1

The Union in Crisis

Pour moi, le Non des Français à la Constitution européenne fut une déception immense. Il rafaiblit le rôle du Parlement de Strasbourg et ruine pour longtemps l'espoir d'une politique étrangère commune qui permettrait a l'Europe de s'opposer aux tendances impérialistes des Etats-Unis. (Günter Grass, interview in *Le Nouvel Observateur*).

... il y a une solution bien claire désormais pour que la nation, notre cher refuge, évite de n'être qu'une nostalgie : c'est de travailler à la construction d'une véritable Union des nations européennes. Mais que de temps perdu .. (Jean Daniel, Editor of *Le Nouvel Observateur*)[1]

1.1 THE CONSTITUTIONAL CRISIS

Europe is in crisis, but the crisis is hardly new. At its heart is the tension between contending political and economic visions of the EU, a simplified characterisation of which is as follows. At one end of the political spectrum lies the notion of a federal or confederal union with strong democratic institutions representing the collective voice of Europe's citizens; at the other is De Gaulle's *l'Europe des patries*, an association of sovereign states loosely assembled into a single market with the aim of promoting greater efficiency. The corresponding economic spectrum has at one end supporters of a Union-level economic government with both a central monetary authority and a strong fiscal authority, one with powers of taxation and responsibility for ensuring growth, full employment and harmonised levels of educational, health and welfare provision. At the other end are those whom I refer to below as supporting a 'banker's Europe', perhaps with a single currency, a Central Bank and mechanisms for regulating competition and external trade, but where

[1] For Günter Grass, see *Le Nouvel Observateur*, Paris 27 October-7 November 2005; for Jean Daniel quote see 'Autocritque?' *Le Nouvel Observateur*, Paris, 9–15 June 2005.

almost all powers are assigned to the national level. Early federalists such as James Madison or Alexander Hamilton[2] would have found these issues familiar.

Today, these tensions have grown to such a degree that they now threaten the European project. Politically, Europe is constrained by the increasingly difficult task of reconciling the conflicting interests of growing number of member-states. The vision of a united supranational Europe with strong federal institutions has faded. The EU's political class is perceived today as defending strictly national interests. In Britain, even the staunchest Europeans feel compelled to repeat that the EU is not, and will never become, a super-state, when a multicultural federal state is precisely what needs to be built. Economically, the architecture of Europe is lopsided and incomplete; the sovereign functions of setting monetary and exchange rate policy have – in the Eurozone – been ceded to a Union-level European central bank, while national fiscal policy has been constrained by the Maastricht Treaty rules. The failure to put in place a Union-level Treasury with an adequate federal budget, approved by the European Parliament, left a major hole in the Treaty. Fiscal conservatism has resulted in sluggish growth and persistently high unemployment in the core states. The central theme of this book is that if the European project is to survive and grow, it must become economically and politically Federalist.

---

*The **European Council (or Council)** is a quarterly meeting of heads of Governments and should not be confused with the **Council of Ministers** (for example, Foreign and Finance Ministers meet monthly). Under the proposed Constitution, an elective President, acting as Chair for both Council and the Council of Ministers meetings, would have replaced the unwieldy 6-month rotating Presidency. While unanimity would still have been required for major decisions, many less important matters would have been subject to Qualified Majority Voting (QMV) using a weighting system more representative of member-states' population than that used under the Nice Treaty.*

*The **European Parliament** cannot initiate legislation, a persevere of the Commission, but it has co-decision power with the Council in the budget and some areas of legislation, and it must approve the Commission's President and team of Commissioners – a power recently used in the 'Butiglione affair'. Under the proposed Constitution, its area of co-decision would have expanded to virtually everything Europe does*

Source: Liddle (2005: 44–5)

Figure 1–1: The European Council, Council of Ministers and the Parliament

---

[2] Madison and Hamilton were authors of *The Federalist Papers*, a set of polemical articles published in New York in 1887–88 about the United States Constitution and the powers to be assigned to the State and Federal levels.

The current political crisis arises from the rejection of the Constitutional Treaty in mid-2005 by French and Dutch voters. While it is possible that some elements of the Treaty may be salvaged if adopted by the European Council, those elements involving fundamental change such as replacing the rotating presidency with a single elected president, extending qualified majority voting and the abolition of some vetoes cannot be saved in this way. Major change will require a new treaty, and a new treaty will require more referendums. In the immediate aftermath of the referendum defeat, European leaders have agreed to 'pause' for a year's reflection. In effect, the business of adapting political institutions to the requirements of running a union of 25 or more members has been postponed – perhaps for years – to enable the political dust to settle. Europe's troubles have been further exacerbated by the row at the June 2005 meeting over Britain's rebate, the CAP and the EU budget, a subject addressed in a separate chapter of this book. Most important, the 'legitimacy' of the whole European project has been put at risk.

When EU leaders signed the draft constitution on 29 October 2004 in Rome, opinion polls showed a majority of French and Dutch in favour and few pundits would have predicted that the treaty would be rejected. But the referendum road is a dangerous one at the best of times, particularly when electorates are disgruntled and potentially volatile. One should recall, too, that turnout is always a factor: for example, a 50 percent turnout means that a change of heart by just 10 percent of the electorate can cause a 20 percent swing, enough to overturn a comfortable lead. In France, it was anticipated that although the two extremes of the political spectrum would vote solidly against the Treaty (joined perhaps by a majority of Greens), the UMP ruling party and the socialist opposition party would produce a clear majority in favour. What was not foreseen was that the revolt in the *Parti Socialiste* would spread, marshalled by such figures as Laurent Fabius, Henri Emmanuelli and Jean-Luc Mélenchon, or that ATTAC[3] would rally an army of young people to their banners. As the late Robin Cook wrote a few days after the referendum results:

> There are warning signs from the recent referendum campaigns,
> particularly from the hostility of the young, that too many people
> already equate the European Union with the pressures that are eroding
> their job security and quality of life. The challenge is to persuade them
> that the European Union is an intelligent way of meeting those
> pressures by forging a continental economy on the same scale as the US

---

[3]   ATTAC (*Association pour la Taxation des Transactions pour l'Aide aux Citoyens*) was originally founded to promoted the Tobin tax, a tax on speculative foreign exchange transactions.

or China. Those who are most worried about globalisation are the very people who should be most supportive of the European Union.[4]

The slogan 'un autre monde est possible' particularly fired the imaginations of young people, often pro-European, but who had borne the weight for more than a decade of high unemployment, growing job insecurity, the reduced pensions and diminishing expectations.[5] When one adds to this already volatile mixture the growing dissatisfaction in France with the Chirac government and populist rhetoric about Polish plumbers and the Anglo-Saxon influence on the Constitution, one has the necessary ingredients for a large protest vote. The 'non' vote was strongest amongst youth as a whole, and within the poorest regions of France; eg, in the Pas de Calais region, over 80 percent voted against the Constitution. A clear majority gave dissatisfaction with the current economic situation in France as their main reason for voting 'non'.[6]

While the case of The Netherlands has strong particularities – the legacy of Pim Fortuijn and Theo van Gogh was to unleash a quantum leap in xenophobia – similar elements were present. In particular, Dutch welfare provisions had been pruned continuously for a decade, the incidence of part-time jobs had increased greatly and the Government of Jan Peter Balkenende was deeply unpopular. Dutch economic growth – always quite closely linked to the performance of the German economy – stopped in 2004 and the country technically entered recession at the end of the first quarter of 2005.[7]

Ironically perhaps, polls conducted after the referendums found a large majority of the French and the Dutch still in favour of building Europe. What voters seem to have contested in both countries is the manner of going about it. Needless to say, whatever the likely impact of French and Dutch rejections, the final demise of the constitution (at the time of writing, still uncertain) is unlikely to do much for promoting the stronger 'social' Europe that many French and Dutch rejectionist voters desire. If anything, the left has been weakened[8] and the hand of centre-right EU 'modernisers' – who wish to promote the free-market model and weaken the notion of a political Union – has been strengthened. On the far right, there has been confused grumbling

---

[4] See Robin Cook 'Europe's secure, well-paid leaders have caused the crisis' *The Guardian*, June 3, 2005.
[5] While the French unemployment rate is currently slightly below 10 percent, youth unemployment is 25 percent.
[6] See Watkins (2005), p 14.
[7] See OECD 'Growth Rates for GDP at Constant Prices for OECD Countries', 13 July 2005.
[8] As David Lawday notes, 'The paradox of France's stunning No vote is that, while it leaves Chirac a lame duck, it damages the divided Socialist Party even more. The PS now faces many years in the political wilderness'; D. Lawday 'A triumph of the right' *New Statesman*, 6 June 2005.

about the euro, notably from the Italian Communications Minister, Roberto Moroni. Although it is most unlikely that any Eurozone state would leave, Britain and Sweden are now less likely to join.[9]

The traditionally federalist Franco-German axis will probably wither with the emergence of politicians such as Angela Merkel, Nicolas Sarkozy and other supporters of Anglo-Saxon market liberalisation. The current British Presidency has set itself the twin goals of decreasing the regulatory burden borne by EU business and furthering the next round of accession talks, particularly with Turkey. While further enlargement is unlikely to be a priority in Paris, Berlin or Rome, deregulation will doubtless find strong support. Monsieur Sarkozy makes no secret of his admiration for Margaret Thatcher, while Frau Merkel's electoral programme claims that growth and employment can best be achieved by granting greater tax relief to German business.[10] In Italy, while Signor Prodi has recently gained ground, victory for the centre-left alliance in the 2006 general election remains uncertain. It is difficult to be optimistic about strengthening European integration at a time when the balance of power in the core states of the EU appears to be shifting to the right.

Since the 'no' vote, there has been much hand-wringing in Brussels – and not a little *schadenfreude* in London – about insufficient constitutional consultation, overcoming democratic deficits, reconnecting the EU to its citizens and so forth. Curiously, only a handful of commentators have dared suggest that such worthy goals can only be realised if the major Eurozone countries can modernise the state, kick-start growth and return to tolerably low levels of unemployment.[11] Complying with the Lisbon agenda (ie, making the Eurozone more competitive by increasing education and labour productivity and streamlining regulation) is only one part of the problem. In this book it is argued that a major constraint on Eurozone growth is not just the private thrift of its citizens, but the public thrift of Governments constrained by the economics of Maastricht and the Stability and Growth Pact (SGP). Europe – and specifically the core states of the Eurozone – will not solve its political problems as long as the present climate of economic insecurity persists.

[9] See Ashley Seager 'Stop the euro – we may want to get off', *The Guardian*, Monday July 18, 2005. Also see Robert Prior-Wandesforde and Gwyn Haache (2005) European Meltdown: Europe fiddles as Rome burns' London, HSBC.

[10] Such is the influence of right-wing economics in the CDU that Angela Merkel's nominee for Finance Minister, Paul Kirchhof, has even suggested introducing a highly regressive 25% 'flat rate tax'.

[11] See for example Will Hutton, 'My problem with Europe' *The Observer*, June 5, 2005. Although the OECD saw the referendum outcome as closely linked to Europe's poor growth performance, it merely reiterated its call for balanced budgets. See Larry Elliot 'Reform and cut rates …' *The Guardian*, May 25, 2005.

1.2 THE UNEMPLOYMENT CRISIS

At the time of the referendum campaigns, my wife and I were living in Italy. For us, the front page of *La Repubblica* on 2 June 2005 provided the perfect anecdotal illustration of the disconnection between EU politics and economics. The two main headlines read: 'Plebiscite in Holland goes against EU Constitution' and '[Italian Budget] Deficit, alarm in Brussels'. The Dutch had just voted down the Constitution, and yet the Commission was still preaching its deflationary message to a country entering recession.

> *Since the mid-1970s the character of the Western European labour market has been undergoing fundamental change, in which the prevailing feature has been growing insecurity. It is an economic insecurity that has become pervasive. Those looking back at the economic history of the second half of the twentieth century will note that the cherished objectives of the post-war era became perceived as 'costs' to be avoided in the last two decades of the century.*
>
> (Guy Standing, 'The new Insecurities', Gowan and Anderson [eds] (1997: 203).

Figure 1–2: Unemployment and Insecurity

It is true that there are structural obstacles to reducing Eurozone unemployment. Starting a small business in Italy is a bureaucratic ordeal and takes far longer than in Britain. In France, not only are start-ups difficult, but there are no UK-style 'one-stop' labour exchanges to ease the task of finding work. The French labour code has 30 pages describing the lengthy and costly procedures for dismissing an employee. In Germany, hopelessly outdated legislation still limits opening hours, thus inhibiting the growth of part-and full-time employment in the service sector. Nevertheless, removing structural rigidities in the labour market (for example, moving to Danish-style employment protection) can only be part of the answer. In the absence of positive business expectations and buoyant demand, entrepreneurs will be reluctant to invest in new plant and equipment. Without such investment, labour productivity will not increase and growth cannot proceed. Nor is the current overvaluation of the euro relative to the dollar helpful; since Eurozone members cannot devalue individually, they must cut wages in order to retain their profit margins.

To understand why 'flexible wages' is not the key to restoring full employment one needs merely to reread Keynes. Writing in the aftermath of the Great Depression, Keynes famously argued that the level of aggregate demand,[12] not flexible wages, must ultimately determine growth and

[12] 'Aggregate demand' means total private, public and foreign demand for a country's final goods and services.

*Keynes published the **General Theory of Employment, Interest and Money** in 1936 at a time when the industrial world was gripped by the Great Depression. Millions of workers were unemployed while factories everywhere either were closed or else operated at under-capacity. The dominant economic orthodoxy (which Keynes called 'classical' economic doctrine) held that as long as market forces were allowed to operate without hindrance, full employment would be restored automatically. If this did not happen, it must be the fault of 'inflexible' labour markets (ie, trade unions) and imprudent government – a view still echoed today.*

Keynes argued that cutting wages could not cure unemployment but, on the contrary, would serve to reduce total (or 'aggregate') demand for goods and services, in turn leading to a lower level of income and employment. Nor could full-employment be restored by cutting interest rates (ie, by making money 'cheaper' to borrow), particularly if interest rates were already low. The key to understanding the ups and downs of a capitalist economy, he argued, was 'expectations'. If industrialists' expectations about future growth prospects remained bleak, they would be reluctant to invest; ie, pessimistic expectations could become self-fulfilling.

The cure, therefore, lay in the State's willingness to kick-start the economy by investing in public works to create jobs. Once economic momentum was regained, private sector expectations would turn buoyant and industrialists would resume investing, thus opening the gates to more employment and growing incomes, which would drive growth forward. In the USA, Roosevelt's New Deal put Keynesian policies into practice, but the Depression was not fully overcome until the advent of rearmament and the Second World War. From 1945–1970, Keynesian thinking was dominant in the Anglo-Saxon world, and governments used fiscal policy (variations in taxation and spending) to 'fine tune' the economy; ie, to achieve a balance between promoting growth and full-employment while keeping inflation low. But in the 1970s, floating exchange rates, rising inflation and falling growth rates led many economists to abandon Keynesian ideas.

Figure 1–3: Basic Keynes for Non-Economists

employment. Wage flexibility (aka, cutting real wages) may result in falling aggregate demand and thus exacerbate unemployment. In many US universities – where most of the world's economic textbooks and economists are produced – Keynes's doctrines are treated as the dated relic of a bygone age. Still, Keynesianism is still alive and well in US government circles. Successive administrations, Republican and Democrat alike, have 'primed the pump' of public and private spending through a combination of increased borrowing and reduced taxation. The Federal Reserve Bank (the US's Central Bank), in marked contrast to its Eurozone counterpart, aims not merely to keep inflation in check but to promote growth and employment.

This does not mean that the policy mix adopted by Washington has been ideal. Following the collapse of the stock market bubble in 2001, the US economy has avoided prolonged recession for two main reasons. First, huge Federal tax cuts and a housing price bubble have combined to underpin consumer spending. Secondly, the world's insatiable appetite for holding dollars (often using them to purchase US companies) has permitted Americans to prolong their spending spree, importing goods from abroad more quickly than the US can sell its own exports to foreigners. As argued below, reducing the huge US deficit without provoking world recession is one of the main challenges of our time.

Comparing US and Eurozone economic policies raises a paradox. American economists regularly deride the Eurozone for being too *dirigiste*, stuck with old formulas and insufficiently attuned to market-friendly policies. Typically, the reaction from many Eurozone countries, starting with France, is that the European welfare model must not be sacrificed on the altar of neo-liberal orthodoxy. In truth, Eurozone macro-economic policies are far more orthodox than those of the USA. Keynesian demand management may not be a politically correct phrase in Washington but it is still practised. By contrast, in France and in Italy, Keynesian policies disappeared in the early 1980s, while in Germany such policies never took root.

A particularly depressing aspect of the recent referendum campaigns is that despite much discussion about the need to preserve Europe's social model and the evils of globalisation and free trade, almost nothing was heard from either side about the macro-economic policies and institutions of the Eurozone, which are the focus of this book. The 'yes' camp appeared smugly satisfied while the 'noes' appeared to eschew rigorous debate about economics. The key point is that anybody who wishes to understand why Europe is in crisis must start with the Eurozone's baleful record on growth and employment, a record which is largely explained (as argued in a later chapter) by the decidedly non-Keynesian nature of the Eurozone's monetary and fiscal arrangements.

The view that the Eurozone's political crisis is largely attributable to poor macro-economic policy, if true, raises a further paradox. Europe's crisis has reinforced the hand of centre-right politicians, those most influenced by the economic theories of the Reagan-Thatcher period. For example in Germany, Angela Merkel's insistence that job creation can be achieved by cutting taxes on business, thus raising profits and investment, ignores the fact that the corporate sector is currently enjoying bumper savings.[13] The centre-right in Europe favours balanced budgets over Keynesian pump priming; it favours the notion of Europe as free-trade area over that of political integration and the emergence of a more federal Europe. This suggests that a 'modernising' agenda

---

[13] See 'The corporate savings glut' *The Economist* July 9th 2005.

for Europe will concentrate on labour-market flexibility (or 'wage cutting') and other supply-side measures rather than boosting investment through a demand-led fiscal strategy. If so – and unless there is serious public debate about economic strategy – the medium term outlook for the Eurozone is poor. As long as the Eurozone continues to perform poorly, political disaffection both within and without (including that in Britain) will grow.

1.3   THE HISTORICAL ROOTS OF THE EUROPEAN PROJECT

How far is history to blame for this crisis? The roots of the European Union lie in the two great wars of the twentieth century and the crisis of capitalism underlying the conflict. The long slaughter in the first half-century – some 50 million military deaths at least – was Europe's 'civil war', as Eric Hobsbawm[14] has called it. Barely twenty years of peace separate the First and Second World wars. It was an uneasy peace at best; Italy and Portugal succumbed to fascism, as did Spain, ravaged by civil war. In Germany, war in the streets hardly ceased between 1919 and 1933. After that, Germany was ruled by Hitler's particularly vicious band of thugs while, in the East, the egalitarian promise of the Bolshevik revolution turned into a nightmare of Stalinist forced collectivisation and party purges. Out of all this turmoil, the 'post-war compromise' in Europe arose like a phoenix, an implicit agreement under which Europe agreed to resume its place in the world capitalist order under American tutelage while the United States agreed to the development of a welfare state under Christian- and Social Democratic tutelage.

In almost every village square in Europe including Britain, there is some list of names of those who gave their lives. They serve as a reminder both of the ill-placed patriotic fervour which sent men off to war and of the fact that Europe's most murderous century has been followed by a lasting peace, the peace that so many politicians had promised in the name of democracy, freedom, world brotherhood and similar inspirational phrases which, in the absence of economic and political integration, were quite empty. Today we have achieved a degree of integration that, in borderless Europe, makes the notion of a third Great War unthinkable.

True, a decade ago Yugoslavia disintegrated with much violence, but the Balkan countries were themselves largely constructs of the two great wars and of the Cold War that followed. Yugoslavia was the exception that proved the rule. War between France and Germany today is no more likely today than war between New York and California. For the current generation of

[14] See Hobsbawn (1995).

Europeans, this truth is self-evident. For them, the promise of Europe is no longer negative – the absence of war – but rather a promise of growth and jobs, prosperity with equity, strong educational, health and welfare provision and a decent pension. But European unity has been late arriving; the idealism that once inspired the project has faded. Economic and political circumstances have changed.

Perhaps it was easier to build Europe during the Cold War, when the American and Soviet standoff provided neutral space in which to erect a shelter for those caught in between. Europe is not just about unity; it is about developing industrialised market economies with a strong dimension of social provision and inclusion. The post-war settlement, built upon an anti-fascist coalition of Christian-Democrats, Socialists and Communist, involved a trade-off: Europe would not join the Soviet camp, but the politics of the centre-left would inform its reconstruction. Western Europe became – somewhat evenly between the Nordic States, Germany, France and Southern Europe – a 'social-market economy'. Both America and the Soviet Union accepted this formula implicitly; it was in America's interest to keep Europe part of 'the West', while the USSR was far too exhausted by the war to do more than hang on to the main territories its armies had captured from the Reich.

The Cold War divided Europe into a large, resource-rich and American-funded western region, and a smaller eastern region, largely Moscow's clients. As the western half prospered, in part because of the Marshall Plan, its social model became more distinct. The region of Western Europe that gradually coalesced into a Common Market and later into a monetary union was initially well defined geographically; Europe could not move eastward to its pre-war frontiers as it has today. The political divide provided the natural boundaries for what was at fist the six members, then nine in 1973 and twelve after 1986. Even at fifteen member-states after the adhesion of the Nordic entrants in 1995, political deepening was feasible and the project could prosper. But a confederation of 25 states with as many different official languages greatly strains the political notion of 'ever closer union', even under the most favourable circumstances.

1.4 EVER-WIDER UNION?

Ever-wider Europe was always a project in danger of faltering – particularly if the promise of growth, full employment and generous funding for new entrants is not met as is most certainly the case today. Jacques Attali's words in 1994 are worth recalling:

The first choice available to Western Europeans ... would be to apply the Maastricht Treaty without enlarging the Union before making it irreversible. This would mean that the Twelve were progressively setting up a genuine federal Union with a common currency, a common defence system and a common foreign policy... After that ... a genuine employment programme could be launched; while at the same time housing, urban renewal, transnational communications and telecommunications schemes could be started on a continental scale, costing about 5 per cent of Community GDP.[15]

That the Single European Act (1986) and the Maastricht Treaty (1992) were being drawn up as the Soviet Bloc disintegrated is perhaps fortuitous, but it is certainly not without irony. The end of the Cold War was the concluding chapter in Europe's great division. In 1992, Maastricht seemed to promise a new dawn. At the same time, the drafters of the Treaty were cautious men for the most part imbued with a rudimentary and traditional view of how economies work, much influenced by the fact that since the mid-1970s growth had faltered and inflation had accelerated. Smitten with the new economic orthodoxies of Anglo-Saxon monetarism which, stripped of its erudite and largely incomprehensible jargon, is little more than what bankers know to be the common sense of 'sound money', they drew up narrowly restrictive rules for Economic and Monetary Union, or EMU. Europe would have a Central Bank and thus a monetary policy modelled on that of the *Bundesbank*. Brussels would have a miniscule budget by the standards of any federal or confederal system, whether the USA, Canada, or even tiny Switzerland. Member-states would be responsible for fiscal policy, but their room for manoeuvre would be tightly constrained even after EMU. Within this straightjacket, the only co-ordinated macroeconomic policy that would emerge was one of co-ordinated stagnation.

1.5   FLAWED ECONOMIC INTEGRATION

Over a decade ago, after Maastricht but well before EMU, the Cambridge economist Wynne Godley wrote:

> European countries are at present locked into a severe recession ... Yet the interdependence of the European economies is already so great that no individual country ... feels able to pursue expansionary policies on its own ... The present situation is screaming aloud for co-ordinated

---

[15] Jacques Attali, 'A Continental Architecture' in Gowan and Anderson (1997), p 346

reflation, but there exists neither the institutions nor an agreed framework of thought which will bring about this obviously desirable result... If there were an economic and monetary union ... co-ordinated reflation of the kind which is so urgently needed could be undertaken only by a federal European government. Without such an institution, EMU would prevent effective action by individual countries and put nothing in its place.[16]

Sadly, stagnation bordering dangerously close to deflation is precisely what the core states of the Eurozone – Germany, France and Italy who together account for 70% of its combined Gross Domestic Product – have experienced for much of the past decade. That does not mean the integration project should be consigned to the dustbin of history. Far from it; the EU is in many important respects a great success story. Its internal market is huge, it has a major trading currency, its exports are sold everywhere and its companies are amongst the world's most powerful. Not least, compared to the United States, the EU's social indicators are enviable; it is a leading force in promoting environmental sustainability, in providing aid to poorer countries, in promoting human rights—the list of positive attributes is a long one. Few would dispute these achievements, but many wonder whether Europe, faced with the ever-mounting pressures of globalisation, can continue to prosper.

The Constitution made the European Charter of Human Rights legally binding. Inter alia, the Charter embraces:

- *The right to freedom of Assembly and Association, 'which includes the right of everyone to form and join trade unions for the protection of his or her interests';*
- *The right to Information and Consultation (within Article II-27) which states 'workers or their representatives must, at the appropriate level, be guaranteed information';*
- *The right of Collective Bargaining Article II-28), which states: 'workers and employers, or their respective organisations, have ... the right to negotiate and conclude collective agreements ... {and} to take action to defend their interests, including strike action'.*

Source: Liddle (2005), Box 4.3, p 33

Figure 1–4: The Constitution and Human Rights

In Washington today, Europe is seen as ageing and infirm; addicted to welfare; unable and unwilling to provide for its own defence. This view may be a

---

[16] See W Godley 'The Hole in the Treaty' in Gowan and Anderson (1997: 176).

temporary aberration reflecting little more than the conservative ideology of the current US administration. More likely, though, the view is symptomatic of a deeper rift between America and Europe. For, like Europe, America has moved on politically from the consensus of the immediate post-wear years. America's version of the social-democratic model effectively ended in the mid-1960s when Lyndon Johnson chose not to fund it through increased taxation. Instead, the combined burden of the Great Society programme and the Vietnam war led to inflation. Inflation led to the collapse of the Bretton Woods system of fixed exchange rates and then, aggravated by two oil shocks in the 1970s, to an economic crisis that was to usher in Ronald Reagan in 1980, and then George H W Bush. The rise of the Republican right set off a social and political revolution, one characterised by the dismantling of social protection and the return to pre-war levels of economic inequality on the one hand, and the consolidation of a populist constituency on the other. Successive Clinton administrations in the 1990s could not reverse a tide which, in 2004, produced an extra 10m Republican votes and brought to power arguably the most right-wing US administration for a century.

As for Britain, Tony Blair's alleged European sympathies have hardly dented the legacy of Thatcher. For the British, who for the most part still consider 'Europe' to lie across the Channel, Brussels is the butt of endless tabloid tales about silly laws, bloated budgets, immigrant invasions and assorted threats to British sovereignty. More worrying is the apparent rise of Euro-scepticism elsewhere – arguably nearly everywhere – in the Union. The Constitution – a sometimes turgid and long-winded document largely concerned with legal and administrative matters – was rejected in France and The Netherlands in a climate of deep social malaise. Had referendums been on offer in Germany and Italy in mid-2005, it is probable that these would have produced a similar result. The European project is at a crossroads. Its achievements, however notable, are much diminished by a climate of economic uncertainty whose spread has become a pandemic.

One needs to recall Europe's achievements before asking what has gone wrong and why. Above all, one needs to recognise that in those fields where Europe does speak with one voice, it wields very considerable power. Those who suggest that the EU is merely an agency for spreading free-market fundamentalism and accelerating globalisation, or that its social model has lost meaning, or that its trade policies work unremittingly against relieving the plight of poor countries and fostering sustainable development – in short that the EU is a right-wing plot – have lost touch with the political reality of the early 21st century. On issues as diverse as human rights, climate change and nuclear proliferation, the single voice of the EU has been a far more effective force for progressive change than have the isolated voices of its constituent members. Even on foreign policy and development co-operation, areas in which the EU is relatively weak, Europe has begun to take a stance independent of the United States – notably over the Iraq war, in furthering the peace process in the Middle East, and in debt relief for Africa. True, the EU does not yet speak with a fully integrated voice and one can hope its progressive voice might be more forceful. But it is undeniable that the relationship between the EU and the USA has changed profoundly over the past three decades. Although Europe cannot (and should not) aim to match US military power, economically and politically, Europe is beginning to stand up for itself.

CHAPTER 2

European Dream or Nightmare?

By the 1990s, the European generation who had been attracted by the 'American dream' were being replaced by those who saw no special attraction, and no special virtue, in the American way of life. For this generation of Europeans, the USA became a less positive force – no longer an exotic and successful cousin, more an old, powerful and sometimes arrogant uncle. After a century in which the USA said something decidedly new to the world, and offered something decidedly new to millions who joined the country, the special appeal of America to Europeans had run its course. (Stephen Haseler, 2004, p 60)

2.1 EUROPE'S SUCCESSES

Two generations ago, almost everyone would have agreed that the average US citizen was far better off than his or her European counterpart. America in the mid-20th century was the land of plenty, a land combining unmatched physical resources with a culture of opportunity, entrepreneurship and hard work to make it by far the world's richest and strongest industrial power. Today, the truth of this statement is no longer obvious. Most EU citizens feel as well off as their US counterparts, and many would argue that the 'quality of life' in the EU is higher than in the USA. From Sweden to Spain, EU citizens enjoy not just high income levels but high levels of education, excellent public services, job security, long holiday entitlements, health care and retirement benefits which are enviable by US standards. Moreover, Europeans enjoy greater income equality, more stringent environmental standards and far lower rates of violent crime.

All this has not happened by chance. The EU-15 – recently expanded to 25 – is today the world's single largest unified market with a population in 2005 of 455m and a GDP of 9.3 trillion euros, slightly greater than the USA. Not only are EU consumers very nearly as prosperous as those in the US, but EU trade with the rest of the world is booming. Over the past three decades, labour productivity has on average grown faster in the EU core countries than in the US. In consequence, the average French or German worker produces about the same value of output per hour as his or her American counterpart. Contrary to popular mythology, Europe's 'welfare state' does not hold it back – the evidence is that higher levels of education, greater job security and universal health and retirement benefits are key to the European success story.

True, Europe still punches below its weight politically. Nor, despite taunts from US neo-conservatives like Robert Kagan,[1] will Europe ever attempt to duplicate US military might. Economically, though, there is no doubt the EU is a major player. The euro is now the currency of 12 of the EU-15 (the accession states will start joining in 2007), and is rapidly challenging the US dollar as a major trading currency. Since its launch it has confounded its critics and become far stronger than the dollar, although this is a mixed blessing. The member-states of the EU-15 run a surplus on their current account transactions with the rest of the world, in contrast to the growing US trade deficit. In 2004, Germany overtook the United States in the total value of its exports. Over the past 10 years the EU-15's exports to the rest of the world have increased from 7 to 11 percent of total GDP; in the US, by contrast, the share of exports in GDP over the same period has stagnated.[2]

The evidence of Europe's success in world markets is everywhere: from the traditional dominance of Europe's fashion industry to its recently acquired leadership in such high-tech areas as mobile phones, aircraft manufacture and aerospace. Sixty-one of the Fortune-500 companies are European while only 51 are America.[3] The EU's large trade surplus enables it to export capital to the US. In 2003, net foreign direct investment (FDI) from the EU to the USA was about €31b, or €49b from the EU-25 to the US and €11b the other way.[4] This flow of capital does more than merely help sustain the US addiction to consumer goods. The EU is becoming the world's largest creditor, holding not merely US financial assets but buying an increasing share of US business. Much as Britain earned a large income during the 20th century from its overseas assets, so Europe can expect to reap a healthy reward from its assets in the years ahead.

Of course, such optimism must be qualified. Living on rentier income is not a good idea, particularly when Europe's growth and employment performance has been mediocre. The problem here is not so much that it lags behind the

[1] See Kagan (2003).
[2] See Morley et al (2004: 77).
[3] See Rifkin (2004: 66).
[4] See http://www.finfacts.com/biz10/foreigndirectinvestmenteu.htm.

United States, since the unemployment gap is less than commonly supposed. The problem is that unless Europe adopts pro-growth policies, it will be unable to finance the high levels of social entitlement that distinguish it from other rich market economies. Without growth, Europe risks becoming less socially inclusive and cohesive, less egalitarian, less able to support the very things which Europeans claim to value.

Books on the European 'miracle' have recently been in fashion, even if a number of these appear to be aimed mainly at the US market. To the European ear, phrases like 'The United States of Europe' and 'The European Dream' sound a bit overblown. Nevertheless, the EU-15 (even more so the EU-25) has very considerable economic weight in the world; its sheer size, its unified currency, its importance in international trade and its unified voice in key areas enable it to exercise an influence that its member-states acting alone would lack. When the EU sets standards on genetically modified crops, on vehicle emissions or on the disposal of toxic waste, the US and the rest of the world must sit up and listen. It is not for nothing that the former CEO of the General Electric, Jack Welsh, was forced to admit: "We have to do business with Europe, so we have no choice but to respect their law".[5]

The story of General Electric's failed bid for Honeywell Corporation is told at length in T R Reid's recent book and is worth summarising here.[6] General Electric, a long established US manufacturer of electric goods, began to diversify in the 1980s. Under the leadership of its ruthlessly efficient and highly paid CEO, Jack Welsh, GE closed down many of its unprofitable lines, sacked workers and acquired all manner of firms from chemical companies to department stores, from stock-brokerage and insurance to the NBC television network. Under Welsh's leadership, GE boasted 80 consecutive quarters of profit growth; by the late 1990s, GE was reported to be the world's most profitable company and was spending some $300m a week on acquisitions. Just before retiring in 2000, Welsh attempted one more takeover; he offered $45b for Honeywell Corporation, a leading avionics and aero-engine firm. This was one of the largest corporate mergers ever. The deal had the approval of Congress and the US Justice Department, and was the leading story in the financial press when the merger was announced in late October 2000. The one thing Jack Welsh hadn't factored into the equation was DG-Comp, the European Commission's Directorate for Competition, at that time headed by Mario Monti.

Monti's anti-trust record had been formidable. He had fined Daimler-Chrysler €70m for advertising different prices for the same car in different

5 See Reid (2004: 105)
6 See Reid (2004), Chapter 6 for a detailed account of the General Electric saga from which the following paragraphs draw heavily.

member States, and in 2004 he fined Microsoft nearly €500m for bundling together browser software and its operating system. In 2001, DG-Comp was worried that the marriage of GE's aircraft engines and airframe capability to Honeywell's avionics and air-traffic control systems would seriously threaten its European competitors. Following protracted negotiations in Brussels in 1991 – and a public protest by George W Bush that US business interests were not receiving fair treatment – the Commission voted down the merger. Not surprisingly, there was a chorus of protest from American politicians and from the media. But Brussels stood firm; the jewel in the crown of GE's huge corporate empire was lost.

2.2   ENVIRONMENTAL POLICY

In environmental policy too, the EU is making its muscle felt. In particular, British readers will be concerned about such diverse matters as safe food, recycled waste and global warming. In my morning newspaper today, immediately below an alarming piece on melting Arctic permafrost and the ozone layer, was a picture of a UK 'fridge mountain' with the subheading that Britain may not be able to comply with an EU white-goods recycling directive taking effect in late 2005. Below are three examples of environmental policy: food standards, drug standards and the control of dangerous emissions into the atmosphere.

In 2002, the European Commission established the European Food Safety Authority (EFSA). In that year, US soybean exports to Europe were around $1.2b, and 80 percent of soybean production in the US is genetically modified, or what is classed as GMO (Genetically Modified Organisms). Because the EU gave notice in 2001 of a new law requiring that any food containing more than one percent GMO be labelled, US exporters of soybean suddenly wondered about their future.[7]

To quote one EU document, 'GM crops are mainly grown on the American continent: the USA accounts for 70% of worldwide sowings of GM crops, Argentina for 14% and Canada for 9%. Of the 41.5 million ha sown in 1999, 53% were soybeans, 27% corn, 9% cotton, 8% rapeseed and 0.1% potatoes.'[8] Since the law came into force in 2004, farm and agribusiness lobbies in the United States have urged its government to contest the EU law before the

---

[7] This law had been criticised by some environmentalists because it replaces the temporary ban in 1998 on imports of GMO foods to the EU; it had been hoped that this ban would be made permanent.

[8] European Commission, Directorate-General for Agriculture (previously DG VI) 'Economic Impacts of Genetically Modified Crops on the Agri-Food Sector; a Synthesis'; p 5; April 2000.

World Trade Association (WTO). Although Washington recently agreed to give the new law a trial period before bringing the matter to the WTO, it is now clear that the implications of this dispute go far beyond US-EU relations.

The initial temporary ban on GMOs issued by Brussels in 1998 arose because of the failure of US food labelling authorities to trace the genetic origin of foodstuffs. The US Food and Drug Administration (FDA) took the position that genetic engineering was just another traditional breeding method, and reasoned that GM foods should be considered safe. Following the 1998 ban, Australia, Japan and Korea passed laws requiring the labelling of GMO foods. China is reported to be introducing a law along similar lines. At present, US citizens are seeking legal action against the FDA. In short, action by Brussels on GMOs has triggered further action both in the US and the rest of the world.

Another example concerns drugs and chemicals as set out in the EU's REACH legislation (Registration, Evaluation and Authorization of Chemicals) and the 'precautionary principle' embodied within it. REACH was launched by Brussels in 2003 and is due to become law in 2005. As the journalist Mark Shapiro (2004) has shown in a recent piece,[9] REACH represents a revolution in chemical regulation for the $500 billion US chemical industry, overturning practices that were pioneered in the United States. In 1976, the US Congress passed the Toxic Substances Control Act (TSCA) requiring all chemicals introduced after the law took effect in 1979 to be tested. The problem with the TSCA is that 80 percent of all US chemicals were introduced before the Act took effect. Prior to 1979, Europe followed the US model so the TSCA set the global standard.

REACH establishes a new standard. Environmental data must now be produced on some 30,000 chemicals currently sold in the United States and around the world without any significant testing of their detrimental effect on human health and the environment. These include such substances as ethyl benzene, which causes nerve damage; heavy metals like cadmium, an ingredient in some paints and ceramics that can cause kidney failure; and a group of plastic by-products called furans which have been shown to be potent carcinogens and endocrine disrupters. Some of these chemicals have already been found in high concentrations in the blood of Americans and Europeans. They would now have to be removed or replaced. A new European Chemicals Agency would administer the programme from Helsinki.

The REACH directive represents a sea change in the basic philosophy of chemical regulation. The American presumption of 'innocent until proven guilty' has been turned on its head, placing the burden of proof on

---

[9] See Mark Shapiro, 'New Power for "Old Europe"' *The Nation Magazine*, December 27, 2004, on which I draw heavily for section 2–2.

manufacturers to prove chemicals are safe – what is known as the "precautionary principle." REACH includes a requirement that toxicity data be posted publicly on the EU agency's website. Test results that were once closely guarded by chemical companies will suddenly be available to citizens and regulators around the world.

In March 2004, the State Department sponsored a trip by Dow Chemical executives to Athens to lobby the Greeks, who at that time held the EU presidency. On 29 April, the US Secretary of State, Colin Powell, sent a long cable to US embassies in all the EU member states stating that REACH's precautionary principle struck at the heart of the US regulatory approaches toward potential environmental hazards. The State Department added that REACH could adversely affect 'the majority of US goods exported to the EU' (over $150bn in 2003), possibly disrupting world trade.

Never before has an EU proposal drawn such hostile criticism from the US. The fact that policies emanating from Brussels now threaten longstanding American industrial practices shows how profoundly trans-Atlantic relations have shifted. 'We used to have to deal with individual countries,' said a spokesman for the American Chemical Council. 'We'd pay attention to, say, France. Not to be pejorative here, but we wouldn't really pay much attention to what Spain was doing. Having the EU as a single bloc with regulatory authority is a new thing for us.'[10]

The most important question of all is that of environmental degradation and global warming. Because the EU has a Directorate for the Environment, Europe's single voice is far more effective than the isolated voices of member states. Take the issue of taxing aircraft fuel, currently under discussion because air travel is a growing source of CO^2 emissions. This is an example of what economists refer to as the problem of 'collective choice'. No single EU member state can levy an effective tax on fuel unless there is agreement that all states do the same. Hence, if such a tax is to work, it must be agreed at the level of the union.[11]

The environmental issue has gained greater urgency since 2001 when the Bush Administration refused to ratify the Kyoto Protocol. Progress on environmental sustainability is considered one of the three pillars of the Lisbon Council in 2000, although just as in the case of the other Lisbon goals, implementation depends on the actions of the member-states. Under the Kyoto Protocol of 1997, the EU committed itself to reducing its emissions of

[10] The quotations are from Mark Shapiro (2004), p 5.
[11] Ironically, the current requirement that decisions in the Council be unanimous, in the failure of the Constitutional Treaty, makes it unlikely that such a tax will be passed in the foreseeable future.

greenhouse gases by 8% below their 1990 level by 2008–2012. This was supplemented by the 1998 Burden Sharing Agreement between EU member-states setting the contributions by each state to the overall EU target. Although the EU Commissioner for the Environment, Margot Wallstroem, fought very hard to get member states to live up to their commitments, data from the EU Environmental Agency showed greenhouse gas emissions had risen in 2000–2001. The Commissioner strongly criticised member states for not taking sufficient measures. Emissions have since fallen slightly, but the burden of reduction has clearly not been shared equally.

In 2004, the Commission set up an emissions-credit trading scheme; this, it was argued, would ensure the targets were met. Under the scheme, highly polluting countries can buy unused 'credits' from those countries – largely the new accession states – that are allowed to emit more than they actually do. Additionally, Ms Wallstroem announced the latest Environmental Action Programme entitled 'Environment 2010: Our Future, Our Choice', which addresses a broad panoply of environmental issues: clean air, soil protection, the sustainable use of pesticides, protection of the marine environment and waste protection and recycling.

In 2005 the new Environment Commissioner, Stavros Dimas, reaffirmed the EU's commitment to Kyoto. In April he attended the annual session of the UN's Sustainable Development Commission (CSD) in New York, a follow-up on the World Summit on Sustainable Development (WSSD). In particular it addressed actions necessary to reach the goals and targets on water, sanitation and human settlements agreed at the UN's Millennium Summit in 2000. EU representatives presented initiatives to implement these goals, such as the EU Water Initiative, which promotes a new approach to resolving global water problems, and the EU Water Facility for African, Caribbean and Pacific countries supported by funding of the amount $ 250 million. Worldwide, the EU is the biggest donor in the water field, providing €1.4 billion annually. Furthermore, the CSD provided substantial input into the UN Millennium Review Summit in September 2005.

But achieving the most important goal – meeting Kyoto targets – is still uncertain. What is clear is that while Brussels can help set standards in this field, the Commission will need to take far tougher action against non-compliant member states than has so far been politically feasible. The general lesson is that while Brussels in many areas is more progressive than Washington, it still lacks the clout of a federal government.

2.3   An Enviable Social Model

As the American writer T R Reid has aptly observed, while 'welfare' may be a term of abuse in the United States, Europeans by contrast are proud and protective of their social model.[12] The difference between the EU and the US will be apparent simply by comparing the share of State expenditure in total GDP. In the EU, the share of the state in GDP varies between roughly 40–50%, of which about half consists of 'transfer payments'; ie, payments collected by the state but then returned to households in the form of unemployment and disability benefit, medical provision, pensions and the like. In the USA, the Federal Government's share is only about 25%; the main 'free' state service is primary and secondary education while the main transfer payments are unemployment and disability benefit, Medicare and Social Security pensions. Of course, in both the US and the EU (as everywhere else) the state or the local authority pays for public goods like defence, policing, and a basic infrastructure of civil administration and justice. But in the US, in contrast to most EU countries, most social provision is not universal in coverage. The widely cited example is that of health: the US spends around 14% of GDP on all forms of health, about twice the level of the EU average, but its infant mortality rate is considerably higher and life expectancy lower than that of the EU-15.

The essential ingredient of the EU social model is the provision of universal benefits, although there is considerable variation between the EU-15 in benefit provision and its finance – and even more variation if the ten recent accession countries are added, largely due to the legacy of social provision there prior to1989. The main constituents of the EU social model are education, health insurance, unemployment benefit, retirement pensions and comprehensive social services; in addition (though often overlooked) is human rights.

Primary and secondary education is free and compulsory throughout Europe. There are differences of course: the Nordic countries provide excellent and nearly universal pre-school facilities, while Italy provides almost none. Primary and secondary school attendance is universal and compulsory, but school-leaving age is typically 16 (although in Germany it is 18). In Britain and France, school meals are either free or highly subsidised, while Dutch school children generally have no canteen facilities. Most important, some countries stream their secondary school children after age 11 between very academic elite schools on the one hand, and a variety of vocational schools on the other; in others, state schools are comprehensive. In Britain, the state school system

---

[12] See Reid (2004).

competes with a significant private sector, while in Germany private schools are almost non-existent. In recent years, almost all EU states have financed a massive expansion in tertiary education; ie, university, technical college/ university or their German equivalent, the *fachhochschule*. Tertiary education is almost everywhere state-run and funded, although the availability and terms of student grants and/or loans varies greatly.

In 1988, EU member-states initiated the 'Bologna Process' whose aim is to set common standards of academic performance, course duration, joint-degrees and title accreditation across the continent; the goal is to establish a European Higher Education Area by 2010. Equally, the European Commission has initiated three related programmes to aid students and teachers in different areas of education. The Socrates Programme is aimed at general education and harmonises standards, encourages common projects and facilitates teacher and student mobility between the member states. A sub-project, Erasmus, provides grants to nearly a million students studying in other member-states. The Cornelius Programme is aimed at schools and has aided more than ten thousand to develop co-operative programmes and activities. Finally, the da Vinci project is concerned with vocational education and placement; an estimated two hundred thousand young people have been helped to find jobs or do community service in another member-state.[13]

Health provision in the EU-15 is either provided directly by the state, as is the case of the NHS in Britain, or by a state-regulated system of universal health insurance. If you are French or German and visit your local doctor, you'll pay him but reclaim the payment from the State-run insurance scheme. If you are Dutch you'll either qualify and be treated under the state scheme (*ziekenfonds*) or pay compulsory contributions to one of the privately administered insurance schemes. In Britain, which pioneered the NHS, a majority of hospitals are owned and run within the state system. These are funded in part through individual national insurance contributions, a graduated contribution scheme which also covers state pension benefits; at the same time, a large and growing private sector exists in both insurance and the provision of medical facilities. By contrast, Swedish hospitals are generally owned and run by local authorities and private hospitals are virtually non-existent. In 2004, the Swedish government banned further hospital privatisation in order to prevent the growth of an inequitable two-tier system. Although all EU-citizens already qualify for treatment in other member-states, the form-filling can be complicated. Starting in 2006 all EU-citizens will carry

---

[13] For details, see Rifkin (2004: 62).

a common medical insurance card – the size of a credit card – entitling them to 'medically necessary care' in any member-state

2.4 LABOUR MARKETS

Unemployment benefit, labour market protection, pensions and so on differ both between the EU and the US, and between different EU states. (Pensions will be dealt with in more detail in a later chapter.)

All EU countries provide unemployment benefit, although the level of benefits varies substantially between states, as does the nature of employment protection legislation (EPL). Moreover, unemployment benefit is usually accompanied by eligibility for other forms of social assistance, so unemployment regimes are typically quite complex. With such qualifications in mind, some simplified comparisons are possible. Denmark for example has fairly lax employment protection but generous unemployment benefit replacing 70 percent of income and stretching to a maximum of four years; Sweden has a similar benefit level but strong protection. In addition, both countries have tailored legislation in this area to reduce the 'poverty trap'; ie, where taking a job entails a loss in total benefits nearly equivalent to active earnings. In both countries, unemployment rates are low and employment rates high relative to the EU average.[14] At the other end of the scale, employment protection and unemployment benefit are relatively poor in the UK and Ireland, well below the EU average. But unemployment and employment rates in the UK, Ireland, Denmark and Sweden compare favourably to the EU-15 average. Rates of GDP growth in all four countries in 2003/04 were higher than the EU-15 average. Clearly, basic indicators give no clear picture of causation with respect to labour market performance.

Since the 1980s the idea has taken hold that unemployment in the EU is the result of over-generous welfare provision and excessive labour market protection, a view strongly supported in the mid-1990s by the OECD. 'Eurosclerosis' was contrasted with the 'liberal' market in the US (and increasingly the UK) where flexible labour markets and low protection were seen as the essential ingredients of 'the great job machine' – a phrase used extensively in the financial press to underline the vitality of Anglo-Saxon job creation. Correcting the 'supply side' of the labour market meant making labour contracts and working hours more 'flexible', changing hiring incentives for employers by reducing the labour costs through subsidies and tax credits and moving away from providing 'passive' benefits to the unemployed towards

---

[14] Current OECD statistics show the employment rates for 2003 in both Denmark and Sweden to be higher not merely than the EU-15 average but higher than in the USA.

a more 'active' stance designed to get them into jobs – through lowering and shortening benefits (in some cases applying a means-test) and tying benefits to being in work, as in the case of tax credits (negative income tax) schemes. As the ILO's chief economist, Guy Standing, has written:

> The debates on employment in Europe have evolved from the consensus of the 1960s that full employment could be preserved by means of macroeconomic demand management to the point where such views are routinely described as 'discredited'. Having done much to discredit it, the supply-side school of economics initially placed zealous faith in market forces, and then tended to place increasing faith in what has become known as 'active labour-market policy'. (Standing, 1996, p 208)[15]

In the early years of the 21st century, a quite different picture from that painted by the OECD has emerged of European labour markets.[16] Since the mid-1990s, eight EU-15 member-states have experienced an important decline in unemployment: Austria, Denmark, The Netherlands, Luxembourg, Ireland, and the UK. In 2004, unemployment in these member-states was lower than the 5.5% rate recorded for the USA. Moreover, the countries of still high and persistent unemployment (Italy, France, Germany and Spain) are not nearly as 'welfare' orientated as, say, the Nordic countries. On the basis of the current picture, there appears to be no relationship between welfare and unemployment.

The picture that does emerge however is one of tying unemployment benefit more closely to active job-search, although not necessarily making jobs more 'flexible'. For example, both the UK and Sweden have tough 'work tests' for receipt of unemployment benefit. But Sweden provides higher job security and better support for the long-term unemployed than does Britain, and its income distribution is far more egalitarian. The Dutch, although they have tightened up on eligibility criteria, have in essence relied on a strategy of creating part-time employment (particularly for women), unlike the Swedes where these is a strong tradition of full-time work and where the proportion of women in full-time jobs is high.

Germany is currently moving towards putting greater stress on work-based eligibility and decoupling benefit levels from earnings, the so-called Hartz IV agreement. According to *The Economist,* Germany is now one of the most competitive countries in the EU.[17] At the same time, the German situation is

[15] See Guy Standing 'The New Insecurities' in Gowan and Aderson (1997).
[16] For a detailed picture, see for example Andersen, Clasen *et al* (2002).
[17] See *The Economist*, 'Germany's Surprising Economy' August 20–26, 2005

Austria	4.5
Belgium	7.8
Denmark	5.4
Finland	8.9
France	9.7
Germany	9.6
Greece	10.5
Ireland	4.5
Italy	8.0
Luxembourg	4.2
Netherlands	4.6
Norway	4.4
Portugal	6.7
Spain	10.9
Sweden	6.4
United Kingdom	4.6
Eurozone-12	8.9
United States	5.5

Source: OECD Standardised
Unemployment Rates, July 2005.

Figure 2–1: Standardised Unemployment Rates for Selected Countries (2004)

exceptional because of the very heavy burden of transfer payments required to integrate the former DDR and support high levels of redundancy resulting from industrial collapse in the east. Spain, although its unemployment rate is still high, has brought it down substantially in the past decade. France, where reducing unemployment has relied more on traditional remedies such as reducing working hours and subsidising the employment of youth, has been relatively unsuccessful in attaining its goals. The Government under the Dominique de Villepin has pledged to give top priority to cutting unemployment. At the time of writing, few details are available of the new Government's strategy. Given the persistent nature of French unemployment – it averaged 9.2% in the 1980s – it is clear that radical measures will be required.

More will be said on European labour markets in a subsequent chapter. The salient point of the brief review above is that labour markets cannot be considered in isolation from macroeconomic policy; ie, it makes little sense to

> *When the FRG and the GDR were reunited in 1990, the West German Chancellor, Helmut Kohl, decided that the East German currency, the Ostmark, would be exchanged for the Deutschmark on a 1:1 basis. Kohl may have thought this politically expedient, but it proved an economic disaster. In general, the average wage must reflect average labour productivity; ie, an average worker's output. Productivity in the East was less than half the West German level. The 1:1 exchange rate resulted in East German workers being paid approximately the same as their Western counterparts despite producing half as much. This fact, together with the collapse of the Eastern Bloc's Common Market (CMEA), led to the bankruptcy of most of Eastern German industrial firms, further reducing average labour productivity in the East. Special taxes were introduced in the West to finance the East, a transfer estimated equivalent to 4% annually of the West's GDP. Much of the money was needed to maintain the East's consumption and thus was unavailable for new investment. Paying for unification has been a major burden on German finances for 15 years and is one of the key factors explaining poor German growth.*

Figure 2–2: The Cost of German Unification

concentrate on 'active' labour market policy while allowing growth to remain stagnant and failing to create new jobs. As the eminent labour economist Richard Freeman argues in a recent paper, despite much Anglo-Saxon rhetoric to the contrary, there is no evidence that Britain and the USA manage their 'flexible' labour markets better than continental EU member-states.[18]

2.5 EURO-SCEPTICS

Why does Britain appear so much more 'American' in its policies than the rest of the EU? In fact, Britain exceptionalism is nothing new.[19] The UK waited until 1975 to join what was then called the 'Common Market', and it was only with reluctance that it embraced the defining documents of what was to become the EU: the Single European Act and the Treaty of Maastricht. Moreover, Britain and Ireland[20] did not sign the Schengen Agreement on borderless travel, Britain and Denmark opted out of the single currency and until 1997 Britain even declined to ratify the Convention on Human Rights.[21]

---

[18] See Freeman (2004); also see *The Economist* 'Are 5.3m Americans missing from the unemployment figures?' July 30, 2005.

[19] See Hugo Young (1998) on the historical roots of British exceptionalism.

[20] In the case of the Republic of Ireland, it did not sign – and cannot until Britain does—because it wants to retain its open border with Northern Ireland.

[21] Although Britain eventually signed the Human Rights Convention when Labour came to power in 1997, it has refused to comply with the European Commission's Working Time Directive which dictates limits to the working week.

In consequence, the British have a less tangible sense of European unity in the everyday sense of travelling without a passport and without the need to change currency. Nor is the sense of 'belonging to Europe' fostered by the unremitting anti-European propaganda served up in much of the British media and the acquiescence in these attitudes of its political class.

For the past decade, the Conservative Party in Britain has moved from a position of wait-and-see to one of outright hostility to 'Europe'.[22] While Labour and the Liberal Democrats both claim to support the project, Labour has at best been lukewarm. This is true in part because a minority of the Party has always viewed Europe with suspicion, but mainly because Blair has assiduously cultivated the support of Euro-sceptic media owners such as Rupert Murdoch, the Rothermere family, Richard Desmond and (until his disgrace) Conrad Black.[23] Nor are the British Treasury and the Bank of England keen to embrace the euro. Joining would diminish the power of both these institutions.

Nothing better reflects the Labour Government's fear of Euro-scepticism than the sigh of relief in London that greeted the negative outcome of the French and Dutch rejections of the European Constitutional Treaty. The outcome of a British referendum on the Constitution, assuming it took place today, would almost certainly be negative. Before the French result, Britain's main political parties either opposed the Constitution, or supported it on the negative grounds that the Government's red lines over matters of sovereignty had been respected and that 'ever closer union' was dead. Unlike the French who lament the insufficiently 'social' nature of Europe, the British feel themselves more prosperous for having distanced themselves from their EU neighbours. It seems to matter little that continental Europe is Britain's largest trading partner by far, and that British prosperity rests at least in part on being Europe's leading financial centre.

Doubtless, the mood of disenchantment in Britain – and its recent spread to France, Italy and Germany – would be different were the core Eurozone countries still experiencing the high growth rates of the 1960s, or even those predicted just before the world recession of 2001. Since then, continued economic stagnation, growing job insecurity and the dismantling of 'unaffordable' social welfare nets has resulted in a major rightward lurch throughout the Eurozone.

The political alarm bells, which one could hear well before the French and

---

[22] While much 'Euro-scepticism' on the right of the Tory Party and UKIP appears to be based on little more than crude chauvinism, a coherent ultra-Thatcherite position is Connelly (1995) whose book is more intellectually cogent than its vulgar title suggests.

[23] A revealing treatment of this (and related) issues is Beckett and Hencke (2004).

Dutch referendums, are now sounding loud and clear. For a variety of reasons, 'Europe' has become less popular. The Swedes rejected the euro in part because they feared it would threaten their social provisions. (Swedes are as proud of their welfare state as the British are of their National Health Service.) Germans are unhappy with the costs of reunification, high unemployment and the budgetary cuts imposed by the Schroeder government. The Dutch dislike the fact that they have kept within the 3% budget limit imposed by Brussels while their larger neighbours have not. The French are deeply divided about embracing an Anglo-Saxon free-market model, which 'non' campaigners argued was entrenched in Giscard's constitution. Most of all, Europe worries about immigrants, who are perceived as threatening 'national' values, over-burdening welfare services and undermining jobs.

2.6 EUROPE'S NEW RIGHT

It is not merely in Britain that 'immigration' is a burning political issue. The fear of immigrants – from Eastern and Central Europe, Asia and Africa – is on the rise everywhere. In Austria, Belgium, Denmark, France, Germany, Italy, The Netherlands, Norway, Portugal and even Switzerland, the political right has recently prospered by preaching a mixture of extreme populism and xenophobia. Clearly, there is no one explanation for this phenomenon. There is no easy correlation between the rightward shift and, say, national income decline or aggregate unemployment (eg, Switzerland is rich and has low unemployment). The new European right is heterogeneous: followers of Pim Fortuijn 'list' in The Netherlands and Umberto Bossi's *Lega Nord* in Italy have distanced themselves from Le Pen's *Front Nationale* in France and Haider's *Freiheitlichen Partei Oesterreichs* in Austria. Populist parties draw upon a spectrum of voters, and their supporters would find the term 'fascist' as repugnant as did the supporters of Mrs Thather in Britain two decades ago.

But the parties of the new right do share broad characteristics. Not only are they fiercely anti-immigrant; in general they favour minimalist government, severe cuts (if not outright abolition) of welfare expenditure while opposing the supra-national institutions of the EU. Their support appears to be drawn predominantly, though not exclusively, from sections of the working- and lower-middle classes whose prospects of secure employment and upward mobility appear increasingly at risk. This is particularly true in rural areas, and in regions where industry has declined precipitously and amongst less educated and unemployed youth.

While social exclusion is part of the explanation, it is far from the whole story. A further reason is what might loosely be described as the new *malaise* about traditional political parties. Doubtless, some of the supporters of new right are protesting against what they perceive as the comatose state of the traditional parties of the centre and centre-left. In the Netherlands, the rise of the LFP (*Lijst Pim Fortuijn*) had much to do with disrupting the near-permanent post-war consensus between the three traditional parties: the VVD (Liberals), CDA (Christian Democrats) and PvdA (Labour). Whether in The Netherlands, Switzerland, Austria or Denmark, traditional parties are perceived by many to have become indistinguishable: the centre-right accepts supra-national Europe while the social-democratic left increasingly accepts a neo-liberal pruning of the welfare state in the name of sound finance.

A further element of the rightwing backlash is that Europeans perceive their future as increasingly less secure. Detailed surveys of support for Le Pen's 2002 first-round victory revealed a large majority of voters citing their main concern as 'insecurity' while 'immigration' came far behind. 'Insecurity' is one of those terms that is difficult to define; nevertheless, it describes a recognisable social pathology of known causes.

For example, UK aggregate unemployment may be low, but what lies beneath the statistics is the near collapse in the past 20 years of male industrial unemployment, the rise of the casual service sector and the growing social division between school dropouts and those who have access to (increasingly privatised) secondary education. Not just in the UK, but also in Europe as a whole there appears to be emerging a disaffected and rootless underclass and a growingly fearful middle class. It is but a short step from disaffection and fear to the demonisation of immigrants and asylum seekers. The recent bombings in Madrid and London have helped ratchet up the fear factor.

Finally, there is an ideological dimension to social exclusion. Unlike settler societies such as Australia and the USA, Europe lacks an ideology of assimilation. 'Send me your poor' says the Statue of Liberty in New York, with the concomitant dream of assimilation and upward mobility. Europe, by contrast, has traditionally exported its poor. Where, exceptionally, Europe has admitted them, immigrants in some countries have been treated as *gastarbeiters*. In the 21st century where civil war and starvation sweep whole continents and ecological upheaval threatens, Europe will need to take in its fair share of permanent political and economic migrants and accept that the benefits of so doing outweigh the burdens.

2.7   DEMOCRATIC DEFICIT

The American economist Paul Krugman once remarked, 'All the main things that are most directly on people's minds now in the developed world involve macroeconomics.' Sustainable growth is indeed crucial: without it, the EU will be unable to sustain its social-market provisions – most seriously, the provision of universal and generous retirement pensions. Equally, the EU is paying the political cost of continued stagnation, unemployment and the erosion of social benefits, all of which have led to growing disaffection with the European project amongst its citizens. To be sure, the failure of the Constitutional Treaty will not lead to the collapse of the European project. The EU will continue to operate under the rules of the Treaty of Nice until such time as the European Council works out limited changes; in the much longer term, it is possible that a new Inter-Governmental Council (IGC) will be convened. By contrast, rejection of the Constitution in a UK referendum, assuming one were to take place, would almost certainly see a change in Britain's EU membership status, causing the UK to drift further towards a mid-Atlantic version of the American model.

A related issue is that of the so-called democratic deficit. Making good the 'democratic deficit' is not merely a question of strengthening the European Parliament or making 'Brussels bureaucrats' more accountable. Bureaucrats in Brussels are no different from their colleagues in Paris or London, and it is politicians, not bureaucrats, who are meant to be accountable. But it is difficult to see MEPs exercising greater authority as long as the lack of a pan-European vision and the reluctance of citizens to participate in EU elections undermine the Parliament's legitimacy.

The Stability and Growth Pact was strong as regards price stability, but failed to deliver the intended fuller employment, and the agreement to weaken it is not likely to resolve the problem. A bigger budget or further borrowing power for the Union could be further federal steps, as could a more Keynesian co-ordination on member states' budget balances. But the fundamental weakness may well be the lack of democratic federal power to counterweigh the centrifugal pull of member state governments ... (John Pinder 2005, 14–15)

Figure 2–3: Democratic Deficit and Economic Policy

The core of the problem is that, increasingly, major decisions about Europe are negotiated between the member-states at meetings of the European Council or 'summits' as they are called in the popular press. What the public sees is crude horse-trading between politicians. Deals are done, typically behind closed doors, in which the interests of the member-states appear far more important than the long-term interests of the Union. Britain's recent refusal to give up its rebate and France's stubborn defence of the Common Agricultural Policy are two obvious examples. In the words of one historian, 'Diplomacy more than democracy continues to be at the heart of the running of the union'.[24]

There is a further reason why the EU needs to recover its economic health. For more than half a century, the US has served as the economic locomotive of the world economy and – as the old adage has it – when the US sneezes, the rest of the world catches cold. Since the economic downturn in 2001, US growth has appeared to recover. More recently, though, US job creation appears to have stalled and the economy may slow. Just as in Britain, a house-price bubble has bolstered US consumer demand in the US. Today, there are clear signs that the bubble's expansion is coming to an end. In itself, this would not be deeply worrying were consumer indebtedness at home not mirrored by a large and growing overseas debt. The rest-of-the world absorbs a dollar debt currently growing at over $600b a year. Recession in the US could provoke a loss of confidence abroad resulting in a flight from the dollar and a dramatic contraction in the world economy. The EU is the only economy large enough to offset such an outcome – to provide the economic locomotive to replace that of the US. EU growth is not merely necessary for Europe; it is vital to sustain momentum in the rest of the world, not least in the poorest trade-dependent countries in need of equitable and sustainable growth.

But Europe, now a major economic power and apparently with a promising future, is losing its way. The following chapters examine the economic foundations of the Union. The main arguments in these chapters are central to this book, namely, that although the EU is a world-class economic power, the weakest link in the Union's structure is its macro-economic institutions and policy – specifically, the highly orthodox economic policies adopted by Brussels and the core member-states since the ratification of Maastricht in 1992, and more specifically since the launch of the euro in 1999.

---

[24] See Ginsborg (2001), p 309.

CHAPTER 3

European and American Economic Performance

'It is not too farfetched to say that Europe chose never really to recover from the two worldwide oil-shock, anti-inflation recessions of the decade 1973 to 1982. Europe seems content to return to sustainable growth rates at lower and lower rates of utilization, without ever recapturing the ground lost in those recessions. With chronic double-digit unemployment rates in several members of the EU, the policy might be described as cutting out of the economy large fractions of the population, buying their acquiescence by welfare-state transfers, and then blaming the "structural" unemployment on the transfers. ... I am not enthralled by the recommendations I heard ... that the US follow the European example and gear monetary policy exclusively to price stability. This orientation of monetary policy has been very costly in Europe, and it is likely to be even more costly if it is enshrined as dogma by the Maastricht Treaty' (James Tobin 1994).[1]

3.1 Prosperity: Europe v America

Is the EU as rich as the USA? The term 'rich' means different things to different people. It can be a stock of wealth, an annual flow of cash, a state of well being extending beyond mere income and so on. Economists usually speak of Gross National Product (GNP) or Gross Domestic Product (GDP)[2], and when making international comparisons they use *per capita* GDP; ie, GDP per head. The absolute size of China's GDP is larger than that of many 'rich' countries,

---

[1] Quoted in Bibow (2004: 1).
[2] The distinction between GNP and GDP merely involves excluding transfer payments and short-term capital flows from abroad. Recently, the term 'Gross National Income' (GNI) has gained currency at the World Bank; while this looks at national income from the 'income' rather than the 'output' side, none of these distinctions needs detain the reader.

but China's GDP per head places it in the lower-middle income range, in the company of El Salvador and Swaziland. Equally, whether one converts China's currency into dollars (or euro or whatever) at the official exchange rate (OER) or at the purchasing power parity (PPP) exchange rate affects its world ranking. On a PPP basis, the average Chinese citizen is many times richer in US dollar terms than using the official exchange rate; in terms of relative ranking, the use of PPP raises China from 136 to 119th place amongst the 2002 countries ranked by the World Bank in 2004

At first glance, a comparison of the relevant numbers supports the view that Americans are richer than Europeans. When Gross Domestic Product (GDP) per head is compared[3], the average level in the EU-15 is about 70 percent of that in the USA. For 2003 using official exchange rates, the figures at current prices are $27,535 for the EU-15 and $38,093 for the USA.[4] Moreover, over the past decade, US growth has been higher than that in the EU, while average unemployment has been lower. However, such international comparisons need careful qualification. Average GDP per head is generally thought to measure 'prosperity' – although as every first-year economics student knows, GDP per head is a poor proxy for 'well-being'. Because household income distribution is less equal in the United States – basically the top 5 percent of households received a far higher share of GDP in the USA than in the EU – comparing average income per capita is misleading.

The 'median' is the middle figure in a ranked array while the mean is the arithmetical average. Think about how you would compare island A whose three families have an annual income of $1000, $1000 and $10,000 with (egalitarian) island B whose three families all receive $3500 per annum. On island A, the median (middle) income is $1000 but the mean income is $12000/3 = $4000. On island B, the median and the mean are both $3500.

Figure 3–1: Mean and Median

For example, while the average American may be richer than the average Swede or German, the median American may be poorer. Moreover, just as taking the EU-15 'average' hides the difference in income between, say, the average German and Greek family, so the US average hides the difference between, say, the inhabitants of California and those of Mississippi.

---

[3]   GDP per head is normally compared internationally using a PPP (Purchasing Power Parity) exchange rate rather than using the official exchange rate (OER); the PPP exchange rate is that which equates the cost of a typical consumption basket in a pair of countries.

[4]   See European Central Bank *Monthly Bulletin*, July 2004.

The comparison of average income per head is misleading in other ways, too. The EU spends a lower proportion of GDP on health care than the USA but benefits from universal coverage and better health (as measured by life expectancy and infant mortality). Climate and distances mean that the average American spends more per capita on energy consumption. Equally, America spends more on questionable 'goods'; ie, defence, police and the like. A far higher proportion of young Americans are incarcerated, and thus are not registered as unemployed. In short, international comparisons of standards of living, unemployment and so on must be treated with caution.

3.2   Effort, Productivity and Employment

A most important consideration is that a higher proportion of the US population is at work than in the EU, and that Americans work longer hours than Europeans. This was not always true. In 1960, average hours worked were about the same in the USA as in Germany, France and the Benelux countries. Today, the data show clearly is while that average American worked about the same number of hours in 2001 as he or she did in 1979 – just over 1800 hours per year – the average European works fewer hours. For the Eurozone, the average number of hours worked per year has fallen from about 1750 in 1979 to about 1500 today.[5]

If one looks at labour productivity (output per worker), workers in the core European countries produce about the same as their US counterparts per hour worked.[6] What is crucial is that Europeans enjoy this high productivity in the form of more leisure – shorter working hours, longer paid holidays and better services. Americans work longer hours, produce more output per year and enjoy this in the form of higher household income. Some economists have argued that this is a matter of social choice; ie, that if Americans work more hours than Europeans, this reflects a different rate of trade off between extra income and extra leisure (what economists term 'leisure preference').[7] It can equally be argued that inequality in the USA leads to higher levels of relative deprivation. Inequality, and the related absence of social safety nets and trade unions, pushes Americans to attempt to earn more today in order to pay for current *and* future consumption. Americans may wish to work shorter hours,

[5]   See OECD *Employment Outlook*, July 2002.
[6]   Jencks (2002) for example finds that per capita GDP per hour worked is much the same in Germany, France and the USA. Note, however, that until the late 1990s labour productivity had grown faster in the core EU countries than in the USA for nearly two decades. Since 2000, however, US labour productivity growth has exceeded that in the EU-15.
[7]   Adair Turner is a leading proponent of this line of argument; see Turner (2004).

but may lack the means of implementing such a collective decision. The average European who by contrast benefits from more progressive political parties, stronger trade unions and a higher level of social provision can afford to enjoy extra productivity in the form of extra leisure.

When such differences are taken into account, the 'prosperity gap' narrows quite considerably. Some economists have argued that the gap is quite small and perhaps even zero.[8] In short, one cannot say that the average American is one-third better-off than the average European. That a smaller percentage of Europeans work and those working may enjoy shorter hours may be a 'benefit' that simply isn't recorded by the market. More leisure is quite acceptable as long as EU labour productivity is high and not stagnating. Labour productivity determines how much we can afford to pay ourselves, regardless of whether that pay takes the form of disposable income or of state services. After all, Europeans have fought hard to get a high level of job security, longer paid holidays and more favourable state pensions – indeed high levels of social and economic infrastructure provision.

	1990–95	1995–2000	2000–2003
US	1.1	2.2	2.5
EU-15	2.4	1.5	1.4

Source: (Turner 2004: 3); OECD Labour Productivity 16-Feb-2005;

Figure 3–2: Comparison of US and EU-15 Labour Productivity growth
            (figures are annual %)

From the mid-1970s to the mid-1990s, EU labour productivity grew faster than in the US.[9] However, looking at recent trends in productivity growth, the European picture seems less bright. Since the mid-90s, US labour productivity growth has caught up and overtaken that of the EU.[10] Comparisons for the past 15 years appear in the figure below. Such comparisons explain in part why there is such concern that the EU is 'falling behind' and that clear targets – such as those of the Lisbon Programme – must be adopted if the EU is to 'catch up'.

[8] A good discussion appears in Boltho (2003); quoting work by Robert Gordon, Boltho suggests the 'gap' may be closer to zero. Per contra, some have argued that the gap is even larger than the figures suggest: See Bergstrom and Gidehag (2004).

[9] See Mishel, Bernstein and Schmitt (2001).

[10] For a review of different measures of productivity and their relevance to 'who is better off?', see Turner (2000). According to the Kok report, EU labour productivity growth over the period 1996–2003 averaged 1.4% in contrast to 2.2% in the US, largely because of the slowdown in the growth of EU investment per head.

Has the recent sprint in US labour productivity been true for the whole US economy? Some particularly interesting findings emerge when productivity figures are disaggregated by sector. One study concludes that relative to the United States, 40% of the UK productivity gap and 70% of Germany's gap is explained by differences in productivity in the wholesale and retail distribution sector. Another study finds that 90% of the jump in productivity in the US is explained by the entry of new firms into wholesale and retail distribution – Wal-Mart, Office Depot, Circuit City and so on.[11] Moreover, almost none of the gain is explained by innovation by existing firms. This suggests that for all the Lisbon discussion of the need to invest in human capital and devote a higher share of GDP to R&D, it is "stack 'em high, sell 'em cheap" operations – particularly where accompanied by a strong aversion to trade-union entry – which account for the US productivity spurt. Recent American productivity gains, it would seem, are mainly about the spread of the Wal-Mart model.

Obviously there are a number of reasons why EU countries will not want to fully imitate this path. First, the US doubtless possesses a natural advantage in terms of low population density and greater opportunity for green-field investment than do the EU core countries; America has the space to accommodate an ever-growing sprawl of suburban shopping malls interlinked by vast expressways which Europe does not. Secondly, the relative strength of both labour and small-business interests is far greater in Europe. Most important, European city dwellers – and a higher proportion of Europeans live in cities and towns than in the US – are more likely to resist the destruction of local social organisation which the disappearance of small retailers entails. This is not to say that the retail sector cannot be modernised; large EU companies currently dominate food retailing in France, Britain and even high-density Holland. But it seems likely that the EU will preserve a different balance between 'modern' and 'traditional' retailing from that in the USA. For all these reasons and more, the current EU obsession with 'catching up' is ill-judged and needs qualification.

With respect to employment, a lower proportion of the European workforce available for work is in employment; ie, the 'employment rate' is about 65 percent in the EU-15 versus 71 percent in the USA – and the gap is even more striking for women.[12] Part of the explanation lies in the fact that the relative absence of social safety nets in the USA forces more Americans – particularly poor Americans – into work. This is particularly true for women and for school leavers.

---

[11] See for example O'Mahoney and de Boer (2002) and van Ark et al. (2002).
[12] See Kok Report (2004), Annexe 1. The Lisbon target for 2010 is 70%, but the Kok Report doubts this target will be met.

But the main concern about the EU's lower employment rate is demographic. As life expectancy rises in the EU, the employed population will need to 'support' a growing number of pensioners. It is estimated that while each retired person is 'supported' by nearly four workers today, in 20 years' time this figure could fall to only two workers; ie, that the 'dependency ratio' could rise from 20–25 percent to 50 percent. Such an outcome is obviously undesirable since it would both raise pension provision and related social spending while lowering the EU's potential growth rate. The 'pension' question is the subject of a separate section.

Furthermore, there is little doubt that over the past decade or more, the average unemployment rate (ie, the proportion of the workforce involuntarily out of work) in the EU-15 has been higher than that in the United States. What is particularly striking about this comparison as shown in the accompanying table is that unemployment in Europe has been growing.

	1974	1983	1996	2004
USA	5.5	9.5	5.4	6.5
France	2.8	8.3	12.3	9.6
Germany	2.1	7.9	8.8	9.9
EU-15	2.8	9.8	10.8	8.9

Source: Turner (2001), p 139; Eurostat 2005

Figure 3–3: Historical unemployment rates for selected OECD countries

The use of average figures hides important differences between countries and regions. For example, the unemployment rates of Austria, Denmark, Ireland, Sweden, The Netherlands and the UK in recent years have been lower than that of the USA.[13] Equally, there are fears in the USA that the current upswing in the business cycle is bringing a jobless recovery 'creating greater problems for Americans than the sluggish job performance of Europe in the 1990s created for Europeans'.[14]

---

[13] There are significant differences between Eurostat conventions defining unemployment and those used by the US Department of Labour; in general, these conventions serve to widen slightly the unemployment gap.

[14] See Freeman and Rodgers (2004) who argue that the US job creation record in the most recent upswing of the business cycle is the worst in living memory.

3.3   Economic Growth?

A related question is whether the EU has been growing more slowly than the US? If so, can one speak of 'Euro-sclerosis', as do neo-liberal economists who contrast the low-growth, highly taxed and over-regulated economies of the old world with a dynamic and highly productive USA.

	1980–95	1995–2000	2001–2004
US	2.9	3.6	2.5
EU-15	2.1	2.4	1.4
US and EU-15 growth per head			
US	1.9	2.3	1.5
EU-15	1.8	2.1	1.4
Source: (Turner 2004: 3); OECD 16-Feb-2005;			

Figure 3–4: US and EU15 GDP growth rates

The answer to the first question is quite straightforward. The EU-15 has been growing more slowly that the US, although the gap is less than commonly thought. The average annual GDP growth rate for the EU-15 over the period 1980–95 was slightly lower than that for the US: 2.1 percent versus 2.9 percent. For the period 2000–2004, the figures are lower still: 2.5 versus 1.4 percent. But because population growth in the US is higher, the difference in growth per capita (ie, in the growth of prosperity) is almost negligible.

Nevertheless, comparisons aside, the figures for the EU-15 are disappointing. The salient point is that the large Eurozone countries – Germany, France and Italy – have not just grown more slowly; they have stagnated. In 2003, Germany, France and Italy experienced several quarters of zero or negative growth. Negative growth and very low inflation put these countries at risk of deflation. In 2004, French and Italian GDP growth was under 2 percent and German growth in the last quarter of 2004 was fractionally negative. In early 2005, both Italy and The Netherlands seemed to be entering recession. These are worrying figures at a time when the US economy had clearly come out of recession. The core states of the Eurozone have done poorly for over a decade. Private household demand has remained weak and has not been offset by buoyant public sector demand. The 'inflationary expectations' of the 1980s have been replaced by the prospect of continued stagnation. It would take little to fall into the Japanese trap of 'deflationary expectations' – a very dangerous situation indeed and one to which I return presently.

3.4 'EURO-SCLEROSIS'?

Broadly, there are two quite different views about the slowdown in EU growth. One, favoured by right-of-centre pundits, is that Europe is over-regulated and its workers prefer welfare to work. The left-of-centre view is that the EU's political class has been far more prudent in matters of economics than their US counterparts. In particular, the European Commission (EC) and the European Central Bank (ECB) have imparted a 'deflationary bias' to macro-economic policy making: notably in having the ECB focus entirely on inflation and in constraining member states' fiscal policy to stay within the limits set by the Stability and Growth Pact (SGP). In economic jargon, these (much simplified) views are said to be 'supply side' and 'demand side' focussed respectively.

The essence of the supply side argument is that EU countries are over-regulated, leading to rigidity in starting new businesses, in hiring and firing workers and, more generally, a culture of dependency on a nanny state. Today, this view of Europe is widely held in the USA, even in 'progressive' intellectual circles.[15] The ascendancy of neo-liberalism during the Reagan-Thatcher years led to its leftward spread in the 1990s, notably, many 'New Democrats' under Clinton and 'New Labour' supporters under Blair who believed that shrinking the state would improve efficiency by enabling market forces to play their full role. Just as Clinton's economic policy was shaped by its fear of financial markets, so in Britain, Gordon Brown virtually froze public sector spending during the first two years of his tenure as Chancellor after 1997.[16] Brown has also excelled at lecturing his colleagues in the rest of Europe on the importance of flexible labour markets; he argues that this is one of the reasons – together with prudence and a rules-based monetary policy – why Britain has one of the lowest unemployment rates in the EU.

There is an element of truth in the supply side argument. As industrial production has shifted from developed to developing countries, so new growth of income and jobs has become increasingly dependent on a dynamic services sector. In a number of core EU economies, starting a small enterprise is a time-consuming business: it is regularly reported in the UK that young French

[14] In the words of one US academic specialist on the EU, the problem with Germany is that it has 'burdened itself and the Eurozone with its inflexible labor laws, high production costs and a bloated welfare bill'; Dinan (2004), p. 304.

[16] For a readable and very perceptive analysis of Brown's record as Chancellor, see William Keegan (2004).

entrepreneurs stream across the channel where setting up shop requires days rather than weeks. Equally, however strong the German economy may be as an exporter of manufactured goods, its service sector remains relatively small by the standards of the major OECD economies. The growth of the service economy has been constrained in core Eurozone countries both by a lack of consumer confidence, and by over-regulation and the high cost of employing low-skilled labour. In the UK, by contrast, a major source of growth has been the rapid expansion of the services sector. Part of this growth comes from the low-wage services sector; eg, jobs in cleaning and catering. At the other end of the spectrum, the highly remunerative financial services sector in Britain now accounts for about 30% of GDP, twice that of manufacturing.

Although some countries need more flexibility, it is seriously misleading to argue that low job growth in the EU is fully or even mainly explained by 'inflexible labour markets' – a view that became the new orthodoxy when enunciated in the 1994 *OECD Jobs Study*. In an important econometric study, Schmitt *et al* (2001) suggest that the empirical evidence does not support the traditional OECD view. Supply side rigidities such as inflexible labour markets do not appear to be nearly as important as the Keynesian notion of insufficient aggregate demand in explaining the Eurozone's inability to increase income and employment.

For one thing, US joblessness has risen in recent years and the current economic recovery has generated far fewer jobs than in the past, leading commentators to speak of a 'jobless recovery'.[17] Nobody would suggest that US labour markets are over-regulated, so 'inflexibility' cannot be the explanation in this case. For another, if one compares US and EU employment figures disaggregated by age group and gender, much of the 'employment gap' is explained by Europe's lower proportion of employed women and young people.

When employment rates between men aged 25–54 (prime age workers) are compared, there is no significant difference in EU-15 and USA. The differences are among women, and younger and older men. With respect to women, the higher US employment rate is explained by the fact that US families purchase a higher proportion of traditional household activity in the market; eg, domestic cleaning, the preparation of meals and child care. For young men, two influences are at work. Young middle class men in the US who progress to further education are more likely to have part time jobs than their European counterparts; equally, they are likely to find a job more quickly upon finishing their studies. At the same time, a significant proportion of young working-class men in the US are removed from the labour pool altogether through

17 See Freeman and Rodgers (2004).

incarceration. Amongst older men, the difference in employment rate appears to be attributable largely to earlier retirement in the EU than in the US.[18] Finally, there are methodological problems in comparing unemployment statistics compiled by Eurostat and the US Department of Labor; different definitions of unemployment appear to explain between one-half and one percentage point of the gap.

An important and highly undesirable feature of greater labour market flexibility is that it correlates with growing income inequality in the primary distribution of household income; ie, the income distribution before tax. One of the results of the OECD's 1993 *Employment Outlook* was that the less wages are regulated by state intervention or by trade-union collective bargaining agreements and the more rapidly wages respond to changes in market forces, the greater is the gap between the average income of the first decile (poor) and ninth decile (rich) of households. The best examples of unregulated or deregulated wage-markets in the OECD group are the United States and Britain: these also score near the bottom of the table in income inequality.

But there are other ways of reducing unemployment. Sweden, Denmark and Austria all combine relatively low levels of unemployment with relatively high levels of national wage bargaining. In short, the evidence suggests flexible labour markets are not correlated with attaining higher growth with low unemployment; rather, deregulation leads to greater income inequality. In short, the so-called cure is worse than the disease.[19]

A better explanation of the Eurozone's high unemployment is provided by the fact that the reduction in government spending required to meet the Maastricht criteria has resulted in a fall in investment. Indeed, in the late 1990s the figures showed the share of public investment in the EU economies to have fallen by nearly one-third in the previous decade.[20] Lower public sector investment has meant lower private sector growth, and lower employment growth. According to one study, within the Eurozone a 1% fall in the investment share in GDP leads to a 0.7% rise in unemployment.[21]

3.5 EUROPE AND AMERICA'S DEFICIT

At a global level, one must remember that the relatively favourable growth record in the USA is facilitated by its large Government budget deficit – in

---

[18] An excellent short analysis is Freeman (2004).
[19] On this issue see Dore (1994).
[20] See Holland (2005).
[21] See (Soukiazis and Castro 2004: 21) 'Every one percentage point increase in the growth of the investment ratio is responsible for 0.7 percentage points decrease in the growth of unemployment rates in the EU countries for the period 1980–2001'

2004, it was 3.6% of GDP – generated under George W Bush. Because both the US Government and the private household sectors spend more than they save, this gap is reflected in a large and growing external trade deficit – 5.3% of GDP in 2004 and forecast to be over 6% in 2005 – that must be financed from abroad. (Incidentally, the US ran a trade deficit even when the budget was in surplus under Clinton!)

Since the US dollar is still the world's main reserve currency, the world's Central Banks, all of which hold dollar reserves, in effect lend money to the US. So too do countries like Germany, Japan and China which, because they run a trade surplus, can export capital to the US. This lending is facilitated by the fact that European and Asian households are generally net savers – although the same is not true for the UK where, like the US, growth is financed in part by foreign savings. By definition, a trade deficit in one part of the world must be offset by a surplus somewhere else since, overall, the sum of the world's financial flows must balance.

Thus, recent US growth has been made possible not just because Government and consumers in the US spend more than they earn, thus keeping demand buoyant, but because EU governments are prudent and households spend less than they earn. This basic principle is often forgotten in comparing the US and EU growth records. The fact that the euro has been allowed to rise freely against the dollar has shifted part of America's burden of adjustment to the Eurozone. China, by contrast, has kept its currency closely aligned with the dollar, either by means of a currency peg or, recently, in moving to a 'managed float' while carefully limiting the extent of its revaluation. Its Central Bank accomplishes this trick by selling its own currency for dollars as required, as does Japan's. In the words of one economist:

> In 2003–4 the US currency was only prevented from freefall by governments in the Far East being prepared to accumulate seemingly endless piles of dollar assets, as a counterpart to export surpluses. By the end of 2003 overseas governments held 1.474 trillion in dollar assets equivalent to 13% of US GDP.[22]

The ECB has followed orthodox free market principles, allowing the euro to appreciate as the market sees fit. This is in keeping with banker's interests; European bankers like a strong euro; their non-euro liabilities depreciate in relation to their (largely) euro denominated assets, thus making them richer.

The conventional wisdom is that the cheaper dollar will eventually bring about adjustment: a cheaper dollar means that imports are more expensive for US consumers but US exports are cheaper for the rest of the world. The problem

[22] See Glyn (2005) p. 13.

here is that for 'adjustment' to take place, a combination of two things must happened. First, US consumers must reduce their expenditure on foreign imports – tighten their belts – in order to free resources for exports. Second, the rest of the world must be able to absorb the US deficit, currently $650b and rising by a net yearly figure of $150b. But belt tightening in the US means slowing US demand, and thus growth – a policy which risks slowing the world economy. By contrast, absorbing annual US exports of $800b means faster world growth and, particularly, faster Eurozone growth. Hence, Eurozone growth is required not merely to reduce European unemployment, but to counteract the danger of world recession posed by the US external deficit.[23] World trade deficits and surpluses could in principle be settled by careful policy co-ordination between the regions concerned, a role Keynes envisaged for the IMF at the time of its founding in 1944. In practice, this role has been relegated to free markets and to central bankers.[24]

Below, one further cost of excessive Eurozone caution is discussed – namely, the danger of deflation. Despite Europe's relatively strong performance in many areas, an obsession with squeezing inflation rather than promoting growth can prove very expensive.

3.6   WHAT IS DEFLATION?

In 2003, the IMF[25] reported that Germany, the locomotive of the EU economy, might soon join Japan in the deflation league.[26] Since 2000, Germany's GDP growth rate has been barely positive and Italy has fared nearly as badly; France has grown slightly faster, but unemployment has remained stubbornly high. Germany and Italy experienced negative growth in the final quarter of 2004, as did Italy and The Netherlands in early 2005. In the Eurozone (EU-12) since 2000, inflationary pressure has gradually declined. For 2004, the Eurozone

---

[23] See Godley, W and A Izurieta (2005). Since U.S. imports are growing steadily at about US$ 250 billion per year and exports at about US$ 100 billion, a correction of the current account, without a recession in the U.S., would require the rest of the world to absorb about US$ 800 billion of exports ($650+$250–$100 billion). But this would be impossible without a significant world economic acceleration.

[24] The latest view circulating in Bush circles is that the US trade deficit, far from being generated by excessive US consumption, is the result of a 'word savings glut' accommodated by the US current account deficit; ie, the direction of causation runs in the opposite direction. That this view is at odds with IMF 'belt tightening' orthodoxy – an orthodoxy dear to the heart of the same people who speak of the world savings glut – should be obvious.

[25] See IMF (2003).

[26] See Paul Krugman 'Is the world stumbling into an economic quagmire?' *New York Times*, May 27, 2003; also The Economist, The Economist (2002) 'Of debt, deflation and denial' Oct. 10, 2002.

annual inflation rate was 1.7% – and only 1.4% where food end energy prices are excluded.[27]

When consumer demand stagnates and unemployment remains high, the economy has excess capacity exercising downward pressure on prices. As stagnation becomes prolonged, prices may start to fall pushing the economy into reverse. The last time this happened in Europe was in the 1930s. Households postpone their consumption in the expectation that prices will fall further. Net creditors gain; net debtors – typically households with mortgages and small enterprises that depend on bank loans – lose since they experience a rise in the real value of debt. Moreover, as prices fall, firms find that their real wage bill rises since money wages cannot readily be cut. Firms lay off workers, increasing unemployment and weakening aggregate demand still further.

Keynes pointed out nearly 70 years ago that to counter deflation, a Central Bank must ease monetary policy by lowering interest rates and pumping more cash into the economy. Nevertheless, he added, monetary policy alone cannot cure the problem. Nominal interest rates cannot fall below zero, at which point monetary policy ceases to be effective. Moreover, even if the Central Bank prints money, households may simply hold the extra cash in the form of increased savings: in economists' parlance, the economy will be caught in a 'liquidity trap'. In short, neither the market on its own nor the Central Bank can cure the problem of recession, particularly if recession turns to deflation.

A robust and sustained monetary and fiscal stimulus is needed to get the economy moving again. Even the straight-laced Bank for International Settlements (BIS) has called for less emphasis on fashionable supply-side reform and more on expansionary demand management.[28] But the EU's political class remains mesmerised by the monetarist and supply-side economic ideology of the 1980.

One doesn't need to travel back to the 1930s to find an example of deflation. Since the Japanese property bubble burst in 1989, that country's GDP has remained stagnant. Following a decade of stagnation, Japan slipped into deflation after 1998. According to the OECD Observer,[29] deflation has become entrenched with prices in 2004 falling for the sixth successive year. The Japanese Government lowered interest rates to nearly zero over a decade ago, but this failed to induce a sustained rise in economic growth. Instead, Japan's once enviably low rate of unemployment has slowly risen. Today it stands at over 5% percent, a historic post-war high by Japanese

---

[27] See OECD Consumer Price Index, 30 March 2005.

[28] See William Keegan 'Sinking US dollar "could drag the world economy under"', *The Guardian Weekly*, July 10–16, 2003.

[29] See OECD Observer 'Japan's economy: firming up? March 2005.

standards.[30] Moreover, attempts to jump-start the economy using traditional fiscal stimuli have had little success.[31]

Until 1998, successive Japanese governments were politically unable and unwilling to run large fiscal deficits.[32] Since the Asian crisis, the deflationary danger has been recognised and the public deficit, used mainly to finance public works, has been the largest of any OECD country.[33] It recently peaked at nearly 8 percent of GDP, but this has failed to produce sustained growth. Although the 2004 growth rate was positive as a result of strong activity in the first quarter, in subsequent quarters output fell. Moreover, because the deficit has been financed by borrowing, Japanese public debt is high (over 100% of GDP) and debt service is a heavy burden. Such growth as there has been appears to have been due to rising demand for Japanese exports from the rest of Asia, mainly China. That the domestic economy remains flat is perhaps not surprising since – unlike the USA and UK – the public deficit is partly offset by strong household savings and an overvalued yen.

The most important lesson for the EU is that a decade of stagnation can produce 'deflationary momentum'. One should not forget that after the Great Crash of 1929, the US economy dragged its way through much of the 1930s with falling prices and high unemployment, defying the efforts of Roosevelt's New Deal to prime the fiscal pump and renew growth. In Europe during the 1930s, countries put up tariff barriers and engaged in competitive devaluations, effectively exporting their unemployment. This was a game in which there were no winners. Ultimately – and paradoxically – it took war production and the imperative of post-war reconstruction to re-launch growth. Today, after nearly a decade of stagnation in the Eurozone's main economies, the parallel is painfully obvious.

3.7   WEAKER FISCAL SYSTEMS

One reason why advanced economies have avoided deflation since the inter-war depression is because they enjoyed a robust fiscal system. Throughout the

[30] Because of the way Japan's unemployment is measured, 5% is probably is a serious underestimate.

[31] While nominal GDP growth remains flat, falling prices mean that real GDP is growing at the rate of deflation.

[32] In the early years until 1997, the deficit gradually grew to 4%, but the Japanese Treasury stepped in and insisted on a hefty tax increase, promptly killing what little growth there was in the economy. Much the same thing appears to have happened in 2004 when the authorities cut back drastically on public investment.

[33] The OECD (Organisation for Economic Cooperation and Development) comprises 30 members; all 'developed' economies.

post-war boom-years until 1973, Keynesian policies were the norm and came with in-built fiscal stabilisers. During an upswing with incomes rising, a progressive tax structure resulted in money being siphoned off to Government; in the downswing, money was pumped back into the economy as fiscal revenues fell and unemployment benefit kicked in to boost private consumption.

With the erosion of the Keynesian consensus in the EU, today's Socialists and Social Democratic parties have joined Christian Democrats and other right-wing parties in their adhesion to monetarist orthodoxy.[34] At Ministries of Finance throughout Europe, it has become part of the received IMF wisdom to assert that a government 'cannot spend its way out of a depression'. Jim Callaghan first used the phrase in 1976 when Britain was in IMF receivership. Gordon Brown repeated the same anti-Keynesian dictum in his speech to the Labour Party Conference in 1997 (although whether he believes it is questionable). The IMF decrees canonically that all external payments crises stem from excessive Government spending and that such spending 'crowds out' private investment. Hence, the all-purpose IMF remedy is to cut spending. These policies were applied to Latin America in the 1980s and to East Asia and Latin America in the 1990s; more recently they have resulted in near economic collapse in economies as diverse as Indonesia and Argentina.

Two further factors have undermined fiscal stabilisers. First, economic deregulation and tax cuts of the Reagan-Thatcher era have increased the size of the informal labour market and made tax incidence less progressive. Tax cuts first became news in the USA in 1970s with the tax revolt by the middle class in California, leading one prescient economist to theorise a 'fiscal crisis' of the state.[35] Under the Reagan administration and later under Thatcher in Britain, tax cuts helped redistribute income to the better off while, at the same time, allegedly boosting growth. This erosion of progressive taxation was perhaps most marked at the end of the 20th century in Britain. In the name of labour market 'flexibility', a growing percentage of the labour force found itself in non-unionised low-wage employment, often of a casual nature; such labour could more readily be shed during the downswing of a business cycle. A recent study of total tax incidence in Britain shows it to be regressive; the total effective rate of tax paid by the richest quintile of households is 34% while that of the poorest is 42%.[36]

Second, the huge growth of international capital markets and financial deregulation has made it far more difficult for governments to pursue

---

[34] For an excellent discussion of the corrosive effect of monetarism on New Labour in Britain, see John Grieve Smith (2001).

[35] See O'Connor (1973).

[36] See Lakin (2003).

counter-cyclical Keynesian policies. World foreign exchange trading in 2004 is approaching \$2 trillion a day, three times its 1989 level.[37] Where the international financial market perceives a government deficit as 'unsustainable' the result is usually a large capital outflow; ie, a speculative attack on the currency. In France, the memory of the Mitterand Government's disastrous attempt in 1981–82 to reflate the economy along Keynesian lines is nearly as painful as that of Black Wednesday is in Britain.[38]

3.8   DEFLATION AND CURRENCY APPRECIATION

When the Eurozone countries locked into the single currency on 1 January 1999, they greatly reduced the EU's vulnerability to the sort of capital market shock that occurred in France and the UK in 1992. Reducing the output variability caused by shocks is thought to promote faster growth; this was one of the main arguments in favour of the euro. But Maastricht (1992) and the subsequent Stability and Growth Pact enshrined in the Amsterdam Treaty (1997) have acted as an economic straightjacket on growth.[39]

Amongst mainstream economists raised on the market orthodoxies taught at US graduate schools from the 1970s onwards, deflation is a dirty word; the market is assumed to be self-regulating.[40] Governments merely need to pursue sensible, rules-based monetary policy and all will be well. The drafters of the Maastricht Treaty of 1992 were not all conservative economists; indeed, many were respected public servants imbued with the noblest motives. But for these men, memories of the inflationary decade that followed 1973 were still fresh. So, too, for *Bundesbank* officials was the folk memory of the German hyperinflation of 1923. The European Central Bank's brief to target 2 percent inflation or less contrasts unfavourably with that of the US Fed, which by statute must consider both inflation *and* employment. Fiscal policy, too, was constrained. Member states signing Maastricht who wished to accede to the single currency were obliged to lower their budget deficit to 3 percent of GDP and their total public sector borrowing to 60 percent of GDP.

In 1992 such deflationary rules were arguably defensible on the ground that in the run-up to the 1999 euro-launch, 'sound money' was necessary to minimise the danger of speculative attack on Eurozone currencies by the international capital market. Today these monetary and fiscal rules are not

---

[37] See A Glyn (2005).

[38] See M Lombard (2004).

[39] The ECB and SGP have been criticised by a large number of centre-left economists. See for example JP Fitoussi and Jerome Creel (2002).

[40] An excellent non-technical book on deflation and market fundamentalism is Paul Krugman (2000).

merely archaic but are positively counter-productive. High unemployment and zero growth *are* a recipe for social instability and rising nationalism.

The effect of a stronger euro is deflationary; ie, it slows growth. Between early 2003 and mid-2005, the euro rose over 40% against the dollar. Although the French and Dutch referendum results have brought the euro down somewhat, most commentators agree it is still overvalued. To offset merely this deflationary effect, it is agreed that the ECB would need to cut rates. In June 2003 it cut its main rate by half a percentage point to 2%, a cut which doesn't fully counteract the impact of the strong euro, still less get the Eurozone economy moving. Since 2003, the ECB has refused to ease monetary policy.

But here's the rub: if the ECB cuts the nominal interest rate much more, the real rate of interest will turn negative. Very low short-term interest rates can seriously disrupt money markets as hot capital flees abroad. If, additionally, long-term interest rates fall, commercial bank profits can be squeezed. Squeezing bank profits is risky when the economy faces a downturn and firms may be struggling to repay bank loans. And if deflation sets in, banks can collapse as they did in the 1930s.[41]

One should quickly add that the British Treasury's mantra that 'we do things better' is not entirely convincing. While it true that Britain's GDP growth rate has been higher than Germany's, average Eurozone GDP growth for 1999–2004 *excluding* Germany is about the same as the UK average. Nor has recent UK growth been driven by higher labour productivity. Broadly, growth has been achieved mainly by employing more workers who work longer hours in the low-skill service jobs. Most alarming, Britain's growth – like the US – has been propped up by a wide gap between household spending and income growth in a manner reminiscent of the run-up to the crash of the early 1990s. This argument has been carefully researched by, amongst others, Wynne Godley and Alex Izurieta at the Cambridge Endowment for Research in Finance (CERF). Their work shows that even were the ECB to follow the Bank of England in adopting a symmetrical inflation target, this step alone would not reverse the drift towards deflation. Given Britain's record on labour productivity per hour worked (20% lower than Germany and France), on income distribution (inequality is worse only in Portugal and Greece) and the fact that UK growth in 2005 is falling, the UK Treasury has little to boast about.

---

[41] Banks typically hold short-term nominal liabilities and longer-term relatively illiquid debt; a deflationary shock raises the value of their liabilities, thus increasing their exposure.

3.9   Structural Reform: necessary but not sufficient

Since the arrival of José Manuel Barroso as the new President of the Commission in 2004, there has been renewed emphasis on 'structural reform'. The list of reforms called for is well known: labour markets must become more flexible, public finances must be put in order and product markets must become more competitive. All are 'supply-side' measures, which the current orthodoxy considers a pre-requisite for restoring dynamism to the Eurozone economy.[42]

Competition in product markets means that member-states must remove remaining barriers to intra-regional trade; these are typically non-tariff barriers embedded in obscure protectionist legislation. So far, so good! Labour market flexibility and public finance reform are more problematic goals. The former means lowering wage and non-wage costs (eg, pension and health insurance contributions) for employers. The latter means cutting state expenditure on public services, typically through forms of privatisation allegedly increasing economic efficiency.

One does not have to be a neo-liberal economist to recognise that specific inefficiencies and abuses exist in EU labour markets.[43] In Germany, occupational disability payments account for 4% of GDP, a greying population threatens to raise the old age dependency ratio within a generation to 35% and state pension transfers are equivalent to 10% of GDP; such trends are cause for serious concern.[44] Nevertheless, this cannot be used as an excuse for the wholesale dismantling of the EU's social model – for the sort of comprehensive attack on public services and labour guarantees which took place in Thatcher's Britain in the 1980s.

First, cutting back on social provision weakens aggregate demand, precisely what is not needed under conditions of potential deflation.[45] Secondly, institutional reform must be negotiated between all parties and seen to be fair; in consequence such reforms take time and cannot be allowed to weaken social cohesion or increase social exclusion. Thirdly, encouraging flexible labour markets usually means abandoning centralised wage bargaining. If and when growth returns, the main supply-side institution for promoting employment while restraining potential inflation (used to great effect in the Netherlands

---

[42] For a highly critical view of the benefits of 'labour market flexibility', see Dean Baker, Andrew Glyn, David Howell and John Schmitt in D. Howell, ed (2004).

[43] For a far more detailed examination of labour-market constraints on growth than provided here, see Andrea Boltho (2003).

[44] See R J March (2003).

[45] A good critique is provided by William Keegan, 'A policy vacuum' *The Guardian*, July 9, 2003.

and Nordic countries) will have disappeared. Finally, rethinking government receipts is just as important as rethinking expenditure.

When deflation threatens, balancing the government budget is not a sensible aim. Neither is it considered sensible in the EU to legislate tax breaks for the very rich, who have the lowest propensity to spend. Governments should be running a well-targeted deficit, in the extreme case financed by printing money (an avenue now blocked by the ECB). Deflationary expectations, once they set in, can only be overcome by a policy of deliberately promoting inflation. Once the danger of deflation recedes and economic growth picks up, not only will revenue rise as employment grows but also new means can be explored of strengthening the revenue side of public finances.

Using monetary policy to control the rate of inflation is called 'inflation targeting'. Whether interest rate adjustments and/or money supply targets are an effective way of doing this is a much-debated question among professional economists. The guru of monetarist economics, Milton Friedman, famously remarked that any attempt to fine tune the economy by monetary means was not very sensible because of the 'long and variable lags' involved; ie, because it is nearly impossible to predict exactly how long it will take, say, for a rise in the Central Bank's interest rate to reduce inflation. The 'transmission mechanism' (to use the economist's phrase) of monetary policy is complex. True, large econometric models of the macro economy have improved since Professor Friedman spoke. But economies change, the financial sector becomes more sensitive to what is going on abroad, large companies rely less on bank credit, financial intermediation becomes multi-layered and so on. We can be reasonably certain that, *ceteris paribus*, a large and dramatic rise in interest rates will eventually slow down the economy and help contain inflation; by contrast, the precise impact of raising rates by 50 basis points is a different matter.

In any case, average inflation has been quite low in the OECD countries for well over a decade. There are three main reasons why this is so. First, globalisation has given rich countries access to a range of manufactures produced abroad more cheaply than at home. The obvious example is the huge expansion in developed country markets of imports from China (eg, the American retailer Wal-Mart buys 80 percent of its products from China) – an expansion currently fuelling populist demands for trade protection in both the US and the EU. Secondly, the widespread application of information and computer-based technology (ICT) has made products and services cheaper. Computers chips are ubiquitous: they help run everything from washing machines to mobile phones to my daughter's I-Pod. A mere fifteen years ago I could not have sat in an office in Italy writing this book on my laptop, still less checked OECD and Eurostat data on the Internet. Nor could my wife and

I have booked Internet tickets for €70 from London to Turin and back. Finally, wage costs have been contained in Europe in part by wage moderation agreements, in part by deregulation and in the main because a large pool of unemployed increases the perceived personal costs of unemployment. In the USA this 'reserve army' may be smaller, but the pool of low-wage unskilled labour is larger and is regularly topped up by new waves of green-card-lottery immigration.

Above all we need to ask whether mild inflation is really a bad thing? Why does the ECB, or for that matter the Bank of England, set the inflationary target at two percent rather than, say, five percent? Most economists will try to convince you that there is something called NAIRU – the non-accelerating inflation rate of unemployment – such that the less unemployment we have, the greater the danger of inflation and thus the greater the need to keep inflationary expectations to a minimum. The problem with this argument is that the relationship between unemployment and inflation is exceedingly hard to pin down, so NAIRU is at best a vague concept and at worst positively misleading. High inflation – anything much over 20 percent – is certainly a bad thing since it raises the spectre of even higher inflation, disrupts firms' planning and penalises families on fixed incomes and non-protected, low-income workers. But moderate inflation – the sort of 3–5 percent level characteristic of the port-war years of economic boom – is perfectly acceptable.

One reason moderate inflation is beneficial is because it redistributes income from creditors to debtors; in laymen's terms, it eats away the debt burden of your mortgage at the expense of bankers and building societies, and mortgage debts is for many households their largest liability. It also eats away Government's debt burden. For another, it helps lubricate the labour market. Workers – quite understandably – resist any attempt to cut nominal wages. But as average productivity differentials between industries and/or regions change, so too must average wage levels. (The contrary view, that wage levels and productivity can be fully untied, led to near industrial collapse and prompted massive income transfers in the former GDR after German unification.). Under conditions of moderate inflation, nominal wages in declining industries can be held constant, enabling real wages to fall. This principle is particularly important under a unified currency such as the euro. Since member-states can no longer adjust to external shocks by varying exchange rates, either wage rates must adjust or else labour must migrate. Central bankers and Finance Ministers, especially in the Eurozone, speak endlessly of the 'fight against inflation' as though it were a serious threat. Arguably, Europe needs more inflation, not less.

The above discussion is part of a wider debate – or perhaps 'debate' is too polite a term – on public finance. In Britain, such was the hysteria of the tabloid press over 'tax and spend' prior to the 1997 election that Gordon Brown's first two years as Chancellor were marked by the most extreme fiscal caution at a time when the need for public expenditure on Britain's threadbare public services was painfully obvious. Nobody can disagree with the principle of keeping public finance on a sound footing, although nobody quite knows precisely how 'sound' public finance should be. Ministers of Finance in general believe that it means 'pleasing the financial markets'; while Central Bankers believe it means 'balancing the books' – as though an economy functioned like a bank.

The basics of public finance are pretty straightforward. When the economy is in recession, Government should aim to spend more than it receives; in the upswing, it should do the contrary. To a degree, the economy does this automatically through 'fiscal stabilisers'; in a downswing tax receipts fall as people get poorer and public spending on such things as unemployment benefit rises, while the opposite happens in an upswing. Over a full business cycle, typically about 7–8 years, the books should balance in the sense that Government's share in a growing economy should not change radically. Equally, Government should be concerned about how future claims on finance (eg, pensions) are to be met, so some sensible forward planning will be required.

There are two ways to raise money: Government can either increase taxes or it can borrow from the public – the third option, printing money, is normally reserved for extreme emergencies. Raising direct taxation (income and corporation tax) is never popular, so over time governments have shifted increasingly to indirect taxes such as VAT which, while less progressive, sweeps in a lot of money. A few right-wing economists have argued that lowering personal taxation will raise work incentives and thus total tax revenue – a principle famously suggested by Arthur Laffer and codified in Reagan-Thatcher economic dogma – but the empirical evidence suggests otherwise. George H W Bush was correct in dismissing the Laffer curve as 'voodoo economics'.

Two criticisms are levelled at increased public borrowing by orthodox economists. First, it is said to be imprudent. If the stock of public sector debt is too large, servicing the debt can place a major strain on public coffers. This is true, say, in a country like Italy where pensioners hold large amounts of government debt and public revenue collection is weak and uneven. It need not be true where the stock of public borrowing is at a manageable level and fiscal administration is strong. Second, it is claimed to be ineffective, because it causes an opposite offsetting reaction in the private sector. One version of this argument – kown by economists as the 'Barro-Ricardo hypothesis' – says that private households will anticipate that extra borrowing for extra public expenditure today must mean higher taxes tomorrow, and so will react by reducing private expenditure. This is no more than a hypothesis unsupported by evidence. Another version of the argument is that extra public borrowing, because it raises interest rates, 'crowds out' private investment. Although this has become received wisdom in many textbooks, the evidence for 'full crowding out' is weak since, often, public borrowing is used to finance expenditure – on health and education, on economic infrastructure – which fosters private investment. Building a new hospital for example creates a range of private sector activities – from construction to catering – while improving the health and productivity of the local workforce.

The upshot of all this is that the need for low inflation and 'sound public finance', while self-evidently correct at one level, can be quite misleading when one examines the detail. True, a highly indebted country with shaky public finances may need to 'get its house in order'. But it is not self-evident that the core Eurozone economies, whose problem is low growth and high unemployment, need to keep inflation under 2 percent and maintain a zero budget balance over the cycle. What constitutes sound public financial policy depends on circumstances.

Between 2003 and 2005, Herr Schroeder announced various tax cuts aimed at boosting industrial profits and consumer spending. But because German households, unlike their British and American counterparts, cannot be coaxed into becoming net debtors in order to boost consumption, the danger is that a modest tax cut may simply raise household savings further. More generally, once taxes are slashed it is difficult to raise them again, thus weakening the fiscal system.

What is needed today is a massive and sustained fiscal stimulus, a Government-led boost to demand in Germany, France and Italy of the order of 2 percent of GDP. That such an injection would breach the SGP goes without saying. In the words of *The Economist*:

> The euro has … suffered from misconceived efforts to restrict countries' fiscal freedom. The recent emasculation of the stability and growth pact, which sought to limit euro members' budget deficits to 3% of GDP on pain of swingeing fines, is welcome. Even without the pact, countries such as Italy would have only limited fiscal freedom, because of the scale of their debts; but Germany and France might have benefited over the past few years from a larger dose of fiscal expansion.[46]

---

[46] See 'And now, the euro' *The Economist*, June 11th 2005.

The SGP rules need to be amended accordingly, a step that the ECOFIN[47] agreement of March 2005 has fudged (see pp 79–80). For such a policy to be successful, moreover, public spending will need to rise not merely in Germany but in all those Eurozone countries whose economies are stagnating. This is why the co-ordination of macroeconomic policy between member-states is so important. These are matters dealt with in greater details in the next chapter.

Equally, deflation is the reason the EU needs broad tax harmonisation. The argument that because US states have different tax regimes, the EU can do the same is quite misleading. US macro economic policy is steered by a Federal Government whose share of GDP is above 25%; by contrast, 'federal' spending in the EU represents just under 1% of members states' combined GDP. Moreover, the Brussels budget contains no built-in tax stabilisers. Tax competition amongst member states weakens EU public finance as capital flows from high- to low-tax regions. Broad agreement on levels of corporate tax and personal tax for the super-rich is a desirable policy goal. But this goal is resisted fiercely by the UK Treasury and the UK's financial service sector.

3.10 BUSH IS A CLOSET KEYNESIAN

The irony of the EU's situation is that in the USA, the home of conservative economics and free market orthodoxy, Government has provided a tremendous monetary and fiscal stimulus to the economy. George W Bush has pursued the sort of defence-linked Keynesian policies combined with non-Keynesian protectionism used by Ronald Reagan, inventor of the hugely expensive Star Wars programme.

In late June 2003 the Fed lowered the prime rate to 1%, the lowest in 45 years, but since then it has raised rates slightly. The Fed knows that lowering long-rates could hurt the banking sector; indeed, any further cut in short-term rates could damage US money markets, which account for nearly 25 percent of the total money supply. This is the main reason its Chairman, Alan Greenspan, backed the Bush tax cut and extra spending which raised the deficit to nearly 5%.

It may be of great concern that the 2003 Bush tax cuts chiefly benefited the rich and selected industries and that extra public spending went largely to defence.[48] But consider the policies in detail. In June 2002, Bush passed a farm

---

[47] ECOFIN is the acronym of the Economic and Finance Committee of the EU Council; the Committee is made up of the member-states' Finance Ministers who meet monthly in Brussels.

[48] For a stinging critique of the Bush tax cut, see Paul Krugman (2001). As Alex Izurieta at CERF Cambridge has pointed out, the defence spending has a multiplier of only unity as opposed to a multiplier of four for social spending.

bill raising agricultural subsidies by 80%, or nearly USD 200 billion over 10 years. He has asked Congress for a USD 1.4 trillion tax cut over the same period. In his State of the Union message in January 2002, he asked Congress to raise defence spending by USD 50 billion, the largest rise in two decades. However poorly targeted, the sheer magnitude of these fiscal stimuli suggests the US still knows how to prime the economic pump. As Keynes famously remarked, under conditions of incipient deflation, Government should create employment even if it means hiring workers to dig holes and fill them up again.

The EU response has been pitiful. The ECB has continued to focus on inflation while allowing the euro to drift upwards, thus transferring much of the burden of US adjustment to an already stagnant Eurozone. The Finance ministers have agreed to a slight relaxation in the SGP – the fundamentally deflationary Maastricht rules stay in place. Enthusiasm for 'reform' continues to focus almost exclusively on the supply side, chiefly on encouraging labour market 'flexibility'.

The Japanese experience of the past decade shows monetary policy plus erratic and poorly-targeted fiscal stimuli cannot kick-start a large economy— indeed, once deflation actually sets in, not even large fiscal stimuli can do so. Under conditions of potential deflation, it is patently absurd to aim at a balanced budget for each member state. Nobody – least of all the financial markets – believes that loosening the German and French fiscal purse strings will lead to hyperinflation under current conditions. Neither the IMF nor the BIS are particularly progressive bodies, but they do know that action is needed. Sadly, their warnings have been ignored. The ECB and the EU's Finance Ministers continue to defend a policy based on the economics of Herbert Hoover.

As the President of the European Investment Bank, Willem Buiter, put it wryly:

> Anti deflationary policies involve tax cuts, increased transfer payments or higher public spending on goods and services. They will tend to be politically popular. It is, therefore, somewhat of a mystery why a political programme that makes economic sense and should be politically popular does not get implemented. (Buiter 2004: 70)

The EU is thus at a crucial juncture. Although still nominally committed to the post-war political settlement that institutionalised the welfare state and guaranteed near full-employment and strong social safety nets, the settlement is in danger of unravelling. Politically, the EU has concentrated on widening the union rather than on deepening its federal structures. Giscard's compromise constitution did little more than codify the *status quo*. Its initially modest federalist proposals were almost wholly abandoned in favour of what Perry Anderson has aptly termed 'a hierarchy of nation states ... without a summit'.[49] Economically, the EU's adherence to neo-liberal orthodoxy, reinforced by the Anglo-Saxon posturing and free-market fervour amongst the new accession states, has blocked the adoption of economic policies that might reverse the drift towards deflation.

The founding fathers of a united Europe hoped for more than merely a free trade area; their vision of a 'social' Europe formed the bedrock of the post-war settlement. They knew full well that high unemployment and low growth leads to social instability and xenophobia. That was the fundamental lesson of the 1930s, a lesson ignored at Maastricht and which, if unheeded in today's economic climate, could prove exceedingly damaging if not fatal for the European project.

---

[49] See Perry Anderson 'Force and Consent' *New Left Review* 17, Sept-Oct 2002.

CHAPTER 4

Maastricht Economics

In a system of the kind envisaged at Maastricht, national
macroeconomic policy becomes a thing of the past: all that remains to
member states are distributive options on – necessary reduced –
expenditures within balanced budgets, at competitive levels of taxation.
...The single obligation of the ... European Central Bank, more
restrictive than the Charter of the US Federal Reserve, is the
maintenance of price stability. The protective and regulative functions
of existing national states will be dismantled, leaving sound money as
the sole regulator, as in the classical model in the epoch before Keynes.
(Perry Anderson, 1996, p 130)[1].

4.1 A REFERENDUM ON THE 'BRUSSELS CONSENSUS'?

Tempting though it may be for people like me who supported the Constitution,
one cannot dismiss all those on the French Left who voted *non* as loonies,
nostalgic for France's pivotal role in Europe or clamouring against the evils of
globalisation and neo-liberalism. The main Eurozone economies have
experienced low growth, high unemployment and shrinking social benefits for
the better part of a decade. French unemployment has stood around 10% for
two decades, Germany's unemployment is comparable, Italy is in recession and
the 'Dutch miracle' has collapsed. Little wonder voters are disillusioned.
Rekindling an economic debate about the future of Europe is an urgent task;
it will last well beyond the 2005 referendums and needs far wider public
discussion.

Several years ago, Joseph Stiglitz's best-seller on globalisation popularised
the notion of the Washington Consensus, an orthodox policy recipe of
government financial stringency and market deregulation applied by the IMF

---

[1] See Perry Anderson, 'The Europe to Come' in Gowan and Anderson (1997).

to developing countries, the roots of which lie in the monetarist doctrines of the 1970s given prominence during the Thatcher-Reagan years. Today, economists are asking whether this consensus has not crossed to Brussels and Frankfurt?

The reader may well ask 'what's wrong with a bit of financial prudence; or for that matter, making labour markets more flexible?' Understanding what's wrong needs a further brief explanation of orthodox theory, so bear with me. Orthodox economic theory tells us that an economy can only grow in a stable, non-inflationary environment where unemployment is at its 'natural' rate. (The 'natural' rate is often called the 'non-accelerating inflationary rate of unemployment', or NAIRU for short.) In consequence, even the smallest hint of inflation requires a firm response, a task best entrusted to an independent central monetary authority. By contrast, fiscal policy (taxation and government spending) is of minor importance and best left to the operation of fiscal stabilisers built into the tax system. On this view, a combination of wise monetary policy and fiscal prudence must produce eventually growth. If not, it is because of institutional rigidities such as national wage bargaining, employment protection legislation, expensive benefit schemes and the like; in short, too much welfare. In the (critical) view of one academic commentator:

> Because the advent of EMU diminishes the scope for adjustment through the demand-side – given that monetary policy is 'Europeanised' and fiscal policy is constrained by the SGP – it necessarily puts more of the burden of any adjustment on the supply-side (Iain Begg, 2002, p 23)

The economic architecture of the EU fits this orthodox picture well. The European Central Bank (ECB) is a monetary giant, surrounded by member-states constrained by the SGP and reduced in size to 'fiscal dwarves'.[2] The Brussels budget is tiny – just under 1% of combined European GDP compared to 25% in the USA – and since it must balance by law, it is useless as a fiscal instrument. Unlike the US Fed, which attempts to strike a balance between inflation, employment and growth, the ECB focuses entirely on inflation. According to Brussels orthodoxy, if the core Eurozone countries are not growing, it is because they continue to flout the SGP rules, while maintaining unaffordable levels of employment benefit, excessive protection and so on. If governments were sufficiently prudent – balancing deficits in the downswing of the business cycle with surpluses in the upswing – there would be no problem budget balance. Indeed, given that government transfer payments

---

[2] The phrase is from Fitoussi and Saraceno (2004).

automatically stabilise the economy over the cycle, the business cycle is self-correcting and there is no need whatever for discretionary fiscal policy at national level.

Two elements complete the picture. The SGP zero-deficit rule means that in the long term, government borrowing must fall to zero. There is no room here for publicly funded pensions, generous unemployment benefit and universal state-led health provision; the State is reduced to pure night watchman. Add to this an EU Competition Commissioner whose role is to see that 'uncompetitive public enterprise' (eg, transport, energy and telecoms) is privatised and one gets something close to a Thatcherite dream. This is what the French mean when they speak of sacrificing the European Social Model to Anglo-Saxon free-market economics.

The alternative is to widen the remit of the ECB to make it more like the Fed and to scrap the SGP, leaving more room for member-states to follow discretionary fiscal policy. Equally, some form of 'fiscal federalism' will need to be adopted, if only to achieve an acceptable degree of co-ordination between monetary and fiscal policy and room for counter-cyclical investment. This might ultimately take the form of an expanded EU budget along the lines originally proposed by the MacDougall report in 1977. Meanwhile, the EU should at very least have the power – like the US Treasury – to raise funds in the international capital market, a power delegated to the low-profile European Investment Bank (EIB) in order to fund much needed expenditure on social and economic infrastructure. Such a fund was first proposed in the 1993 Delors White Paper, and more recently as a 'rainy day' fund in the 2003 Sapir Report. The latter, incidentally, recommended redirecting finance used for the Common Agricultural Policy towards promoting growth in the new accession states, but Sapir's report to the Commission was ignored.[3] Instead, the Brussels budget is capped, it must balance each year by law and Brussels cannot borrow money on the international market.

The economic architecture of Europe is asymmetric and deeply flawed; unless the problem is addressed, the Eurozone risks continued stagnation; under such conditions the Lisbon goals cannot be met, confidence in the euro will be undermined and popular discontent will rise. Those Euro-sceptics in Britain who feel vindicated should remember that over half of Britain's trade is with the Eurozone. If only for this reason, the French (and Dutch) referendum results are of vital importance to us all.

---

[3]   See MacDougall Report (1977), European Commission (1993) and Sapir et al (2003). The latter is discussed in detail in Chapter 9.

4.2 POLITICAL AND ECONOMIC CRISIS

Table 4.1 shows the how the components of aggregate demand have grown since the mid-1990s for the EU-15. At the outset of the period, growth was constrained as countries tightened their budgets to meet the Maastricht convergence criteria as a condition for joining the euro. In 1999–2000, there was a slight spurt in growth, but this slowed with the world slump in 2001. Since the adoption of the Lisbon Strategy in 2000, average annual growth of the EU15 has been of the order of 1.5%, or half the value envisaged for the decade. Low investment has been the main factor slowing economic activity; for the first four years of the new decade this rose by an average of less than 0.5% per year. Private and Government consumption have not been buoyant either, growing at around 2% per annum; enough to keep the EU moving forward, but not enough to rekindle investment growth. Exports, buoyed by growth in 2004, have grown at an average annual rate of just over 3%. Poor growth and persistent unemployment tend to be bedfellows. Average Eurozone unemployment in early 2005 stands at 8.8%, barely down on the 9% figure recorded in 2000.[4]

Component	1996–2000	2001	2002	2003	2004
GDP	2.7	1.7	1.0	0.8	2.3
GDP Eurozone*	2.6	1.6	0.9	0.5	2.1
Private Consumption	2.7	2.0	1.2	1.4	1.9
Government Consumption	1.7	2.5	3.2	1.9	1.9
Investment	4.3	0.4	-1.5	-0.1	2.9
Exports	7.8	2.9	1.6	0.6	7.0
Imports	8.3	1.3	1.1	2.4	6.9

Source: Eurostat (2005), Real GDP Growth Rates; Euro-memorandum Group (2004), p 6.

* Eurozone figures differ marginally from those of the EU-15; demand components refer to the EU-15.

Figure 4–1: Growth in Components of GDP of EU-15; (annual % changes)

The Eurozone figures mask significant discrepancies between countries; good performance in countries like Ireland, Greece and Austria contrasts with the

[4] See OECD Quarterly National Accounts Database; 13 May 2005.

poor performance of the Eurozone's core countries. In 2003, Germany, France and Italy experienced several quarters of zero or negative growth, which together with very low inflation put these countries at risk of tipping into deflation. In 2004, French and Italian GDP growth was under 2% and German growth in the last quarter of 2004 was fractionally negative; in 2005 first quarter data for Italy shows it to be slipping into recession.

In 2003, the IMF[5] reported that Germany, the locomotive of the EU economy, might soon join Japan in the deflation league.[6] Since 2000, Germany's GDP growth rate has been barely positive while France and Italy have fared little better. Germany and Italy experienced negative growth in the final quarter of 2004. In the Eurozone since 2000, inflationary pressure has gradually declined. For 2004, the Eurozone annual inflation rate was 1.7% – and only 1.4% when food end energy prices are excluded.[7] In 2003, in response to the Broad Economic Policy Guidelines (BEPG) issued by the Commission that year, UEAPME, the representative body of Europe's Small and Medium Size Enterprise issued an uncharacteristically strong warning:

> UEAPME recognises the importance of stable prices for the economy and the efforts made by the ECB in the past to ensure this. However, high inflation rates are not the problem at the moment and we ask the ECB to use the room for an interest rate reduction for a more proactive approach towards the monetary environment: Low levels of demand (private consumption and investments), decreasing oil prices and the strong Euro are reducing the pressure on inflation. High inflation differentials between member states make it necessary to rethink the inflation targets in order to avoid the danger of deflation at the lower end of the scale. If deflation happens, monetary policy will lose most of its instruments, therefore, everything has to be done in order to avoid it from the start.[8]

4.3 POLICY RESPONSES

Over the 2001–2003 downswing the ECB cut rates from 4.75% to 2%, where the rate still stands today. In contrast the more pro-active Federal Reserve Bank

---

[5]   See IMF (2003).

[6]   See Paul Krugman 'Stating the Obvious' May 27, 2003; also *The Economist*, 'Of debt, deflation and denial' Oct. 10, 2002.

[7]   See OECD Consumer Price Index, 30 March 2005.

[8]   UEAPME (*Union Européenne de l'Artisanat et des Petites et Moyennes Entreprises*) 'European Commission's proposal for the BEPG 2003 or shortcomings of Europe's economic policy; Position paper on Broad Economic Policy Guidelines 2003', Brussels, 3–6–03.

(the US Central Bank or 'the Fed' for short) cut rates in the downswing from 6% to 1%.[9] Moreover, the ECB has refused to budge despite evidence from the OECD that the Eurozone's monetary transmission mechanism is slower than in the US; ie, that a *more* proactive monetary policy is required in the Eurozone to achieve the same effect as in the US.[10]

The problem is not merely that the ECB is too cautious. Many economists consider the ECB's narrow focus on inflation as one reason for the stagnation in the Eurozone core states since 2001[11]. (By contrast, the US Fed focuses on getting the balance right between low inflation, low unemployment and growth.) Germany, France and Italy account for the greatest part of Eurozone output. While there is a certainly a case for looser monetary policy—— particularly when core Eurozone states are at risk of deflation – monetary relaxation alone will not guarantee growth.

Monetary policy in the Eurozone is set centrally by the ECB. By contrast, fiscal policy is set both at EU level – the EU budget – and, far more importantly, at the level of the individual member states. The EU budget is capped by the 1992 Maastricht Treaty at 1.24% of combined EU Gross National Income (GNI)[12], while actual expenditure is slightly less (1% of GNI) and the bulk of the money goes on the Common Agricultural Policy (CAP) and structural funds. Moreover, the EU's annual budget must balance by law. This makes the central budget quite useless for counter-cyclical policy, the burden of adjustment falling entirely on fiscal policy in the member states.[13]

Fiscal expenditure by the member states is constrained by the provisions of the Maastricht Treaty (Article 104.3) and the Stability and Growth Pact (SGP), enshrined in the Amsterdam Treaty of 1997. According to SGP rules, Eurozone states should not allow their budget deficit to rise above 3% other than in very exceptional circumstances; total public sector borrowing (PSB) should not exceed 60% of GDP and national authorities should aim at budgetary balance or surplus over the business cycle. The '3/60 rule' was enshrined in the Treaty

[9] Since then the rate has risen to by steps to 2.75% (March 2005).

[10] See Larry Elliot 'Brown needs to apply reverse thrust to Reagan theories' *The Guardian*, June 14, 2004.

[11] Detailed evidence, including figures on the weakening of Eurozone domestic demand, is given in Bibow (2004). For a critical discussion of the SGP, see Arestis and Sawyer (2002, 2003).

[12] When EMU was first discussed in the 1970s, the Chief Advisor to the Treasury, Sir Donald MacDougall, suggested the EU budget should be about 7% of combined GDP if it was to be used as an effective instrument in correcting the business cycle (MacDougall Report, 1977). The figure of 1.27% was fixed at the Berlin summit of 1999 for the perspective period 2000–2006. The GNI equivalent of this percentage is 1.24%.

[13] See Iain Begg (2004).

as a target to be met for joining the euro. Arguably, the rules could be justified as a sop to the currency markets in the run-up to EMU. By contrast, the 1997 Stability and Growth Pact (SGP) made the Maastricht economic rules permanent and enabled the Commission to take action against offending states.[14] In short, fiscal policy in the Eurozone is severely constrained at EU level by the size of the budget and the legal requirement that it must always balance; at member-state level, fiscal policy is constrained by the SPG.

Because fiscal policy is purely the responsibility of individual member states, the European Commission attempts to co-ordinate fiscal goals by means of the Broad Economic Policy Guidelines (BEPG). These were first issued in 2000; they are meant to provide a set of short- and medium-term policy goals for Eurozone countries and are revised periodically. (In parallel, employment policy is meant to be co-ordinated by means of the European Employment Strategy, or EES.) Although the BEPG do stress worthy aims such as improving infrastructure, raising employment, investing in life-long education and improving social inclusion, the BEPG are no more than 'guidelines'. The adoption of the Open Method of Co-ordination (OMC) adds to the 'softness' with which member states act.[15] The overall result is a double co-ordination failure. First, there is little co-ordination of fiscal policy between member-states; secondly, since the ECB is shielded by statute from consultation with member-state Governments, there is negligible co-ordination of monetary and fiscal policy.[16]

It has been apparent since 2001 that, in the trough of a business cycle, budgetary deficits in the core countries would exceed 3%. In 2003, first Germany and then France and Italy were reprimanded by the European Commission; legal proceedings were started at the European Court of Justice (ECJ), which in 2004 threw the case back to the Council where a majority of members voted against sanctions. Given that the Maastricht Treaty and SGP are embedded in the Constitutional Treaty, it has become ever more necessary to come up with a 'workable' SGP or else drop any pretence of making it legally binding. At the time of writing, Finance Ministers of the EU-25 have reached a patch-up compromise over Luxemburg's very modest proposals for reforming

---

[14] Determining whether a country has breached the rules is one of the functions of ECOFIN, the Council of Economic and Finance Ministers of all EU member states. Full ECOFIN meetings are usually preceded by a meeting of 'narrow' ECOFIN; ie, Eurozone member states.

[15] Sapir (2003), whose views on EU macroeconomic policy are quite different from those presented here, agrees that the BEPG and the 'open method' of co-ordination are very weak tools.

[16] Since Nice, the ECB President can sit in on meetings of the Eurozone meetings of ECOFIN; hence one might speak of 'nominal' co-ordination.

the Pact. The ECB and many finance ministers who are members of the Eurozone's ECOFIN, meanwhile, continue to oppose any relaxation of the SGP rules. In the words of William Keegan:

> The debate about the degree to which the Stability and Growth Pact should be relaxed goes on and some progress, though not enough, is being made against the Neanderthal, pre-Keynesian views that still dominate the discussion.[17]

In short, economic policy in the Eurozone states is constrained today by a variety of rules and practices, sometimes referred to as the 'Brussels' consensus:

- A single monetary authority at EU level, the ECB, which is not pro-active, and whose 'credibility' depends on an exclusively anti-inflationary posture;
- the rejection of a centralised fiscal authority in favour of a small EU budget subject to annual balance;
- at member-state level, the Maastricht-SGP rules which cap public borrowing and keep fiscal policy too tight in a downturn and over the business cycle;
- weak fiscal co-ordination between states, no co-ordination between monetary and fiscal policy and the absence of a long-term growth strategy;
- the belief that supply-side measures alone, ranging from flexible labour markets to higher R&D expenditure, will bring private investment-led growth.

4.4 THE EU'S ECONOMIC ASYMMETRY

> *The head of the European Monetary Institute itself .. Alexandre Lamfalussy, in charge of technical preparations for the single currency – in an Appendix to the report of the Delors Committee of which he himself was a member – argued that 'if the only global macroeconomic tool available within EMU would be the common monetary policy implemented by the European central banking system', the outcome would be 'an unappealing prospect'. If monetary union was to work, he explained, a common fiscal policy was essential.*
>
> **(Perry Anderson 'The Europe to Come' in Gowan and Anderson [eds] (1997: 132)**

Figure 4–2: Early Warning

The theoretical underpinnings of these arrangements, much influenced at design stage by the *Bundesbank*, are strictly orthodox – or neo-liberal to use the

---

[17] See William Keegan 'Franc is gone but it's still old Europe' *The Observer*, 20 February 2005.

contemporary phrase. The Brussels Consensus[18] has been aptly described as the application of the Washington Consensus to Europe, a set of principles emphasising, first, balanced budgets and price stability attainable through shrinking the size of the state; and secondly, structural reforms opening the economy to international competition. In the case of the EU, the institutional arrangements of the currency union are uniquely conservative. Power is concentrated in the hands of a fully independent central monetary authority; a Competition Commissioner enforces economic liberalisation; fiscal policy is left to the member-states and constrained by the SGP; and 'accountability' depends at union-level on a Parliament lacking the power either to shape the institutional arrangements of economic governance or to initiate policy.

The basic economic logic of the consensus can be summarised as follows. The ECB controls inflation at EU level through the interest rate instrument. (The ECB's 'two-pillar' policy also includes a money supply target for M3, although this has recently been modified.) Inflation is targeted by statute to remain below 2%, a rate considered to be the irreducible 'core rate' of inflation. Equally, it is assumed that monetary policy has no long-term effect on the real economy. According to this reasoning, monetary policy cannot affect unemployment since this must settle at its 'natural rate', while monetary policy affects growth only indirectly by keeping inflation and thus inflationary expectations under control. Since there is only one goal (low inflation) and one instrument (the repo-rate), the ECB cannot have an exchange rate policy; ie, the underlying theory is that once the 'core' interest-rate is attained, the correct exchange rate will automatically be achieved by market forces.[19]

Nevertheless, because of the one-size-fits-all nature of monetary policy in a monetary union, the monetary instrument must be complemented by fiscal policies tailored to meet the needs of member-states. Differences arise between member states because they are of differing size and strength or because their business cycles differ, or else because unpredictable outside shocks affect them in different ways (what economists call *asymmetric* shocks). According to the theory of the optimum currency area, it is desirable to centralise a part of national budgets at European level, so that if a shock occurs, an automatic fiscal

---

[18] Excellent characterisations of the 'Brussels Consensus' appear in Tamborini (2004) and Fitoussi and Saraceno (2004); the latter refer to the Brussels-Frankfurt-Washington (BFW) Consensus. Also see Irvin (2003), Irvin (2004) and Irvin (2005).

[19] Not only is such a view untenable theoretically since foreign exchange markets regularly overshoot, it means in practice that the ECB has adopted a policy of 'benign neglect' of the euro, allowing it to appreciate strongly against the US dollar. In this, the ECB accommodates the Bush administration's 'benign neglect' of the dollar, justified on the grounds that the free market can be left to solve the US external account deficit.

An **asymmetric shock** is one that does not affect all members of a currency area in the same way. The theory of an optimal currency area suggests the need for a central fiscal authority to compensate for such shocks by means of automatic transfers – if Michigan (USA) suddenly goes into recession, it pays less Federal tax and receives more unemployment benefit. In the absence of a central authority, Michigan would have to mobilise the resources itself – a task which would be made much harder if Michigan's power to borrow was constrained by the Centre.

The **free rider problem** arises where one state uses a public good without paying its fair share. This would become a problem in public finance if, for example, Italy were greatly to increase its euro-denominated public borrowing. Such borrowing, although not inflationary in a manner comparable to borrowing from the Central Bank, would eventually push up euro-interest rates. In effect, Italy might increase its growth by borrowing, but rising interest rates would have a contractionary effect on all other members of the Eurozone. This is the rationale for setting borrowing limits on member-states. Capping annual deficits is one way of limiting borrowing, although even the Delors Report (1989) avoided setting such caps. A good theoretical discussion is De Grauwe (1992).

Figure 4–3: Asymmetric Shocks and Free Riders

transfer can take place to the affected region.[20] (Such a mechanism exists in the United States where if, for example, the state of Michigan is affected by deep recession, compensation funds will flow from the Federal Government). This principle was first taken into account in the MacDougall Report (1977), which had recommended establishing a federal budget equivalent to 5–7% of combined member-states' GDP. However, even MacDougall's very modest degree of fiscal federalism was quite unacceptable to the bankers on the Delors Committee.

If asymmetric shocks are a potential problem, an even greater problem was thought to be that of member-states adopting discretionary fiscal policies. If member states were left entirely free to pursue their own fiscal policy – so the orthodox account goes – they would spend freely, spreading inflation and leaving others to foot the bill; ie, they would become 'free riders'. The centre must impose discipline in the form of a Pact.[21] The SGP restriction on the budget deficit – that it cannot exceed 3% and must balance over the cycle – serves two aims. First, in the short-to-medium term, it constrains member-states to a fiscal stance that leaves no room for discretion; ie, macroeconomic balance over the cycle is governed entirely by the action of automatic stabilisers. (It is the orthodox view that because of the nature of fiscal lags, discretionary

---

[20] See Musgrave (1959); also see Kenen (1995).

[21] The Delors Committee was reluctant to impose fiscal limits on member-states' budgets, although such limits were though necessary to qualify for EMU. It was only in the mid-1990s that the Maastricht qualification rules were re-interpreted to apply after EMU.

fiscal policy often makes the business cycle worse and thus is best abandoned.) Secondly, in the longer-term, the zero budget balance requirement ensures that the size of public debt falls to zero; in other words, that the state – because it can neither borrow nor print money, and is gradually compelled by tax competition to lower taxes – is forced to contract. This division of labour between a strong ECB and fiscally weak member-states provides a 'well-behaved' policy environment in which growth can take place.

In the world described above, deficient demand and unemployment cannot arise; ie, this is essentially the pre-Keynesian world of neo-classicist economics. Rather, insofar as the 'natural' rate[22] of unemployment is exceeded, unemployment arises either because inflationary expectations lead to unrealistic wage demands or else because wage markets are 'inflexible'; ie, wage bargains are too strongly influenced by trade union bargaining at national or regional level. In consequence, much of the debate about the Eurozone's poor performance has concentrated on structural obstacles to the smooth functioning of the free market; notably, labour market rigidities, a welfare regime that discourages work, burdensome taxes on enterprise and so on.

According to the orthodox theory, such problems are all different faces of the same coin; they can be cured by a prolonged period of unemployment that dampens inflationary expectations and weakens trade unions. A corollary is that unemployment may also rise because of excessive charges borne by employers leading to a loss of 'international competitiveness'; however, this too is curable since contracting the state removes the need for such costs. If one completes this picture with trade liberalisation (already achieved), services liberalisation (nearly achieved), a competition Commissioner to ensure the liquidation of public monopolies such as power and railways, longer working hours, lower pensions and so on, then in the words of one commentator "the European Union appears as the neo-liberals' ideal world".[23]

For ordinary mortals, though, this world turns out to be one of unemployment and very low growth in the core states – hardly a world designed to foster the knowledge economy, sustainable growth and social cohesion envisaged in Lisbon 2000. Since the institutions of the European Union were not very democratic to begin with, prolonged unemployment and growing pressure to prune the state, cut welfare, privatise pensions and so on invariably lead to a crisis of legitimacy. This is the crisis Europe faces today. In short, although creation of the euro may be symbolic of the rise of an

---

[22] This 'natural rate' is usually called the Non-Accelerating Inflation Rate of Unemployment' (NAIRU). Orthodox theory posits that although actual unemployment may temporarily differ, in the long term unemployment must settle at NAIRU.

[23] See EPOC (2005) Chap 3, p 17 (prepared by Malcolm Sawyer).

alternative model to that of US capitalism, the completion of EMU is unfinished and unbalanced; without substantial modification, the economic foundation of Europe cannot sustain the European Social Model.[24]

4.5   WHY WAS MAASTRICHT SO CONSERVATIVE?

It is important to distinguish between the advantages of the euro, and the disadvantages of the Eurozone's economic architecture. Creating a common currency not merely reduces transactions costs, making cross-border dealings more transparent and facilitating economies of scale; crucially, a single currency protects the Eurozone from speculative attack by powerful financial markets. This is a considerable accomplishment. By contrast, because of the 'bankers' orthodoxy' inherent in the Maastricht-SGP rules, the full advantages of the euro cannot be realised – which is what is meant by saying that the euro cannot be 'completed'.

The Maastricht economic rules were first conceived in the late 1988–89s at a time when the world was emerging from a period of serious inflation and the ratio of public debt to GDP in many EU countries had grown alarmingly. Having secured the passage of the Single European Act in 1986, the President of the European Commission, Jacques Delors, set up a committee largely composed of central bankers with himself as Chairman to report on the creation of a single currency or Economic and Monetary Union (EMU). Delors knew that the Germans – in particular the *Bundesbank* – was opposed to EMU, and that as a matter of political expediency the architecture of EMU would have to be strictly orthodox. His report was approved by the Council of Ministers' meeting in Madrid in June 1989.[25] But it took the sudden collapse of East Germany to spur political agreement on the euro between Mitterand and Kohl. The fear of a reunited Germany led to French support for a form of EMU carefully designed to assuage the fears of German bankers.

It is against this background that the drafting of the Maastricht Treaty's economic rules must be understood. Moreover, public finances in most of the then 12 member-states had deteriorated. In the early 1980s, countries such as Belgium, Greece, Italy and Ireland had public debt stocks in excess of 100% of GDP and current budget deficits as high as 10% of GDP. Broadly speaking, Germany and the financially stable northern European countries were

---

[24] A number of recent books, perhaps prematurely, have painted the European model in glowing terms relative to the US variant of capitalism; see for example Haseler (2004), Rifkin (2004).

[25] See European Commission (1989) 'Delors Report'; the report was drafted by the Italian economist and Deputy-Director of the Italian Central Bank, Tommaso Padoa-Schioppa.

concerned that their southern European neighbours might continue to run 'unsustainable' budget deficits for which they, the richer countries, might have to pay (see Figure 4–3 on the 'free rider' problem.)

Secondly, economic ideology of the day was still strongly affected by the anti-Keynesian climate of Thatcher-Reagan years and by the belief that economic management should rely on rules-based monetary policy applied by independent central banks.[26] Governments' sole concern – so ran the Washington-inspired orthodoxy – should be to 'get prices right'; discretionary fiscal policy was strongly discouraged and the monetarist doctrine of the Chicago School had gained worldwide influence. The drafters of the Maastricht Treaty were not necessarily monetarists, but like all bankers they believed in 'sound money'.

Thirdly, for two decades policy makers have been obsessed with maintaining the confidence of powerful international financial markets. This first became apparent in 1982 when in France the newly elected Mitterand Government tried to use Keynesian measures to boost growth and employment, precipitating a speculative attack on the franc. Subsequently, France focussed on keeping its currency strong: the *franc fort* policy. Delors himself had been Finance Minister at the time; more than most, he recognised the potential havoc that could result from losing the confidence of financial markets.

The year in which the Maastricht Treaty was signed, 1992, was also a year of chaos in the foreign exchange markets. Currency traders judged that public finances in some countries were overstretched, that inflation might result and therefore that those currencies were vulnerable. The Italian lira was vulnerable because government borrowing was thought far too high; whether the French could bring down their (far smaller) deficit was uncertain. Sterling was vulnerable because it was thought to have joined the Exchange Rate Mechanism (ERM) at too high an exchange rate.

In Britain, the memory of 'Black Wednesday' in September 1992 still rankles. Over a three-day period and at a cost to the Bank of England of nearly £10b in reserves, hedge-fund speculators forced sterling out of the ERM and the Chancellor, Norman Lamont, out of office. The franc and the lira also came under attack. France managed a successful exchange rate adjustment while staying within the ERM and Italy, although forced to devalue, managed to

---

[26] For a succinct summarisation of the 'New Consensus Macroeconomics', see Arestis and Sawyer (2003). Particularly apt is the notion that "the essence of Say's Law holds, namely, that effective demand does not play an independent role in the (long-term) determination of the level of economic activity, and adjusts to underpin the supply-side determined level of economic activity (which itself corresponds to NAIRU). Shocks to the level of demand can be met by variations in the rate of interest to ensure that inflation does not develop (if unemployment falls below NAIRU)." (p 3.)

rejoin the ERM's outer band. The crucial point is that the restrictive Maastricht rules were designed at least in part to assuage financial markets and manage an effective – if unnecessarily lengthy – transition towards the adoption of a common currency in January 1999. They were 'convergence conditions'; it was not until 1997 that they were carved in stone.

In Germany, a folk memory of inflation was coupled with a particular attachment to the *Deutschmark* as a symbol of national recovery. In the post-war context, the stability of the new currency was identified with the miracle years. In the words of one writer, a precondition to entry into the euro was:

'... to ensure at very least that the new currency is 'as hard as' the Mark, by insisting that the institutional arrangements for EMU are identical to those applying for the Mark: independent bank, stability culture, Frankfurt Headquarters... Embracing the euro is thus seen not as an enthusiastic strategy for economic advancement, but rather as a collective price to be paid for economic re-unifications.[27]

From 1993 until 1999, the Exchange Rate Mechanism (ERM) kept Europe's currencies together with reasonable success. But the separate currencies were still vulnerable to speculative attack. Once the currencies locked together to form the euro on 1 January 1999, the risk of financial attack effectively ceased. This is because the euro, like the dollar, is so widely used that a successful financial attack – eg, one forcing a significant devaluation in the short term – cannot be mounted.[28] Nevertheless, this point was ignored when adopting the SGP. Politicians and functionaries have continued to follow the same orthodox strictures. This vital point about the euro – that stability does not derive from any simple notion of 'fiscal rectitude' – is almost entirely absent from public discourse. It is perhaps not surprising that so many Europeans should agree that balancing the books keeps the currency strong. Few politicians dare challenge what seems a commonsense principle of household budgeting. Yet as every first-year economics student learns, while the annual budget of the local baker or grocer needs to balance, that of Government does not, particularly when the economy is in the doldrums and unemployment is high.

A related point concerns 'rules and discretion'. The decline in Keynesian economics has been accompanied by the belief that politicians should have as little discretion as possible in setting fiscal and monetary policy; in economists'

---

[27] See Leaman (2001), p 20; Leaman further observes (p 64) in the years leading up to Germany's great hyper-inflation of 1922–23, the average annual borrowing requirement was 75% – in contrast to the 3% limit impose by the Maastricht Treaty.

[28] Of course if markets sense that the currency is overvalued then, in the absence of Central Bank intervention, markets can gradually force it downward.

jargon, that policy should be 'rules-determined'. A corollary of this view is that 'discretionary' policy leads to fluctuations and macro-economic instability, which in turn reduces growth. The particular lesson drawn is that national counter-cyclical policy can be left to 'automatic stabilisers'; ie, during a recession tax receipts fall more than government expenditure, enabling consumers to spend more and the economy to grow. The general lesson drawn, not surprisingly, is that reducing the size of the public sector will ease the strain on public finances and therefore improve stability and growth. Such views are widely accepted not just on the political centre-right but increasingly on the centre-left and across much of the economics profession[29]

4.6 ECONOMICS: BACK TO THE FUTURE?

Keynesian economics was not suddenly invalidated by the rise of Thatcher-Reagan monetarism of the 1980s. Indeed, it seems ironic that some of the most ardent practitioners of Keynesian policies today are to be found in the United States and Japan. A key plank in George W Bush's strategy to revive the US economy in the wake of the 'burst bubble' depression of 2001 was a huge tax cut designed to boost consumer spending and rekindle growth. Equally, the Japanese were converted to Keynesian deficit spending in the mid-1990s when it became apparent that lowering interest rates to zero was insufficient to spur private investment. By 2003, Japan's budget deficit was 6.5% of GDP, higher than that of the United States.

Keynes's fundamental point was not about 'pump priming' or even 'fine tuning', but rather about the role of the state in undertaking long-term investment designed to boost productivity and keep growth expectations buoyant. Such was the case during Europe's Marshall plan recovery, which gave rise to the German *wirtschaftswunder* and the French *trente glorieuses*. Europe's growth record of the 1950s and 60s was not merely – or even primarily – a matter of 'catching up'; rather, Europe grew because in its core countries, large investments were made not just in manufacturing but in social and economic infrastructure, as reflected in the growth of Europe's public sector share from under 30% in 1950 to roughly 40% two decades later. By contrast, in Britain in the mid-1970s, long-term investment lagged behind that of its continental neighbours, public infrastructure began a long decline and manufacturing investment stagnated.

[29] See for example Fatas, A and A Milhov (2003) for the case against fiscal discretion; there is a large and growing economics literature about the 'size of government', efficiency and growth. For an orthodox view by two leading economists at the EC in Brussels, see Martinez-Mongay and Sekkat (2004). For a journalistic account of 'the end of boom and bust' see Anatole Kaletsky 'Apolitical Economy' *Prospect*, May 2005.

Nor was average annual inflation of 3–4% in the industrialised countries a problem in the 1950s and 1960s: indeed, mild inflation had generally been considered an inducement to growth since it reduced companies' (and Governments') liabilities. But following dollar devaluation and the oil shock of 1973 – and again in 1979 – the West's industrial growth faltered and inflation rose. Arguably, had Lyndon Johnson not attempted to finance both his 'Great Society' programmes and the Vietnam War without raising taxes, Nixon's 'benign neglect' of the dollar, the crisis and dollar devaluation of 1971 and the ensuing collapse of fixed exchange rates might have been avoided.[30]

This aside on economic history is vital to understanding Europe's woes. Today, the US administration has once again adopted a policy of 'benign neglect' of the dollar, just as it did in the 1970s. Discounting the post-referendum blip, over the past several years the dollar has been allowed to depreciate by nearly 50% against the euro. Because most of the major trading countries in Asia have maintained a peg to the dollar (even if China has recently moved to a 'managed float'), the brunt of trade adjustment has fallen on the Eurozone.[31] The ECB, too, appears to be following a policy of 'benign neglect'. There has been little attempt to counter euro appreciation; instead, the ECB continues to focus exclusively on its inflationary remit. The irony is that the euro was intended to protect Europe against the reluctance of the US to follow responsible policies.

For nearly two decades after the Bretton Woods Conference of 1944, floating exchange rates had been unpopular because of their association with the competitive devaluations of the inter-war years. As William Keegan has observed:

> Benign neglect of the dollar in the 1970s was a major factor behind the decision by West German Chancellor Helmut Schmidt and French President Valery Giscard d'Estaing to construct 'a zone of monetary stability in Europe'. This led to the European Monetary System (more popularly known as the exchange rate mechanism) in 1979, without which the Great Leap Forward to the European single currency (1999) would almost certainly not have taken place.[32]

[30] First, there was a realignment of exchange rates against the dollar under the 'Smithsonian Agreement' of 1971; this was followed by the shift to a floating exchange rate system in 1973.

[31] China's recent decision to move to a 'managed float' against a basket of currency has hardly effected its dollar exchange rate. Interestingly, though, China willingness to use its trade surplus to purchase US paper has pushed down US long-term bond yields; in turn, this has constrained the ability of the US Fed to slow the rise in US house prices by pushing up short term interest rates.

[32] See William Keegan, 'Shock as Continent cut adrift by Snow' *The Observer*, November 21, 2004.

Economic theory tells us that under a floating exchange rate regime, monetary policy becomes more powerful than (Keynesian) fiscal policy – a principle dear to the heart of most bankers and Treasury officials. But this principle alone does not explain the ascendancy of monetarism in the 1970s and 1980s.

In the early 1970s, as inflation soared and workers attempted to defend their real wage position, economic growth faltered and social unrest grew. In 1976, following a run on sterling which forced Britain's Labour Government into the arms of the IMF, Jim Callaghan had famously repudiated Keynesianism by declaring that no government could 'spend its way out of recession'. The recession of the late 1970s was one of the factors explaining why Jimmy Carter lost power in the US while, in Britain, Callahan's government faced the 'winter of discontent'. The new decade saw radically conservative governments come to power in both countries with a similar agenda: to reduce trade union power and shrink the size of the state.

Other European countries appeared to resist Thatcherite policies for a time, but their Central Banks reacted to the oil shocks by applying the monetary brakes and squeezing credit. As is now obvious, the Keynesian tradition – so influential in the US and Britain after the war – was intellectually less well-rooted in 'continental' Europe where pro-growth, pro-union traditions were more anchored in the politics of the post-war settlement. This was particularly true in Germany where 'global steering' (as Keynesian demand management was called) was not introduced until 1967 when the SPD became senior partner in a coalition government and passed the Stability and Growth Act (*Gesetz zur Förderung der Stabilität und des Wachstums der Wirtschaft*).[33] Keynesian policies were largely abandoned when fixed exchange rates broke down in the early 1970s. Ironically, the name of the Act was borrowed 30 years later for a decidedly anti-Keynesian Pact.

4.7   THE 'WASHINGTON CONSENSUS'

A further shock to the world economy occurred when, within weeks of the 1979 oil crisis, an interest rate rise engineered by Paul Volcker at the US Fed sent world interest rates soaring. The interest-rate spike set off a chain of events, including the Mexican debt default of 1981, which tipped much of Latin America and Africa into recession and resulted in an unserviceable debt burden. Just when poor countries found themselves facing huge interest repayments,

---

[33] Fritz Schäffer, the West German Federal finance minister from 1949 to 1957, explicitly rejected the notion of Keynesian deficit financing. 'Global Steering' was enshrined in the West German 'Stability and Growth Act' of 1967 (*Gesetz zur Förderung der Stabilität und des Wachstums der Wirtschaft*) ; See Tim Congdon (2004) 'Will the EU's Constitution rescue its Currency' *EU Constitutional Briefing Paper No 6,* London: The Bruges Group.

international credit for these countries dried up, thus forcing them into IMF receivership. The IMF mantra of 'deregulation, deflation and devaluation' became the basis for what would be known a decade later as the Washington Consensus.

The Thatcher-Reagan governments, aided by the IMF, helped spread not just the gospel of monetarism, but of 'supply side' economics: the notion that more can be accomplished by allowing free-market forces to discipline workers and removing barriers to entrepreneurship than by Keynesian-style demand management. Although the intellectual basis of this doctrine was always suspect, supply-side economics gained widespread currency, not least amongst economists in Brussels. It finds expression chiefly in the notions that concentrating on 'labour market flexibility' can cure unemployment and that a demand-management is largely irrelevant and can be left entirely to 'automatic' fiscal stabilisers. These twin doctrines lie at the heart of the Brussels Consensus.

One further factor seems to have played a role in securing the victory of Europe's 'sound money' polices, notably, the success of Clinton's deficit reduction programme after 1992. Deficit reduction is merely another name for orthodox public finance. It became a policy aim of the Clinton administration largely because of the relative power of Wall Street and the Treasury. Anybody who doubts the power of the Treasury (Ministry of Finance) and Central Bankers to determine economic policy in Washington, London or Berlin should study the influence of Alan Greenspan on the first Clinton Administration or of the *Bundesbank* on the drafting of the Maastricht Treaty and the SGP.[34]

What is surprising about deficit reduction in the US under Clinton is that instead of leading to lower growth, it appeared to increase it, thus causing government revenue to rise more quickly than expenditure and producing budget surplus – hailed by some as Clinton's greatest achievement. It can be argued that by lowering long-term bond yields, deficit-reduction fomented growth by forcing US banks to expand credit to the private sector.[35] The point is simply that in the 1990s, while some economists questioned the wisdom of Maastricht and the SGP, supporters of Maastricht could point out that deficit reduction in the United States had been accompanied by a decade of strong growth. And if one claimed that US deficit reduction could not be said to explain US growth, the retort was that neither could EU deficit reduction be said to explain EU stagnation. The answer, in broad terms, is that while deficit reduction in the early Clinton years took place against the background of an economy buoyed by accelerating growth of high technology and a bullish stock

---

[34] On the US see Stiglitz (2003); on the UK see Keegan (2004); on Germany see Leaman (2001).
[35] An excellent discussion of the matter appears in the early chapters of Stiglitz (2003).

market, financial stringency in Europe appears to have fed upon – and contributed to – pessimism about growth.

In the chapter that follows, I return to the Maastricht story and consider in detail the debate over the Stability and Growth Pact. Can the Pact be reformed or should it be scrapped altogether? If it is scrapped, what should take its place? Should the EU adopt a UK-style 'Golden Rule' or should it attempt more radical reform? Should the European Central Bank be restructured? In short, the chapter provides a highly critical assessment of the current economic architecture of the Eurozone and argues that, sooner rather than later, radical surgery is required.

CHAPTER 5

Minor or Major Surgery?

Fiscal policy is the incomplete chapter in the macroeconomic arrangements agreed at Maastricht. The Stability and Growth Pact (SGP) was an attempt to patch it up, but it failed. We need to understand: why? (S. Collignon, 2004, p 1)

5.1 Eight Holes in the SGP

Germany, France and Italy are the key countries that have been unable to live within the narrow confines of the much-debated SGP. Attempts by the Commission in 2001 and 2002 to make marginal adjustments to the SGP proved unsuccessful. The Commission's Financial Affairs Commissioner, Joaquín Almunia, admitted as much by calling in Autumn 2004 for proposals that would 'clarify' the SGP and allow member states to run budget deficits in excess of 3% when experiencing a prolonged period of sluggish growth. A compromise solution defining 'exceptional circumstances' was agreed during the Luxembourg presidency in March 2005, but the basic rules remained fundamentally unchanged. Below are eight inter-related criticisms of Maastricht and the Stability and Growth Pact (SGP).[1]

a) **The 2% ECB inflation ceiling is too low**: Aside from the fact that the ECB's mandate is too restrictive, its 2% inflation ceiling is too low, particularly since the ECB aims to keep inflation in the range 0–2%. As argued in an influential paper by Ackerloff, Dickens and Perry (1996) and again in Wyplosz (2002), very low inflation reduces wage market flexibility and thus economic efficiency. Because money wages are generally inflexible downwards, under conditions of very low inflation, wage differentials cannot adjust to sectoral or regional differences in productivity growth.

[1] Standard academic texts on the SGP are Brunila, A, Buti, M and D Franco [eds] (2001), and Buti, M and D Franco (2005). For a trenchant critique see Wyplosz (2002).

b) **The numbers are arbitrary**: The 3% budget deficit and 60% public borrowing figures are arbitrary limits. These figures are not underpinned by any economic logic; rather, they represent a conservative 'guess' of what limits the financial markets would accept in the early 1990s.[2] This argument has been made by a number of authors; eg, Buiter *et al*, 1993. In 2004 the US trade deficit was 5.3% of GDP; in Japan the 2003 deficit was over 8% and the stock of public sector borrowing represented over 80% of GDP – but in neither of these countries is a dangerous acceleration in inflation likely. Indeed, Japan in 2005 is still struggling to escape deflation; ie, falling prices.

c) **Budgetary limits are no longer necessary**: The rationale for Maastricht was to reassure financial markets and minimise the risk of speculative attack on EU currencies in the run-up to EMU, particularly the weaker ones: eg, lira, peseta, drachma etc. Once the single currency was in place, the risk disappeared. Since there is only one central bank, no Eurozone country can cause inflation by printing money to finance a budget deficit.[3] Nor is there any evidence that government borrowing to finance a deficit 'crowds out' private investment by an equal amount.

d) **The budget deficit is not clearly defined**: The drafters of the Treaty make no distinction between 'headline' and 'structural' budget deficits (the latter netted of cyclical components), or the current and capital budget. The 'basic' deficit, that net of interest payments, is not mentioned. It is unclear whether Maastricht is compatible with a 'golden rule'; ie, maintaining structural budget balance while borrowing for public investment. Because of its vagueness, the Treaty's provisions are nearly impossible to interpret in a court of law.

e) **Attaining budget balance over the cycle is deflationary**: The (implicit) provision that a member state's budget should balance over the cycle is strongly deflationary. Given a deficit limit of 3% in the downswing, to achieve a balanced budget over the cycle implies running a 3% surplus or more in the upswing. Where public non-discretionary investment is included in the budget, this would imply large cuts in expenditure in the good years, over and above 'automatic stabiliser' cuts. Moreover, under a budget balance rule and with monetisation (printing money) ruled out, there

---

[2]   In fact, the 3% deficit limit was arrived at by assuming that anything above a 60% ratio of debt to GDP was unsustainable and that the nominal rate of growth of GDP at the peak of the cycle would be 5%; hence if inflation were assumed to be 2%, the real rate of growth would finance a 3% deficit and public debt would be sustainable. Besides being arbitrary, this logic says nothing about why the budget should be in balance over the cycle as a whole.

[3]   In the bad old days, the Treasury could 'monetise' a budget deficit by selling Treasury paper to the Central Bank, in effect much the same as 'printing money'.

All economics students learn the basic (Keynesian) national income identity which says that National Income (Y) is equal to the sum of its component parts, private consumption (C), total investment (I), government current spending (G) and net exports (X-M); or:

1. $Y = C + I + G + (X-M)$

Moreover, income (Y) can either be consumed (C), saved (S) or taxed away (T); so;

2. $Y = C + S + T$

Substituting the right-hand side of (2) for Y in expression (1), we get:

3. $C + S + T = C + I + G + (X-M)$

Re-arranging expression (3) gives:

4. $(S-I) + (T-G) = (X-M)$

Expression 4 says that the (private) savings-investment balance (S-I) plus the government's budget balance (T-G) must be equal to the external (trade) balance (X-M). The International Monetary Fund is fond of arguing that if the savings-investment balance is in equilibrium (S-I = 0) but the external balance (X-M) is negative, this is **because** (T-G) is negative, hence government must reduce its spending. The difficulty with this view is that the above expressions are identities; nothing can be inferred about causation.

Figure 5–1: The Savings Balance Identity

appears to be no provision for expansion of the monetary base to correspond with real growth. Even the staunchest Friedmanite would blanch.

f) **Budget balance is not a policy variable**: economists will recognise the 'three balance' identity, which says that the sum of the domestic private savings gap and the domestic public savings gap (ie, the budget deficit) must equal the external current account deficit, or:

$$(S-I) + (T-G) = (X-M)$$

As Godley and Izurieta (2004) point out, the budget (T-G) can only cycle around zero as required by the SGP if the sum of the other two balances also cycles around zero. Take a simple example. If at full employment, the UK normally runs a small private savings surplus (S-I) but a larger deficit on external current account (X-M), it must run a budget deficit.[4] This conclusion follows irrespective of Government's fiscal stance. Reducing the

---

[4] Taking the example of Germany, another way of reading this is that given the constraint on Germany's budget deficit (T-G)* and its traditionally large private savings surplus (S-I), it must run a current account surplus (X-M); ie, that the German export-led-growth model is 'forced' by keeping deliberately maintaining an output gap and constraining domestic demand.

budget deficit to zero means, in essence, reducing absorption by reducing national income and employment. Proponents of the SGP ignore this basic economic logic.[5]

g) **The SGP implies reducing public debt to zero**: According to Maastricht and the SGP, public indebtedness should not exceed 60% of any country's GDP and the budget should be in balance over the business cycle as a whole. There are two problems here. First, it is unclear whether the debts ratio refers to gross or net debt.[6] Secondly, the '3/60' rule is logically inconsistent. As noted by De Grauwe (2003) amongst others, if the target budget deficit over the cycle is zero, then public sector debt in the long term must fall to zero.[7] This follows from the assumption that no new debt is incurred over the business cycle and old debt gradually matures and is repaid. Targetting zero public debt might make sense as a way of reducing indebtedness in the short term, but it makes no sense in the long term.

h) **Only the stock of debt matters**: As many economists have pointed out, the object of the Maastricht and SGP exercise was to prevent member states accumulating high and unserviceable indebtedness, thus creating a problem of moral hazard since the ECB might be forced to monetise one country's debt at the cost of inflation to all member-states.[8] The logical solution would be to monitor member states' indebtedness and its sustainability, the latter depending on whether the nominal interest rate was higher than the nominal rate of growth. The Centre for Economic Policy Reform in London has suggested that the SGP be replaced by a 'Sustainability Council' at EU-level whose function would be to monitor indebtedness.[9]

5.2 A GOLDEN RULE FOR THE EUROZONE?

An option widely promoted by Britain's current Chancellor, Gordon Brown, is to model a fiscal and monetary policy on that pursued by the Treasury and

---

[5] The orthodox economic retort is that full-employment income level is illusory; if the economy can be stabilised at a low, non-accelerating inflation rate, this is the 'natural rate' of employment level and the 'output gap' is zero. See for example Alesina et al (2001).

[6] Net debt is defined as Government's total liabilities minus total assets.

[7] This is because the steady state relationship between debt and the debt ratio (the share of public sector borrowing in GDP) is given by $d = b.gY$ where: d is the long-term deficit as a share of GDP; b is the long-term debt share in GDP and gY is the nominal growth rate of GDP. Rearranging, we get $b = d/gY$ – or that provided the long term deficit (d) is some very small number close to zero, b (the warranted PSB ratio) must be close to zero.

[8] 'Monetising' a member state's debt means that the ECB would lend money to the country in question, creating the extra euros itself rather than borrowing them. The likelihood of this happening is negligible since the ECB is prevented by statute from baling out member states.

[9] See CEPR (2003).

the Bank of England. On this logic, the SGP would follow the UK Treasury's 'Golden Rule'. The Rule calls for structural budgetary balance over the cycle. Public borrowing is allowed only for Government capital expenditure, and public indebtedness is capped at 60%. Like the ECB, the Bank of England's Monetary Policy Committee (MPC) has a 2% inflation target.[10] Unlike the ECB, however, the MPC's inflation target is 'symmetrical'; ie, if inflation falls below the target level, monetary policy must be eased. Britain uses monetary rather than fiscal fine-tuning of the economy and, as the above suggests, the policy is 'rules-driven'. Although the budget is required to balance over the cycle, there is no fixed limit on the size of the deficit during a recession.

One advantage of UK arrangements is that the 'independence' of the Bank of England is more apparent than real since the MPC (Monetary Policy Committee) includes economists and financial experts who are meant to reflect on how best to achieve the right balance between growth, low inflation and full unemployment. The Bank of England's *de facto* policy targets are broader than those of the ECB. As William Keegan has written 'The MPC is, in practice, a Keynesian manager of demand in the economy. But no such Keynesian management of demand takes place in Germany and France.'[11]

With regard to fiscal policy, whether a 'Golden Rule' approach provides a genuine alternative model to the SGP is arguable. For one thing, the fiscal corset is only slightly looser—the budget must still balance over the cycle. The only advantages of UK-style policy are the symmetrical nature of inflation target and the provision that investment can be financed by public borrowing. For another, the UK monetary and fiscal policy can be co-ordinated because The Bank of England and the Treasury are each national institutions. By contrast, the EU Central Bank operates at supranational level while responsibility for fiscal policy remains dispersed amongst the Finance Ministries of the member states. Adopting a Golden Rule would not resolve this fundamental design fault.

More importantly, how far is Britain's relatively favourable record of combining growth with low inflation explained by its institutional arrangements and rules-driven policies? Low inflation, whether in Britain or in the EU, has far more to do with globalisation and the explosion of cheap imports from developing countries like China than with Central Bank inflation targeting. As for growth, Britain has been fortunate in that aggregate demand has remained high over the cycle because of increased Government spending

---

[10] Prior to the adoption of the HIPC measure of inflation in 2003, the inflation target was 2.5%.
[11] See William Keegan 'Why Europe's not working' *The Guardian*, May 24 2005.

on public services and buoyant private consumption.[12] By contrast, in the core Eurozone countries, consumers have reacted to the threat of a downturn by increasing domestic private saving. Britain's consumer spending is driven by several factors, which do not figure in the rest of the EU. One is that UK mortgages are tied to short-term interest rates – in contrast to the German *pfandbrief* or long-term mortgage bond; another is the widespread (and deregulated) use of credit cards.[13] At present, though, the 'golden rule' seems headed for trouble. Many economists in Britain have expressed concern about whether the continued expansion of household indebtedness underlying the growth of consumption demand is sustainable,[14] a concern borne out by the slowdown of spending in 2005. At the time of writing, forecasts for the growth of UK GDP in 2005 are being lowered from 3 percent to 1.5–2.0 percent. This means that Treasury revenues will decrease and the budget deficit will grow. More ominously, unemployment is rising – on one estimate, it could reach two million by 2007.[15]

Because the Golden Rule is in danger of being breached, the Treasury appears to have shifted the goalposts by announcing that the current economic cycle began not in 1999 as previously claimed, but in 1997. The years 1997–99 – the first two years of the new Labour government – were years of low spending and financial surplus in which the Chancellor was building his 'prudent' reputation with the financial markets. By stretching it from 1999–2005 to 1997–2005, the Chancellor has guaranteed that the budget will balance over the current cycle. That's all very well, but here's the rub. The economy appears to have peaked in 2005 at a time when the budget is still in deficit. To make the budget balance over the next cycle, Britain would need to be running a surplus now.[16] It is clear that even if the Golden Rule is met for the cycle period which is ending, it will not be met over the next cycle unless public spending is curtailed or taxes are raised. But a cut in public spending in the coming years would not only blow New Labour's modernisation plans out of the water; either a cut or a tax rise would help push the economy into

---

[12] The reader should note that in 2005, public service spending has only just regained its 1997 level when New Labour came to power.

[13] According to Adams (2004), Britain accounts for 75% of total credit card debt in the EU. See Adams, T (2004) 'Give Me Some Credit' *The Observer*, 18 April 2004.

[14] According to Alex Izurieta of the Judge Institute in Cambridge, in 2004 the UK flow of net lending as a percentage of personal income reached an unprecedented level of 17%; he considers a sustainable level to be 5%, implying a fall in net lending equivalent to 12% of disposable income. If this fall happened quickly, it would trigger a severe recession. See Godley and Izurieta (2004).

[15] See Patrick Hoskins in *The New Statesman*, 25 July 2005.

[16] See Heather Stewart 'Golden Brown?' *The Observer*, 24 July 2005.

recession. More generally, Britain's failure even under the most prudent of Chancellors to iron out the business cycle using automatic fiscal stabilisers is a clear warning to those in Brussels who preach the virtues of fiscal automaticity.

In short, although UK macroeconomic arrangements may at first sight seem preferable, whether Britain's success can be credited to the policies of the Treasury and the Bank of England is debatable. Over the period 1999–2005, UK growth has thrived on greatly increased public spending on health and education, buoyant consumer demand, consumer credit underwritten by steadily rising asset prices and foreign direct investment (FDI) into London's financial services sector, a sector now larger than manufacturing. Such a model is difficult to export, particularly at a time when UK growth appears to have peaked and unemployment is once again rising.

5.3   THE SGP AND ENLARGEMENT

The recent accession places further pressure on the Union's economic arrangements; the EU acquired ten new members in mid-2004. Expansion was greeted with much fanfare, even if doubts remain in some quarters about its wisdom. Setting aside geo-political factors, the economic benefits to the core states of enlargement are ready access to a wider market and to cheap skilled labour. The other potential benefit is that high 'catch-up' growth will foster more growth in the core Eurozone, particularly since the new accession states are important trading partners for the core countries. The main costs are extra pressure on the structural funds and agricultural subsidies in the EU budget on the one hand, and on the other the danger that low rates of corporate taxation will draw firms towards the periphery, thus prolonging stagnation in the core states.[17]

Another difficulty is that the large accession countries – Poland, Hungary and the Czech Republic – have high unemployment and budget deficits, although most accession states have a low level of public indebtedness. In order to join the Eurozone, as they must, these countries have to fall into line with the 3% budget deficit rule of Maastricht and the SGP. As Charles Wyplosz (2003) has argued, the application of deflationary policies over a period of several years could bring about a severe recession in the Eurozone's newest members. Equally, the new entrants – particularly the ex-Eastern bloc countries

---

[17] The popular argument that core states 'lose' because of investment migration wrongly assumes a zero-sum game outcome. After all, a large a flow of US investment towards Europe in the post-war period was reflected in increased transatlantic trade, making the US richer, not poorer.

– all need finance to modernise their economic infrastructure. The Sapir Report (2003) recommended, *inter alia*, scrapping the Common Agricultural Policy and redirecting EU budgetary resources to this end; but the recommendation was unheeded.

Enlargement will continue to raise serious questions both for new members and for old. For the new states, a period of prolonged membership of the new Exchange Rate Mechanism (ERM 2) in order to gain Eurozone entry may prove very costly if tight Maastricht-style budgetary controls are imposed. By contrast, if ERM membership conditions are relaxed, the accession states may repeat the success of earlier lower-income entrants like Spain, Portugal and Ireland. All have achieved rapid 'catch-up' growth. Per capita income levels in Spain and Portugal have risen towards the EU-15 average; Ireland's is now well above the average and exceeds that of the UK.

5.4 BRUSSELS: A PAUCITY OF PRESCRIPTIONS

When one looks around for remedies, the prescriptions on hand are hardly encouraging. Although a few Finance Ministers are breaking ranks, ECOFIN appears to believe that sooner or later 'financial discipline' will create a suitable climate for investment and growth. The Brussels Consensus is increasingly seen to rest on little more than a quasi-mystical belief in sound money, akin to the economic philosophy of Herbert Hoover in the 1920s.

Various suggestions have been made about how the ECB might be reformed.[18] But while it is true that its anti-inflationary remit is absurdly narrow, monetary policy alone cannot jump-start the Eurozone economy. The first reason is that the ECB's interest rate is already close to zero in real terms. Because most gross fixed capital formation (investment) is relatively unresponsive to interest rates, cheap money alone cannot cure a recession. As Keynes famously argued, using interest rate policy in a recession is like pushing on a piece of string. A further problem is that monetary policy is subject to notoriously long and variable lags, one of the rare points on which on which Monetarists and Keynesians agree. Moreover, there is evidence that the lags are longer in the EU than in the USA; in short, using monetary policy as a central instrument of policy under current conditions in the EU is deeply problematic.[19]

Nor can exchange rate policy alone do the trick, even if the euro settles for some time at a more realistic rate against the dollar. This is not merely because

---

[18] See for example Fitoussi and Creel (2002).

[19] See Larry Elliot 'Brown needs to apply reverse thrust to Reagan theories' The Guardian, June 14, 2004.

management of the euro (at least downward) is seen as falling outside the ECB's remit. Ironically, Europeans savings have helped the US run huge twin deficits and pursue a policy of benign neglect of the dollar, spurring US investment and growth. Fundamentally, dollar adjustment can only take place if US resources are transferred from consumption into export-orientated investment; ie, if US consumers tighten their belts. But if US consumers are to consume less, Eurozone consumers (and others) must consume more to prevent world demand from contracting.

Assuming that the political will to adjust exists in the US – a heroic assumption[20] – adjustment will take time, caution and co-operation lest it set off a new US recession. Meanwhile, Europe is left largely on its own to shoulder the burden. It is unlikely Asia will accept major revaluation. First, Japan has suffered nearly 15 years of stagnation. Secondly, China is still a poor country and has no intention of drastically curtailing its export-led growth to accommodate the rich, still less of conceding to the sabre-rattling demands of the US Senate.[21] China's recent move to a 'managed float', although clever politics, is for the moment little more than economic window-dressing.[22] Ironically, one way for the EU to engineer a fall in the euro is by engaging in just the sort of 'fiscal irresponsibility' financial markets fear; ie, underwriting a long-term investment programme to create jobs such as that advanced in the Delors White Paper (EC, 1993), agreed at the Essen summit in 1994 but largely abandoned as being too expensive.

Does the Lisbon agenda provide a solution? There is much that is positive and important about the Lisbon (2000) process, not the least as set out in Wim Kok's (2004) report. The goals are well known, and for the most part admirable. It is crucial that the EU should stress quality of life factors including the environment, sustainable development, high levels of education and lifetime learning. Europe cannot become 'competitive' in areas promoting low 'flexible' wages; on the contrary, its comparative advantage lies in reproducing a highly educated workforce, productive precisely because of its social entitlements. Lisbon correctly promotes more employment (ie, less involuntary unemployment), greater labour mobility through better education, more portable pensions and so on.

---

[20] It has been argued that the external deficit of the United States could likely rise to perhaps 10% of GDP towards the end of the decade. See Godley, W and A Izurieta (2004) 'Deficits Which Need a Global Solution', *Financial Times*, 2 December 2004.

[21] See 'US and EU turn up the heat on China', *International Herald Tribune*, May 18, 2005.

[22] In fact, China would well revalue more seriously than at present. Its dollar reserves are huge, and by providing what is in effect a loan to the US it enables the US economy to continue living beyond its means.

While Lisbon goals are integral to social Europe, they do not add up to a growth strategy. The causality is more likely to run in the opposite direction. Only by readopting a Delors-style macroeconomic strategy focussed on investment-driven growth can the Lisbon goals be realised. Unfortunately, macroeconomics is absent from the Kok report; only two paragraphs are devoted to the subject.

5.5   RADICAL SURGERY: THE ECB

It should be clear from the above that marginal tinkering with economic institutions of the EU is not the answer. This is true not merely because the basic economic architecture of the EU is lopsided, but also because Eurozone growth is needed to make resources available to the faster integration of the accession countries as well as to offset the potential deflationary threat to world trade posed by the US current account deficit. In short, even were current economic arrangements not threatened by the EU's political crisis, serious surgery would be needed.

The first criticism of the ECB is that its anti-inflationary remit is too narrow, a view shared by many economists.[23] If the sole objective of the ECB is low inflation, this means the sole objective of EU-wide macroeconomic policy is inflation targeting. The objectives of monetary policy should surely be derived from the wider considerations. A fundamental requirement would be to require the ECB to balance the goals of growth, full employment and low inflation – as does the US Federal Reserve Bank. This can be done either by statute, or by changing the composition of the ECB's policy-making Board. For example, the Bank of England's Monetary Policy Committee (MPC) includes various independent advisors – including notable academics – and membership rotates at regular intervals. Although the MPC does not have as wide a remit as its US equivalent, it clearly does take wider policy goals into account.

The pursuit of multiple objectives by the ECB logically implies multiplying the policy instruments at its disposal. Thus, fiscal and exchange rate policies are required; since the ECB policy instruments are limited, it should logically co-ordinate its policies with member-states to achieve some balanced set of macro policies. Constitutionally, however, the ECB is required to operate in complete independence from member-states, or even from ECOFIN, the European Council's monthly meeting of Finance Ministers.

---

[23] For a particularly trenchant critique of the ECB, see John Grahl 'Europe's Inflexible Bank' *Le Monde Diplomatique*, July 2005.

A closely related matter is the ECB's lack of accountability.[24] Unlike the Fed or the Bank of England, the ECB Governing Council does not publish its minutes nor is any record available of members' voting record. This means that while the European Parliament can debate monetary matters, it has no means of establishing how and why the ECB reaches its conclusions. To a degree, this is mitigated by the fact that the ECB President now addresses the European Parliament and gives monthly press conferences. But the secretive nature of the ECB does little to reinforce its authority; rather, the perceived lack of democratic accountability detracts from its legitimacy. In the absence of an EU level fiscal authority to act as a counterbalance, the ECB is arguably more autonomous than the US Fed or even the *Bundesbank* before EMU.

The constitutional requirement that national governments must not influence the ECB reinforces the view of that body's perceived lack of democratic accountability, while at the same time making it nearly impossible to co-ordinate EU-level monetary policy with state-level fiscal policy. There is evidence that the Central Bank governors sitting on the Governing Council do vote according to the interests of the member-states they represent, rather than determining EU-wide interest.[25] If the evidence is correct, then the political justification collapses for maintaining a Chinese wall between the ECB, member-states and Parliament. There is no economic justification for this wall other than in a world of highly orthodox theory.

5.6 EVEN MORE RADICAL SURGERY FOR FISCAL POLICY

In contrast to the Sapir Report (2003) or the Kok Report (2004), the view advanced here is that the SGP should be scrapped. The institutional arrangements shaping EU macro-policy require major surgery. This is hardly surprising given the theoretical perspectives set out above. In the absence of genuine fiscal institutions at Union level, national fiscal policies should be designed as far as possible to achieve the economic objectives of national governments rather than set artificial limits on national deficits. In the words of Malcolm Sawyer, removing the fiscal straightjacket imposed on member-states 'by no means preclude[s] some co-ordination of national fiscal policies as such co-ordination should enhance, rather than detract from, the use of national fiscal policies.'[26]

[24] A very useful discussion of ECB transparency is contained in Willem Buiter, 'Alice in Euroland', speech at Southbank University, 15 December 1998. Even The Economist leader page argues that the ECB has an 'excessive degree of independence'; see The Economist, 'Less bashing please' July 16–22nd, 2005.

[25] The evidence from a study by Meade and Sheet (2001) is quoted in Arestis and Sawyer (2002).

[26] See EPOC (2005) Chap 3, p 4 (prepared by Malcolm Sawyer).

Two examples will help illustrate the need for flexible fiscal policy at national level. First, let us suppose that Ireland is experiencing rapid growth with 4% inflation and Germany is in recession with 0% inflation while the EU-wide rate of interest is 2%. This would mean that high-growth Ireland faced a negative real interest rate, while low-growth Germany faced a positive one; macroeconomic correction requires Ireland and Germany to apply quite different fiscal policies rather than merely to assume that a correction will be achieved through the operation of automatic stabilisers. Secondly, there is evidence that the link between GDP growth and the budget position varies considerably between member states. Buti et al (1997) find that a 1% slowdown in economic growth would raise member-states' budget deficit by 0.5% on average, but by up to 0.9% in the case of The Netherlands and Spain.[27] If a given slowdown in growth has a different impact on the budget of individual member-states – say, because of differing employment effects and hence a differing impact on expenditure and receipts – the imposition of a common fiscal constraint makes no sense. What does make sense is to replace the SGP with appropriate institutional arrangements for monitoring the size of member-states' indebtedness; ie, establishing a Sustainability Council along the lines described above.

Assuming the SGP is abolished, the problem of poor fiscal co-ordination amongst core states remains. The Broad Economic Policy Guidelines are wholly inadequate; some EU-level fiscal authority is required. Several authors[28] have proposed setting up a European Stabilisation Fund (ESF) which, broadly speaking, would resemble an IMF facility. The fund, possibly administered by the European Investment Bank (EIB), would be financed by borrowing on the international market; loans would be disbursed in the event of a serious economic downturn, whether in one or several member-states. Each state would be required to draw up a contingency plan for its use in recession, and equally to draw up a plan to offset overheating; these would allow rapid reaction to excessive expansion or contraction by an amount equivalent of up to 2% of the member-state's GDP. In principle, the ESF would supplement – and substantially strengthen – the operation of automatic stabilisers at national level.

The EIB should equally be used to promote long-term public investment at EU level; the accelerated development of common infrastructure as envisaged by the Delors White Paper (1993) in such areas as telecommunications, transport and research as a vital part of Europe.[29] Doubtless, this can be done

---

[27] See Buti et al quoted in EPOC (2005), Chap 3, p 4.

[28] See for example the 'rainy day fund proposed in Sapir (2003); and the proposals in the EPOC Report (2005).

[29] For a good discussion of this matter see Holland (2006).

PFIs (Private Financial Initiatives) and PPPs (Public Private Partnerships) are terms first coined at the World Bank and IMF in the 1980s. PPPs most often take the form of PFIs.

Under a PFI, private enterprise assumes most of the cost of building a project, which is then in effect leased back to the public sector at a generous fee. Although the beneficial effect is usually claimed to be an increase in efficiency, in reality it is to move the project off the books of the Ministry of Finance (Treasury) thus reducing the public borrowing requirement and maintaining 'prudence'.

Figure 5–2: PFIs and PPPs

in part though private investment, and common standards assured by means of a regulatory authority. Or, once again, it can be done through the EIB, thus avoiding excessive reliance on Private Financial Initiatives (PFIs) and Public Private Partnerships (PPPs) under which current capital costs are taken off-budget only to reappear as expensive handouts to industry in future. Nobody will quarrel with the greater use of the EIB to promote ecologically sustainable development, whether in the form of renewable energy generation, environmental clean-up or the restructuring of transport systems. Sustainable development – and the supporting research required – features as an agenda item in almost every European summit, and progress here has been one of the genuine success stories of Europe.

A major restructuring of EU economic institutions would enable a variety of other questions to be addressed. One example is the setting of common standards of social welfare and cohesion policies in defence of the European Social Model. While recognising that quite different 'welfare models' exist in the EU, certain minimum levels of welfare achievement should be defined and extended – for instance, in the areas of social security, workers' protection, education and health. Agreement might be reached between member states on spending a certain proportion of GDP on welfare. Equally, some degree of tax harmonisation is called for 'to recover the room for manoeuvre within national expenditure policies which many member states have lost during the last two decades due to increasing pressure on taxes and to tax competition amongst member states.[30] While full tax harmonisation is unrealistic and unnecessary, initiatives in this area would include a common centralised system for the calculation of VAT based on national accounts; a pan-EU system of dividend withholding tax for non-EU residents; the harmonisation of corporation tax

---

[30] EPOC (2005), chap 16, p 6; the call for tax harmonisation is hardly new; the Ruding Report to the Commission in 1992 called for corporation tax to be set uniformly at 30%.

throughout the EU[31] (though not of personal taxation), and the introduction of EU-wide energy taxes, starting with aircraft fuel. As Roger Liddle has written:

> Business would obtain significant cost savings if there was a harmonised corporate tax base across the EU – the rates could still vary between countries but the regulatory burden on business would be much reduced. (Liddle, 2005: 68)

The most important fiscal reform would be the establishment of a Federal EU budget as envisaged in the MacDougall Report (1977). MacDougall's target, it will be recalled, was of the order of 5–7% of combined EU GDP, large enough to be used as an instrument of counter cyclical fiscal policy but much smaller in comparison to the US Federal Budget which represents some 25% of US GDP. An EU Federal Budget is necessary not just to mobilise the resources necessary to strengthen pan-European investment, underwrite the European Social Model and intensify activity in the areas of security and development aid. Crucially, a Federal Budget is needed to redress the asymmetry between centralised monetary and decentralised fiscal policy described above. The theory of public finance – eg, Musgrave (1959) – underlines need for symmetry between monetary and fiscal institutions and policies.

At present, EU fiscal policy is caught in much the same vicious circle as existed in the 1930s: lack of growth leads to budgetary prudence and budgetary prudence leads to even less growth. The current lack of support – particularly amongst the major players – for expanding the EU budget is understandable in light of this situation. Nevertheless, an enlarged budget to be used for counter-cyclical spending is now an essential ingredient for re-igniting growth in the core states on the Eurozone. Let us assume agreement could be reached on the MacDougall target of 5 percent. A figure of 5% of combined GDP could be achieved by making member-states' contributions a progressive percentage of their GDP and incrementing contributions in stages – say, by 0.5% per annum between the present and 2012.

Obviously, funding this level of expenditure will require radical changes on the revenue side. The current system comprises the original or 'first own resources' (revenues from the common external tariff plus agricultural levies representing some 10–15% of the budget); the lion's share comes from member-

---

[31] It has been suggested that a multi-tier corporation tax be adopted according to a country's per capita income level; see EPOC (2005), chap 16. A 'withholding tax' for income from capital earned by non-residents exists in the USA and is being adopted by the EU.

states' VAT-based consumption revenue as well as their contributions from GDP. At present, VAT-based claims are inter-regionally regressive, placing a greater proportional burden on poorer member-states where consumption accounts for a larger share of GDP than in richer states. GDP-based claims, known as the 'fourth resource', account for just under half of total revenue; these claims are neither regressive nor progressive. Existing arrangements could be replaced using a unified GDP-based revenue raising system based on a progressive tax schedule, a variant of the 'modulation coefficients' based GDP contribution proposed by Spain in 1998.[32]

Finally the EU, like the US Federal Government, should be allowed to borrow. This would entail the abrogation of Articles 268 and 269 of the Maastricht Treaty requiring the annual EU budget to balance and to be financed entirely from 'own resources'. EU-level deficit finance would be justified in two cases; notably, where long-maturation investment was required in research or infrastructure on an EU-wide basis whose beneficiaries would be future generations; and secondly, where such finance was required for EU-wide stabilisation; ie, for a European Stabilisation Fund as described above.

5.7 RELEVANCE FOR A SOCIAL EUROPE

To resume, many people – particularly on the left – think of Maastricht and EMU as incompatible with Keynesian-style public spending. Precisely the opposite is true. It is because Europe does now have a world currency that it is protected from speculative attack. This is the main reason why Keynesian-style policies can be made to work, despite globalisation. Equally, the single currency obviates the need for policing current budget deficits. Unfortunately, at precisely the time expansionary fiscal policies have become possible and vital in the EU, political opinion has swung rightward and fiscal orthodoxy has become entrenched.

Economic stagnation in the Eurozone is now more than a decade long. The Japanese experience is instructive about how great a fiscal and monetary effort is required to overcome 'deflationary expectations'. The Eurozone remains dangerously vulnerable to this malady; it certainly cannot afford the cost in terms of economic output foregone – not to mention the political costs – of failing to act.

Calling for a more pro-active Central Bank and making marginal

---

[32] In order to raise revenue equivalent to 5% of combined EU GDP, the EPOC Report calculates that country-specific progressive tax rates (proportional to per capita GDP) would range between 0.95% of GDP for Latvia to 5.25% for Italy and 11.35% for Luxembourg. See EPOC Report (2005), chap 16, Table 18.1.

adjustments to the SGP of the sort agreed in 2005 are mere window-dressing. Implementing the social agenda of Lisbon is necessary and desirable, but attaining the Lisbon goals will be as much the effect as the cause of faster growth, and such a goal is incompatible with the EU's current economic institutional design. The cost of low growth and high unemployment has not been confined to the economic sphere; the evidence of its political impact is everywhere. The roots of this political backlash are complex, but few will doubt that the politics of a high-growth Europe with jobs for all would dispel the gloom on offer. Achieving high growth and low unemployment calls for radical surgery. Growth with equity is no pipe dream; today, it is crucial to making the Union work.

CHAPTER 6

Inequality versus Welfare

Today's filthy rich are wealthier, healthier and more secure than ever...
I know a tycoon who recently passed to his son, tax free, a business
worth more than £300m. This is commonplace. It seems remarkable
that any high roller these days resorts to fraud to enrich himself. It is
possible to bank such huge sums legally that criminality seems
redundant. (Max Hastings 'They've never had it so good' *The Guardian*,
August 6, 2005.)

6.1 INCOME DISTRIBUTION: THE NEO-LIBERAL LEGACY

To those who assert the superiority of the Anglo-Saxon model in delivering growth
with relatively low unemployment, one retort is to point to the growth in
inequality in countries like the United States and Britain. The distribution of
income in the US is the least egalitarian of any of the major industrialised
countries. This was not always true. The policies introduced under Roosevelt's
New Deal in the 1930s improved the lot of the poor, the Second World War
brought full employment and the post-war period saw further strides in reducing
the extreme inequalities that characterised US capitalism in the early 20th century.
But the neo-liberal revolution of the Reagan-Thatcher years with its emphasis on
economic deregulation, reduced taxation and the rolling back of the state reversed
this trend. Indeed, the rising trend in inequality continued through the end of
the twentieth century, unchecked by the Clinton administration in the US and
only recently addressed by the Blair Government in the UK. In terms of creating
greater income inequality, the Anglo-Saxon model has been truly revolutionary.

In a recent article, Paul Krugman[1] points out that over the past 30 years
the US income distribution has become as unequal as it was before the Great
Depression. In broad-brush terms, this shift is explained by the fact that the

[1] See Krugman (2004).

rich – the very top percentiles of the household income distribution – have become very much richer than before. By contrast, income has stagnated for the vast majority of Americans while the bottom twenty percent (the lowest quintile) is actually worse off. In 1970 the top 100 CEOs were paid about 40 times as much as the average worker; in 2000 they were paid about 1000 times as much. At the same time, median family income in 2000 was barely higher than it was in 1970, while at the bottom of the pyramid unskilled workers saw their position worsen.

It is instructive to look at this phenomenon more closely. In the years 1970–2000, the share of the top 10 percent of households – the 9th or 'top' decile – rose from 23 to 44 percent. This is a startling figure. It means that most of the increase in US national income over the past 30 years has been captured by the top decile. Moreover, within the top decile, the inequality in income distribution is as striking as for the population as a whole. The 11-point gain in the share of national income going to the top decile has not been shared out equally. Far from it; the share of the lower half – from the 90th to the 95th percentile – has remained nearly flat, with the gain concentrated in the top 5%, and amongst these in the top 1%.[2] US Census Bureau data confirm this trend and show that despite a GDP growth rate of 3.8% in 2004, only the top 5% of households experienced real income gains; incomes for the remaining 95% were flat or falling.[3]

Moreover, the combination of rising remuneration in the form of share-options, capital gains and other forms of asset appreciation, plus laxer inheritance tax, means that America's wealth distribution looks increasingly like its income distribution. An unequal distribution of wealth helps propagate the transmission of income inequality from one generation to the next, thus re-enforcing the hierarchy of privilege.[4] Krugman's warning is worth quoting:

> The United States did not start as a society that you could describe as middle-class. We were a society with a dominant economic elite. We became a middle class society and thought we had reached a stable state. We were wrong because we have now right back to where we were before … . We can no longer dismiss income distribution as a

2 In economist's terms, the upper tail of the income distribution conforms to a Pareto distribution. Thus, if (hypothetically) the richest, second richest and third richest person are A, B and C, if B were 10 times richer than C, we would expect A to be 100 (10x10) times richer than C. Some economists (eg, Martin Feldstein) regard this as a normal state of affairs and see no problem with the rich becoming richer as long as the poor are no worse off.
3 See 'Life in the bottom 80 Percent' *The New York Times*, September 1, 2005.
4 Following in Meade's footsteps, see Stiglitz (1969) for a model of the relation between patterns of inheritance and the distribution of assets and of income.

minor issue. In the United States it is now of the same order as economic growth in determining the standard of living of ordinary families. (Krugman, 2004; 79, 88)

6.2   Is the EU more egalitarian?

In comparison with the United States, the EU is more egalitarian, the obvious point being that the EU has higher standards of welfare provision that are funded from a more progressive tax system; with a couple of exceptions, this is true for the EU-15 member-states. While most people – or at least Europeans – would agree that a level of inequality comparable to that in the USA is undesirable, the question is whether the EU can sustain its welfare state?

A few would argue that the welfare state is a bad thing; too much welfare and bureaucracy blunt individual initiative and choke off the entrepreneurial spirit. *Per contra*, supporters of the welfare state hold quite different views about its future. Some argue that globalisation, particularly the pressure of ever-greater international competition, means that the 'EU welfare model' must inevitably be undermined; an eminent advocate of this view is John Gray.[5] Others point to the diversity of 'models' within the EU itself while noting that a number of northern European countries outperform the US in terms of welfare, employment and growth. Still others point to a universal tendency for the income distribution to worsen in recent years. Below I examine the merits of such arguments.

6.3   Measuring Inequality

An aside is necessary for the non-technical reader. There is a voluminous literature on the definition of inequality as well as on methodology and measurement problems.[6] For present purposes, a quick review of the Gini coefficient and the Kuznets hypothesis will suffice.

The graph in Figure 6–1 plots the percentage of households from poorest to richest on the horizontal axis and the percentage of national income on the vertical axis. The curve on the diagram is called a Lorenz curve.[7] In a perfectly egalitarian world, the bottom 20 percent of households would receive 20% of national income, the bottom 40 percent would receive 40% and so on. The diagonal line represents perfect equality. In the real world, of course, the Lorenz

[5]   See John Gray 'For Europe's sake, keep Britain out' *New Statesman*, Monday 19 May 2003.
[6]   The classical short text on this subject is Amartya Sen (1973).
[7]   The diagram is from http://william-king.www.drexel.edu/top/prin/txt/factors/dist4.html

plot lies below the diagonal; eg, the bottom 20% of households receive (say) 5% of income, the bottom 40% only 15% of income and so on. What matters for present purposes is that the Gini coefficient is defined as the ratio of the dark-shaded area under the diagonal to the total area under the diagonal. The total area is the sum of the dark-shaded and light-shaded areas. The greater the inequality, the greater the 'bulge' in the curve relative to the diagonal line, the higher the value of the Gini coefficient. A country with a Gini coefficient of 0.40 is far less egalitarian than one with a Gini coefficient of 0.20.[8]

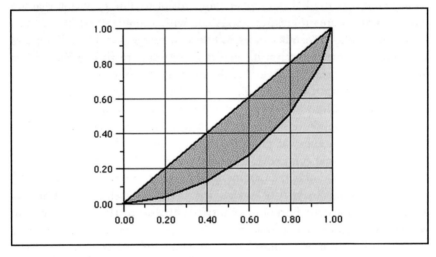

Figure 6–1: A hypothetical Lorenz Curve

A second point worth reviewing here is the 'inverted-U' hypothesis associated with the work of Simon Kuznets. In the 1960s, Kuznets suggested very poor countries (where the vast majority lived at subsistence level) might have a relatively egalitarian distribution. But as a country grows richer, Kuznets speculated, inequality and thus the Gini coefficient can be expected to increase. Eventually, though, middle-class prosperity will trickle down to everyone and the Gini will fall. In short, if one plots the Gini coefficient for a country over time, the result will resemble an 'inverted-U'. While no firm conclusion has ever been drawn from the many studies attempting to test Kuznets's assertion, economists have continued to use the 'U' and 'inverted-U' as a convenient

---

[8]   The astute reader will note that two countries could have an identical Gini coefficient but that the curves could differ in shape; say, one having a pronounced bulge at the lower end of the distribution while the other has a bulge at the high end. For this reason, other measures such as the Thiel coefficient and the decile ratio are used to in place of or to supplement the Gini coefficient, but we need not pursue the matter here.

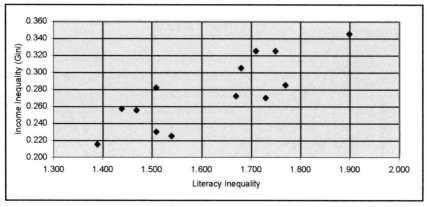

Figure 6–2: Income Inequality and Literacy for Selected OECD countries[9]

illustrative device when speaking of how the Gini coefficient might change over time.

It has become fashionable in recent years to extend the Kuznets hypothesis to the case of rich countries, which although they became more egalitarian in the post-war period up to the late 1970s, have since become less so. Hence the curve we are interested in is shaped like a 'U' rather than an 'inverted-U' (see Figure 6–3 below).

The orthodox economic explanation of why inequality has increased in recent years can be summarised roughly as follows. With economic growth increasingly driven by information and communications technology (ICT), the labour market in the 'knowledge economy' attaches an increasing premium to high levels of education (human capital) and these workers command a growing premium relative to unskilled workers. As a result, the wage differential between skilled and unskilled grows. Where labour market flexibility exists, income inequality increases. Alternatively, where the welfare state attempts to set a lower limit on wages, unemployment grows.

There are two reasons why the orthodox view is mistaken, or at best misleading. In the first place, falling unskilled wages may simply reflect a mismatch between the supply and demand for low-skill jobs. In the United States where the level of education is lower than the EU, a larger number of workers chase unskilled jobs resulting in low wages. In much of the EU and particularly in Germany and the Nordic countries, fewer workers do unskilled jobs; in consequence, unskilled and semi-skilled labour is more highly rewarded. Such a conclusion appears to be borne out by examining the

[9]   The countries in Figure 6–2 from left to right are DK, NOR, NL, DE, SWE, FIN, BE, AUS, IRL, CH, UK, CAN, USA; source Morley *et al* (2004: 54).

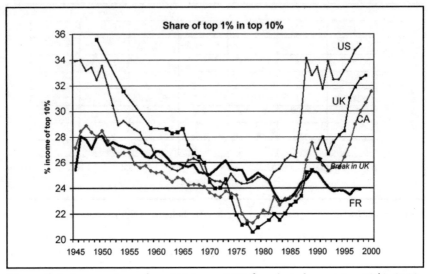

Figure 6–3: Income share of top 1% in top 10% for selected countries, 1945–2000

relationship between income and literacy inequality shown in Figure 6–2. In the second place, the rise of inequality in the US in the past 30 years seems to have more to do with what has happened at the top end of the income distribution; ie, with the rise of the super-rich.

The relevance of the above suggestion – that Gini coefficients are 'U-shaped' over time because of the gains of the super-rich – will be apparent from the Figure 6–3, which plots the coefficients for the post war period in the USA, Canada, the UK and France. The coefficients plotted are a special case of the Gini: the Pareto-Gini, showing the share of income of the top 1 percent to the top 10 of income earners.[10] A U-shape emerges clearly in three of the four cases.

What Figure 6–3 shows clearly is a fall in inequality until the late 1970s. Thereafter, inequality rises sharply again in the Anglo-Saxon countries (USA, UK and Canada) while it remains stable in France. The plot appears to confirm Krugman's assertion that the post-war compression in the US distribution has been reversed with the share of the top decile rising to levels last seen in the 1930s – and that inequality within the top decile has increased greatly.

But the evidence above does not seem consistent with the conventional theory ascribing the new inequality to changes in the gap between skilled and unskilled. This is not to deny that unskilled workers have suffered a worsening income position. In the US and the UK as we have seen, the bottom quartile

[10] The diagram is from Atkinson (2003).

has lost out in both relative and absolute terms. Rather, Figure 6–3 suggests that by far the most important factor in explaining growing inequality is the growth in the income share of the top decile – and even more, the growth of inequality within the top decile. In the 'liberal' Anglo-Saxon countries since 1980, the poor may have become slightly poorer, but what is striking is that the very rich have become so much richer.

6.4 INEQUALITY AND WELFARE

When discussing inequality, one must distinguish between income distribution before taxes and transfers (sometimes called the 'market' distribution) and income distribution after taxes and transfers. It is conventional when comparing countries to use the latter.[11]

That European countries are in general far more egalitarian than the United States is apparent from Figure 6–4 below showing Gini coefficients measured on a comparable basis for the US and the EU-15.[12] The most egalitarian countries (those with the lowest Gini values) are, unsurprisingly, the Nordic group; at the other end of the table one finds the USA and the UK where inequality has grown significantly since 1980.[13] The highest EU values are for Portugal and Greece; given that these two countries are the least developed in the EU-15, this is not surprising.

What is particularly interesting about the recent studies, however, is its concern with the question of whether the European welfare states are becoming more unequal. Whether one accepts the 'knowledge economy' hypothesis or even the more general argument that globalisation has undermined the foundations of the EU welfare state, the logical conclusion would be that inequality in the EU is growing. Several studies therefore have looked at the change in Gini coefficients over time for countries and country groups.[14] If inequality were growing, we would expect to find a U-shape time-plot for

[11] Equally, until recently, pre- and post-net transfer data was not available for the EU. This has been remedied with the development of the EUROMOD dataset, developed at Cambridge to estimate and compare the effects of taxes and transfers on personal and household income across the EU-15.

[12] The Gini calculations refer to the mid-1990s and are based on the Luxembourg Income Study (LIS) household data, 1979–99, the most recent attempt to measure income using a standardised definition. For details, see Smeeding (2002). Ginis for Portugal and Greece, excluded from the Smeeding study, are taken from Papatheodorou and Pavlopoulos (2003) whose data is from the Consortium of Household Panels for European socio-economic research (CHER);.

[13] Although Smeeding (2002) uses several measures of income inequality besides the Gini coefficient, I have ignored them since they all give roughly the same country ranking.

[14] *Inter alia*, see Smeeding (2002) and Atkinson (2003).

Sweden 1995	.221
Finland 1995	.226
Luxembourg 1994	.235
Netherlands 1994	.253
Belgium 1997	.255
Denmark 1997	.257
Germany 1994	.261
Austria 1995	.277
France 1994	.288
Spain 1990	.303
Ireland 1987	.328
Italy 1995	.342
UK 1995	.344
Greece (CHER, 1999)	.362
Portugal (CHER, 1999)	.375
EU-15 average	*.288*
USA 1995	.372
Source: Smeeding (2002); Atkinson (2003).	

Figure 6–4: Gini Coefficients by Country

individual or grouped Ginis. Other than in the case of the USA and the UK, no conclusive evidence of such a relationship is found.

It would appear that growing inequality is above all a political phenomenon, attributable to the policies followed by specific right-wing governments rather than a deterministic attribute of globalisation. This point emerges clearly when looking at the UK under Thatcher in the 1980s. In the period 1984–90, the Gini coefficient for the UK rose by 10 points. This change was larger than for any other OECD country. The 1990 UK Gini was nearly 7 points higher than the highest value recorded in the 1960s.[15] Not only did inequality increase more rapidly in the UK than in the USA in this period, but there were differences in its root causes. In both countries the rich grew richer; in the UK however, a combination of de-industrialisation, a steep rise in unemployment and the assault against trade-unions and welfare means that the poor grew poorer faster in Britain than in the USA.

[15] See Atkinson (2003).

The assault on welfare in the UK was not just a matter of bashing organised workers. Government statistics for the period 1980–2000 show the number of children in poverty having risen from 1.4m to 4.4m and the number of pensioners with less than half the average income doubled.[16] By the end of the century, not only was Britain less equal than other EU states at a comparable average income level, its social and economic infrastructure was in tatters. It is important to add, however, that since 2000 the Labour Government in the UK has made some progress in reversing these trends.[17]

6.5   INEQUALITY BETWEEN WELFARE STATES

It has been convenient so far to treat EU welfare states as if they were all much the same. Clearly, they are not – as the spread of Gini coefficients suggests. Several questions arise here. First, do inequalities across the EU-15 arise from differences between member states, or are inter-State differences swamped by intra-state differences? Second, is there a discernible typology of EU welfare regimes and, if so, how might this illuminate trends in inequality – or for that matter, trends in productivity and total employment which bear strongly on inequality?

The nature of inequality between different EU states and regions is important because the guiding principle of policy in Brussels has been to reduce the divide between richer and poorer member-states and their regions. The lion's share of the Union's 'own resources' is spent on the Common Agricultural Policy (CAP) and the Structural Funds. The CAP, whatever one thinks of it today, was set up on the principle that predominantly industrial member-states should aid their poorer, predominantly agricultural neighbours. By the same logic, the Structural Funds targeted extra resources at the poorer regions of the EU.

Within EU member-states, the distribution of income after taxes and transfers is – with the exception of the two poorest states – more egalitarian that that in the USA. Hence we would expect the average Gini coefficient for the EU-15 to be lower (more egalitarian) than for the USA. By contrast, if one looks at income variance within the EU as a whole – say, as measured by the difference in regions accounting for the top 10% of incomes and the lowest 10% of incomes, the regional income disparities in the EU are very wide indeed – considerably greater than in the US.

For example, Bavaria in Germany and Inner London in the UK are amongst the richest regions while Voreio Aigaio in Greece and the Portuguese Azores the

[16] See for example Gordon and Townsend (2000).
[17] See Toynbee and Walker (2005).

EU's poorest; the former have an average income more than twice as high as the latter.[18] Such regional differences reflect the fact that the accession countries have generally been much poorer than the EU 'core' – not just the Eastern and Central European states joining in 2004 but Portugal, Spain and Ireland who joined in previous rounds. And although accession countries are amongst the fastest growing in the EU (eg, Ireland) the catching up process takes time. The United States has been an integrated economic unit far longer than has the EU.

But several recent studies have found that inequality is most marked within member states, not between them. As one of these studies concludes:

> None of the indices show that more than 7.8% of overall inequality is attributable to the between-group component. In other words, more than 92% of overall EU inequality is attributed to income disparities within member states.[19]

Such a finding suggests that poverty reduction sponsored by Brussels could be better targeted. It is already self-evident that the provision of subsidies to crops rather than farmers is, from a redistributional perspective, spectacularly inefficient. It is perhaps less evident that member states, rather than throwing money at specific sectors and regions, might benefit most by introducing incentives to modernise their welfare provision, expand education and health care, reduce poverty amongst children and pensioners, alleviate long-term unemployment and enforce progressive taxation regimes (starting with combating tax evasion by the very rich).

This does not mean, obviously, that all regional policy is a bad thing. Clearly, there will be cases when large-scale investment is required in regional economic and social infrastructure. But such investment is best carried out in the name of regional growth, not under the misleading banner of poverty reduction. The current climate in Brussels of anti-Keynesian macro-policy and deregulatory micro-efficiency targets does not augur well in this respect.

6.6 DIFFERENT MODELS OF 'SOCIAL EUROPE'

The notion of the 'European social model' is of course no more than a convenient abstraction that in reality groups together quite different non-convergent welfare regimes. A number of social theorists have hypothised a typology of welfare regimes in the EU, the best known perhaps being that

---

[18] See Morley *et al* (2004); note that there are 71 European NUTS-1 regions whose average size is approximately the same as the States of the US. (NUTS, not the best of Brussels acronyms, stands for 'nomenclature of territorial units for statistics).

[19] See for example Papatheodorou and Pavlopoulos (2003: 15)

proposed by Gørsa Esping-Andersen (1990) as summarised below:
"Esping-Anderson distinguishes between three broad welfare regimes termed social-democratic, corporatist and liberal. Right (neo-liberal) parties champion market-led, minimalist welfare states, and they side with employers against work-time limits, encouraging long work hours. Social Democratic parties champion 'solidaristic' welfare and work-time policies encouraging fewer work hours, but also higher, more uniform, and equitable employment levels that limit aggregate reductions in hours. Finally, Christian Democratic parties and their conservative-welfare legacies have fostered male-breadwinner work and widespread labor-market exclusion. Recent reforms of such regimes of 'welfare without work' combine part-time female employment, work-sharing with resistance to Sunday opening and the '24-hour economy' to produce the OECD's lowest work-hours."[20]

This classification helps illuminate a number of crucial differences in the thrust of welfare and labour market policy. At the (neo-) liberal end of the spectrum, one would expect a Britain to do poorly in equality; the shrinkage of the welfare state and reduced direct taxation has meant that the difference between the income distribution before and after taxes and transfers is less pronounced than elsewhere (although it is still more pronounced than in the US). The UK's deregulated labour market promotes a combination of more MacJobs, higher earnings differentials, longer working hours and a higher employment rate than in most other EU countries. Means-tested benefits tend to reinforce social stratification.

Nor did the emergence in the UK of a Social-Democratic government in 1997 immediately reverse this trend. New Labour's reluctance to raise taxes on higher incomes, its US-style emphasis on 'welfare-to-work' and the shift to means-tested benefits and tax-credits, all helped foster a higher employment rate and force women into the labour force, but at the cost of greater wage differentials and less job security. Only after 2001 did New Labour address the depth of poverty in the UK, particularly amongst the young and the elderly.[21]

The Esping-Andersen distinction between Social-Democratic and Christian-Democratic welfare regimes is particularly illuminating. Social Democratic regimes – exemplified mainly by the experience of the Nordic Countries –may emphasise shorter working hours, but their policies encourage greater labour force participation and a higher employment rate. Generous non-means-tested welfare benefits not only reduce inequality but facilitate greater female and youth labour force participation. Excellent vocational education, extensive

---

[20] See Burgoon and Baxandall (2004: 3).
[21] According to some commentators, Britain today has developed a 'new' model, liberal but social too, which the rest of the EU can admire. See Pearce and Dixon (2005).

on-the-job training and an aversion to 'second-tier' jobs – all part of a universalistic ethos of social solidarity – minimise the risk of gender- or aged-based social exclusion and the growth of a low-skill, marginally employable social underclass. A strong tax system built on an ethos of 'fairness' (rather than simple equal opportunity) not only promotes intra-generational equity but guarantees intra-generational equity; ie, substantial state pensions without a 'pensions crisis'.

The Christian Democratic welfare model – which Esping-Anderson sees as emerging from the corporatist Bismarkian state – lies between these poles on the spectrum. While more egalitarian than the neo-liberal model, the Christian-Democratic model is patriarchal and family-centred. The state provides limited welfare focussed on generous unemployment benefit and pensions rather than on universal services. Education and health provision is less universalistic. Women's participation in the work force is at best encouraged on a part-time basis; little attention is given to maternity leave, crèche and all-day school provision. 'Social capitalism' has tended to provide earnings-related, transfer-heavy and service-weak social benefits, frequently resorting to early retirement and disability schemes and female labour-market exclusion that invite much scorn and the label "welfare without work" (Esping-Anderson, 1996).

Although a number of studies have suggested a classification of the EU-15 member states along the above (or slightly amended) lines and attempted do draw socio-metric conclusions, I shall not review the work here. Esping-Andersen's work provides a suggestive and illuminating typology rather than a rigorous analytical framework, a typology best served by illustrative examples.

6.7 RESTRUCTURING WELFARE: FINLAND AND THE NETHERLANDS

Finland and The Netherlands are two such examples, the Social-Democratic and the latter Christian-Democratic, both forced to adapt under the pressure of changed circumstances.[22]

Finland is, with Sweden, the most egalitarian country in the EU-15. Its has a highly educated workforce, virtually no poverty, a strong trade-union movement, relatively low work-hours and very low gender discrimination in the labour market. Following the economic shock of the early 1990s caused by the collapse of the USSR and Comecom, GDP growth turned negative and unemployment soared to a peak of 19% in 1994. A number of experiments in

---

[22] These examples are cited in a very useful recent paper by Burgoon and Baxandall (2004).

'work-sharing' were pioneered to bridge the gap while the economy recovered. By 2004, unemployment was just below the EU average, while the total employment rate stood at 68%, well above the average. Public-employment funds were used to defray wages lost as a result of full-time workers shifting to part-time work, in order to make way for unemployed youth. Partial early retirement (with part-time work) was also used to spread jobs, with government supplementing half the wages lost. While the working week was not reduced (as, say, in France), the working week became more 'flexible'. Gender discrimination has been minimised through the provision of excellent crèche facilities and full-day schools.

On the other hand, the Finns have been more resistant to the institutionalisation of part-time work. Burgoon and Baxandall (2004) report that in 1996, part-time work was 11 percent, below the EU-15 average of 17 percent; only 16 percent of women worked part time, half the EU average. Equally, Finnish Social Democracy has been less protective than Christian Democracies of 'pro-social' hours; they are almost twice as likely to work during evenings, night, and Sundays than the EU average. In short, Finnish work-time policies have sought to reduce unemployment, combat labour-market dualisms, and relieve toil, rather than pursue family-centred goals.

In The Netherlands, by contrast, it was recognised in the 1980s that a 'welfare-heavy' system with low female participation and high absenteeism, disability-leave and early retirement was no longer fiscally viable. In a country with the lowest working hours and nearly the lowest (and most gender-biased) employment rate in the EU, reform was necessary – but it has followed a different route from Finland. Reform of the welfare system began in 1982 with the Christian-Democrat-led government under Ruud Lubbers, and continued under Wim Kok's social-democrat-led 'purple coalition' (1994–2002). The main thrust of reform was to move those on welfare back into work. Thus, the eligibility rules for unemployment were tightened and benefits lowered; early-retirement was made more difficult to obtain and disability and sickness benefits were cut. As a result, absenteeism fell and the employment rate rose – although hours worked per-employee increased only slightly

The bias against 'anti-social' hours went largely unchanged, with virtually no change in universal Sunday closure and only limited extension of late-night shopping. Traditional barriers to full-time female employment remained; notably, very limited crèche facilities and the absence of school lunches. In the early 1990s, minimum-wage and social-security entitlements were extended to one-third-time jobs and less, setting the stage for a rapid increase in part-time and generally low-status female employment. While full-time (typically head-of-household) workers saw their working hours decrease, between 1983 and 2000 the proportion of part-time workers rose from 18 to 32 percent, one of the highest figures in the EU. The impact on the labour statistics of the growth of part-time work for women is striking: in 2004, The Netherlands had an employment rate of just over 70%, but the lowest hours worked per week (31) in the EU-15.

These examples provide a useful illustration of contrasting labour-market priorities of Christian- and Social-Democratic labour regimes. Under crisis, Nordic Social-Democratic regimes have tended to expand educational and social service provision in order to underpin the availability of full-time work for all. Work-sharing and/or part time work has been encouraged only as a temporary palliative, the overall aim being to minimise social fragmentation in the form of second-class and/or gender biased part-time jobs. Christian-Democratic welfare regimes, traditionally more reliant on transfers and unemployment compensation rather than service provision, have responded to crisis by strengthening incentives to remain in the work force, notably though tightening eligibility criteria and support for exit. At the same time, their commitment to 'family values' is reflected in strong opposition to 'anti-social' hours and Sunday opening, while the relative absence of strong social services and the low priority given to combating age- and gender bias has resulted in the proliferation of low paid, part-time jobs. Just as under 'liberal' welfare regimes committed to the free play of market forces, little concern appears to be shown for work patterns that increase long-term social stratification.

6.8   The Cost of Foregoing Welfare

We live in a world where globalisation, technical change and the spread of the service economy have already changed patterns of work. In the current century, it is clear that the bulk of employment will no longer be provided by the industrial sector. Fifty years ago, the standard production worker could count on a decently paid and secure job. The promise of the weekly wage packet in skilled and semi-skilled industrial jobs protected by strong trade unions has receded; in its place we see the rise of part-time, semi-skilled work, often at low wages and with little protection.

Moreover, the new service economy generates dualism: in Britain, there is a growing social and economic gap between the highly educated young people for whom jobs, opportunity and money seem to abound, and those stuck in the lowest ranks of society. The apparent classlessness of youth culture masks deep and abiding differences in social inheritance: different educational attainment increasingly defines life chances, not just for the individual, but also for the family group. In future, those who lack the necessary skills or the resources to acquire them may slide into a life of low pay and insecure employment, possibly into the ranks of the long-term unemployed. There is now a considerable body of evidence linking the degree of inequality in a society to the physical and mental health of its citizens. The cost of inequality goes well beyond the failure to fulfil human potential, spilling over into the social pathology of chronic disability, mental disorder and crime.[23]

As Esping-Anderson (2002) argues, in the 21st century we cannot afford *not* to be egalitarian. Not only is the social cohesion afforded by strong public services desirable in principle, it is increasingly instrumental for economic efficiency. Take pensions for example. If each new generation of workers is required to support a larger cohort of retirees, to provide for insurance and health care and for itself to educate of its own children, then each generation must be more productive than the last. But the poorly educated not only have low productivity, they tend to work fewer years – about 10 years less than those with a good education.[24]

Whatever short-term financial constraints may exist on welfare provision by the state, it is nonsense to suggest that welfare provision (starting with universal educational provision) distorts competition and dulls incentives and for that reason should be jettisoned, or at least greatly pruned, in order to give full rein to the market. Those neo-liberals who argue for such a solution believe that welfare needs can be met entirely within the market, and that the role of the state is merely to equip individuals with educational opportunities required for making full use of market opportunities. Accordingly, the state does no more than level the playing field, enabling a meritocracy to flower. Such a view overlooks the fact that it is unregulated markets that generate social risks and perpetuate deep inequalities. The strong social-democratic welfare regime seeks to minimise income inequalities and to provide universal guarantees of social citizenship.[25] Such citizenship is itself a precondition for making good a Lisbon agenda strategy aimed at promoting sustainable development based on investment in education.

[23] See for example Wilkinson (1996).
[24] See Morley et al (2004).
[25] Robert Taylor (2005) puts an admirable case for a strong welfare state in his new pamphlet on the Swedish model. Had I read it in time, the current chapter could have benefited greatly from his insights.

CHAPTER 7

The New Challenges

The British state has avoided the pension time-bomb only by displacing
risk, misery and poverty on to the next generation of pensioners. If
[Continental] Europeans have a problem, it is because they plan to treat
their pensioners properly (Will Hutton 2002, p 235)

7.1 PRESENT AND FUTURE GENERATIONS

The current chapter focuses on two challenges for Europe: competitiveness (the
Lisbon agenda) and the 'pensions crisis'. These have been chosen in part because
so much attention has been devoted to them in the press and in the more
specialised literature. The Lisbon agenda is often cited as being a recipe for
growth. In truth, it is questionable whether either 'making Europe more
competitive' is of overriding importance or that competitiveness alone can
deliver growth. This is not to dismiss Lisbon. On the contrary, the Lisbon
summit will be remembered if only for the fact that it placed 'sustainable
development' high on the European agenda.

The other issue examined in this chapter is the pensions crisis. The question
here is what we can do today to avoid a very serious problem for the next
generation. There is no doubt that all developed countries whose demographic
structure is changing face a serious long-term problem of funding pensions, a
problem that cannot be resolved by privatising retirement provision or
pretending that a return to 'family values' will lead to more children and a
reversal of the trend. Society as a whole will need to save more (and probably
to work longer). For present purposes, it is important to emphasise that higher
productivity and faster growth can help generate that extra savings. While the
provision of pensions at EU level is a distant ideal, fomenting faster growth
and higher productivity is not. So too is improved regulation of pension
provision throughout the Union, thus ensuring that there are common
standards of European entitlement in old age. Clearly, while some EU member

states are doing better than others and cross-country comparisons are helpful, the tendency to pontificate about how 'we' have solved our problem and 'they' have not is decidedly unhelpful.

There are a variety of other challenges facing the EU that are either ignored or insufficiently examined here. Climate change and environmental policy is the most obvious, a subject which although touched upon earlier merits far more attention than it is given in this book. Equally, it would have been useful to include separate sections on European transport and other economic infrastructure, on social infrastructure provision or even on the disappointingly slow development of common political institutions. For present purposes, though, I have chosen to focus on a limited range of topics rather than to skim a wide selection.

7.2 PRODUCTIVITY: WHAT ABOUT LISBON?

Much has been made of the 'Lisbon strategy', a plan approved at the Lisbon meeting of European Heads of State in March 2000 to make the EU 'the world's most dynamic economy by 2010'. Lisbon addressed the fields of economic, social and environment development and emphasised the need for upgrading the educational level of the EU's work force in order improve social cohesion and to boost growth and job creation. A key goal of the strategy was to increase the EU employment rate from 63 in 2000 to 70% by 2010. Equally, Lisbon identifies a 'knowledge deficit' when the EU is compared to the USA. The EU spends 1.4% of GDP on higher education and 1.8% on research and development (R&D); this contrasts with 3% and 2.7% in the US.[1]

The original strategy was prepared by a group of some of the EU's leading specialists in the field of science and growth.[2] More recently Wim Kok, a former Prime Minister of the Netherlands, has chaired a further group of prominent figures to report on the progress of the strategy – hereafter, referred to as the 'Kok report'.[3]

In some circles, the Lisbon strategy has been dismissed as little more than the human face of neo-liberalism, a view which has hardened since Portugal's José Manuel Barroso – a prominent member of the European centre-right and a strong supporter of the 'Lisbon process' – succeeded Romano Prodi as President of the European Commission. But dismissing Lisbon – or in the

---

[1] See Liddle (2005), p 60.

[2] Amongst the persons involved were Maria Joao Rodriguez, Luc Soete and Christopher Freeman, some of Europe's most prominent academics in this area.

[3] In March 2003, the European Council asked the Commission to set up a European Employment Task Force and Wim Kok was chosen as Chair.

extreme case the whole European project[4] – as a right-wing plot is facile and misleading. As the Kok Report admits, the Lisbon strategy was prepared in 1999–2000 when US economic growth was still strong and the notion of the 'new economy' – one immune to recession – much in vogue. Since then, the high-tech bubble has burst and the specialists have had to reassess their optimism about 'human capital' as the force driving economic growth. But then, nobody would disagree with the view that an educated work force is important, no more than with the need for social inclusion and sustainable development.

Equally, as the Kok report points out:

> Whether it is life expectancy, infant mortality rates, income inequality or poverty, Europe has a much better record than the United States. The objective of Lisbon is to uphold this record in an environment where challenges are multiple and growing. [Kok report 2004: 11].

Nevertheless, the report warns that unless the EU's growth rate picks up, Europe's standard of living will be eroded and its system of social provision in work and in retirement will be threatened; it will be overtaken by East Asia sooner rather than later. Expenditure on pensions and health could increase on average to 4–5% of GDP by 2030; looking at demographic trends, the ratio of elderly people to those of working age (15–64) is set to rise from 25% today to 50% by 2050.

With respect to technological progress, environment and sustainability the Kok Report sounds ominous warnings: the EU-15's share of high-tech manufactures is lower than the US, and with expansion to 25 members this gap will widen. The volume of traffic on Europe's roads is increasing, as is pollution. Although EU member states are signatories to Kyoto, greenhouse gas emission targets are far from being met. More generally, the EU needs to complete the internal market, particularly in such areas as financial and other services. And in areas such as corporate taxation, the Report is clear that the EU would clearly benefit from harmonisation of tax rates. Clearly, such issues are of critical importance to the future of the EU.

7.3   LIMITS OF THE KOK REPORT?

In a number of ways the report is disappointing. For example, it is obvious from figures cited by the report itself that the EU does not greatly lag behind the USA in the share of R&D expenditure in GDP. In science and engineering

---

4   See for example Anne Gray (2004).

graduates per 100,000 of population, Europe does considerably better than America. Improving education may be highly desirable, but suggesting that educational investment alone will foment rapid growth does not square with the evidence. And while it may be important to encourage greater cross-border competition in financial services and other areas and to facilitate the growth of small enterprise, the report at times seems to echo the 'deregulation' philosophy which was the mantra of the 1990s; eg, in strongly urging greater use of Private Public Partnerships (PPP).

Equally, it is far from self-evident that Europe needs to become the 'world's most competitive economy', a phrase attributed to Tony Blair. Europe has certainly not lost ground to the USA in terms of foreign trade. Rather, the opposite is true. Germany, the 'sick man of Europe' according to the British press, has become the world's most successful exporter. In contrast to the US, the EU-15 runs a positive current account balance with the rest of the world.

The most obvious shortcoming in the Kok report is that it devotes only two paragraphs to the EU's poor record of macro-economic management. In particular it avoids challenging the economic logic underpinning the SGP; instead it merely 'agrees' with the Commission's decision not to enforce the SGP too eagerly. The Report has nothing to say about the ECB, its interest rate and exchange rate policies and inflation targets – or even about the cap on the EU budget. This omission is deeply worrying, not only because the Lisbon Process is meant to be the central pillar of the EU's growth strategy, but more fundamentally because the causality between growth, technological innovation and the 'knowledge society' is bi-directional. Technological progress is as much a result of growth as its cause – the two go together; and with growth comes a greater capacity to meet the targets which Lisbon rightly sets.[5]

Finally, Lisbon's obsession with EU 'competitiveness' is conceptually unfounded. As Paul Krugman never tires of repeating, neither the USA nor Europe (nor anybody else) is being 'out-competed' simply because international trade is not based on absolute advantage.[6] (Economists will recall that in Ricardo's famous example, although Portugal could produce both wine and cloth more cheaply than England, it still paid Portugal to specialise in wine and trade it against English cloth.) However, it is certainly true that globalisation has led to the relocation of productive activities on a world scale. China and India make many of the clothes we wear, and increasingly too, they

[5] Pisani-Ferry (2005) is one of several economists who argues that far more that merely Lisbon-style reform is required to kick-start the Eurozone, including a more pro-active ECB.
[6] A clear restatement of this principle is contained in Adair Turner's 'Liberal Economy'; see Turner (2001), Chap 1. For the original statement, see Krugman (1999), Part I entitled 'A Zero-sum world?'.

make high-tech products like computer chips. This means that our economies (and theirs) must continuously readapt and retool.

To be competitive, Europe doesn't need to copy the US in producing computer software like Microsoft or energy deals like Enron; nor does it need to 'save money' by cutting back on social provision and environmental protection. Rather, it needs to reinforce its comparative advantage in those areas such as high-quality goods and services at which it excels. Above all, Europe needs to realise more fully the advantages of having a highly educated workforce and to reap the economies of scale and inherent in its own huge internal market.

7.4   Pensions: Does Catastrophe Loom?

In general, Europe can be proud of its pension systems. At present, the average person over 65 receives an income equivalent to nearly 90 percent that of the average person of working age. Nor do pensioners appear to be at much higher risk of poverty than the working-age population as a whole.[7] While average figures hide considerable variation between countries and occupations, citizens of the EU-15 have come to expect an adequate pension as an entitlement. The core issue is the sustainability of the system – how to set aside sufficient resources to fund the retirement of future generations. The sums involved are large: for the EU-15, pensions account on average for 10% of GDP and about a quarter of public expenditure. And every day brings new stories of a looming 'pensions crisis' caused by the combination of demography and government financial mismanagement. Do we really have a crisis?

The argument set out below is that although the EU – more precisely, some member- states – will face very serious pension problems in future, the situation does not amount to a crisis. The ultimate responsibility for pensions lies with member states, and this is likely to remain the case in the foreseeable future. And although Brussels makes no contribution to pensions, its influence is to be felt in two ways. First, much policy advice on reform comes from the Council and the Commission. For example, the Broad Economic Policy Guidelines (BEPG) regularly include advice on pension reform. Most important, the common framework of macroeconomic policy developed by the ECB and the Finance Ministers has a growing influence on how fast Europe grows.

Europe is growing too slowly, and this gives rise to the following paradoxes. First, slow growth and unemployment cause fiscal revenue to lag behind expenditure. Finance Ministers determine that expenditure must be cut,

---

[7]   See Morley, Ward & Watt (2004).

particularly if finances are to be put on a 'sound basis' enabling the pensions crisis to be resolved. Expenditure cutting slows growth and employment creation even more. Secondly, the more one tells individuals they must save to avoid a pensions crisis, the more pessimistic individuals will become about future earnings, thus depressing aggregate demand. The pension crisis is in danger of becoming a variant on Keynes's story of the 'widow's cruse'; in this case, the more the widow saves, the less her savings grow.[8]

Some EU states are richer than others, so we would expect pension provision to vary amongst the EU-15. Even amongst those core states of the EU in which per capita living standards are similar, pension provision differs as it does between different sectors of a given economy. Generally, civil servants earn a modest salary, but in most countries they can normally expect to retire relatively early on a reasonable state pension. In the private sector, top CEOs retire as millionaires; by contrast, in Wal-Mart-style companies where workers are unable to join trade unions, pension provision is meagre. Some part-time workers and self-employed persons, particularly women, may fail to contribute enough to qualify for any form of pension. Provision varies not just according to income status, but according to whether basic state pensions are high or low, whether some state benefits are means tested, how far state pensions are earnings related, and how far state benefits are 'topped up' either by occupational pensions provided by employers and private pensions taken out by individuals. Moreover, there is an important 'gender gap' in pension entitlement. According to one source, 92 percent of men in the UK retire with a full basic state pension in their own right while the comparable figure for women in only 16 percent.[9] In short, within the EU-15, systems and levels of pension provision vary widely.

Nevertheless, pension coverage in the EU-15 is in principle universal, even if levels of pension provision vary quite considerably and methods of funding differ. Broadly speaking, in countries like Italy and Austria, retirement takes place relatively early and state pensions are generous. But the cost to the state is high and current levels of provision are generally agreed to be unsustainable, the most problematic cases being Italy and Greece. This is true to a lesser degree in France and Germany where, although state pensions account for about 60–75% of retirement income, pension commitments represent a smaller

---

[8] The 'widow's cruse' – a story in which no matter how much the widow spent her purse was always full – was used by Keynes to illustrate the point that rising consumption demand raises income, which in turn raises savings. The same logic works the other way: the more people save for a rainy day, the less income (and therefore savings) grows.

[9] Jackie Ashley 'State pensions for all is the only way to end this scandal' *The Guardian*, June 23 2005.

proportion of GDP than in Italy and Greece, and successive governments have taken measures to reform the system. Similar reforms have been made in Benelux and the Nordic countries; in these countries, occupational pensions are generally more important than state pensions. It should be noted that funding state pensions is least onerous in the UK, since that country has the lowest level of state pension provision by far of any EU state enjoying a similar level of per capita income.

7.5 THE REFORM OF PAYG PENSIONS

In most European countries, state pension schemes traditionally have operated on a pay-as-you-go (PAYG) basis, meaning that the contributions of new entrants to the labour force pay for the pensions of retirees. PAYG has the advantage of being simple to administer; since new entrants fund retirees, large pension funds are not required. Moreover, as long as new entrants greatly outnumber retirees – say, by a ratio of 4:1 or 5:1 – and as long as the life expectancy after retirement is not too long, such a system works relatively well. When Bismarck first introduced state pensions in Germany in 1889, new entrants vastly outnumbered retirees; the retirement age was 70 and average life expectancy was 48.[10] But today, not only do people retire earlier and live longer but the number of new workers is falling; ie, the 'dependency ratio' (the ratio of retirees to active workers) is rising. Generous and universal pensions will be unsustainable unless extra resources can be set aside out of higher productivity and faster growth.

One remedy has been to 'fund' pensions; ie, to set aside funds earmarked for making good any shortfall in future pensions. In the past two decades, pension funds in the EU – and more generally the OECD countries – have grown rapidly, although very unevenly. At one end of the scale are countries like The Netherlands and the UK where pension assets (or 'pension funds') represent a large slice of GDP[11]; at the other end are Germany, France and Italy, which still rely mainly on 'unfunded' PAYG schemes. Pension funds are most often managed by the private sector, but funds can equally be managed by the state: Belgium, France and Ireland have all set aside funds since 1996 to help fund the PAYG system. More generally, though, Governments have urged companies and employees to bear a larger share of the burden of pension provision. Nordic countries have long required employers to contribute

---

[10] See *The Economist* 'State pensions in Europe; the crumbling pillars of old age' April 4, 2005.
[11] In 1996, the share of pension assets in GDP was 110% in Switzerland, 90% in The Netherlands and 75% in the UK compared to 2–5% in Germany, France and Italy; see Blommestein (2001).

generously to their employees' pensions; at present, companies throughout the EU are being given tax breaks for setting up their own schemes.

Workers too are being asked to contribute more, or else to accept later retirement and/or less generous pensions. One relatively painless money-saving trick is to index pensions to the retail price index rather than to the average industrial wage since the former typically rises more slowly than the latter. This reform was introduced in the UK under Margaret Thatcher; despite pressure from trade unions, it has not changed under New Labour. Another trick has been to raise the pension levy on workers' wages as was done in The Netherlands in 1997 where it rose from 15 to 18%. Or again, state pensions can be cut – as they will be in Austria from 2005. Or else the retirement age can be raised. Postponing retirement met with fierce opposition in France when first attempted in 1995, but succeeded in 2005 when the number of years in work needed to qualify for a full pension by public sector employees was raised from 37.5 to 40. Germany has not yet taken such a step, but in August 2004, a committee reported that the real value of the state pension should be cut by 10% and the retirement age raised progressively from 65 to 70. Such a reform is obviously deeply unpopular.

7.6   THE PILLARS OF RETIREMENT

If the state is the first 'pillar' of the pensions system, the second and third pillars are the private employer and the individual respectively (or 'social partners' as they are known in the Nordic states). In the late 1990s, the Labour Party in Britain made much of the fact that the UK pension system was largely funded by company schemes; ie, that unlike the situation in (say) Germany with a PAYG-based scheme, British workers could rely on private company pensions to supplement their meagre state pensions. Such company pensions – managed by 'fund managers' and typically split 60/40 between bonds and equities – were financially far sounder, it was argued. Although the public finances of other EU countries might be overwhelmed by an 'unfunded pensions gap'[12], Britain thought itself immune to such risk. Since the stock market collapse of 2001, this argument looked extremely suspect. What is worse, when times were good between 1988 and 2001, it is reported that British companies took a 'contribution holiday' and skipped some £28m in contributions.[13]

---

[12] This 'gap' was typically calculated as the difference in Net Present Value between the stream of all future pensions claims and receipts; when expressed as a percentage of GDP, the gap was huge. Oddly, no one seemed to have calculated the 'health gap' or 'education gap' in a similar fashion.

[13] See Blackburn (2005); for a detailed political analysis of the pensions problem, see Blackburn (2003).

The United States, like Britain, operates a two-tier pension system under which the state pension (social security) is topped up by a company pension. Until recently, most company pension schemes in the US were 'defined benefit' schemes; ie, the company pledged itself to pay a given pension at a given age. Companies are also required by law to report any shortfall in current or future pension commitments. The end of the stock-market bubble led to large shortfalls, and the US Congress passed a raft of legislation giving tax relief to corporations enabling them to cover the deficit with less pain. But the main change has been the shift from 'defined benefits' (DB) towards 'defined contribution' (DC) schemes; the latter in effect lower the level of provision and shift the burden of risk onto employees. Equally, under the latter scheme, the future level of provision the individual can expect remains uncertain. In the USA, President Bush's proposed 'privatisation' of Social Security aims at shifting the entire burden of pension provision and its associated risk to the individual.

The shift from DB to DC schemes is visible in Britain, and to a lesser extent in The Netherlands and some Nordic countries. As part of the move towards lower benefits, companies have uncoupled pension provision from final years' salary. According to The Economist, nearly a million employees have seen their old scheme disappear and their employers' contributions slashed, resulting in an annual loss to UK pensioners of up to £1.6bn.[14]

There are three obvious difficulties with privatising pension schemes. First, it places an impossible burden on the current generation of workers who must both save for their own (privatised) pension and contribute towards the PAYG scheme supporting current pensioners. This is the basis of the short-term case against Bush's plan to privatise Social Security in the USA.[15] Secondly, as Turner (2004) points out, as the dependency ratio grows, the capital value of redeemable pensions will tend to fall; ie, because the number of young people available to purchase savers assets will be falling in relative terms. This means quite simply that regardless of inflation, by the time today's worker cashes in his/her pension, its value will have fallen.

The third and more fundamental problem is that individuals cannot be counted upon to make optimal decisions about their own retirement, even assuming they are well informed about the risks associated with different forms of saving; eg, building societies, mutual funds, bonds, balanced investment portfolios and so on. Not only does the state have more and better information, it has a longer time horizon. Individuals are notoriously poor at setting aside money for the long term, particularly if their income is relatively low. Moreover, since there are significant economies of scale in pension provision,

---

[14] See The Economist (2005) cited above.
[15] See P. Krugman 'Slanting Social Security', The New York Times, 11 March 2005.

it makes sense to make collective provision for pensions. The economist and Nobel Laureate, Kenneth Arrow, made the theoretical case for universal state-funded pension provision in his seminal work forty years ago.[16]

In summary, EU member-states face a pension problem of varying degrees of seriousness. In recent years, different EU countries have sought various ways of reducing the state's exposure to this crisis; ie, the potentially unsustainable claim on the state's resources. Traditionally, employers have been asked to shoulder a larger share of the burden – but for various reasons have been reluctant to do so. Employers have typically argued a higher contribution reduces their competitiveness at a time when they are becoming increasingly vulnerable to the pressures of global competition. Nor is it likely or desirable that the brunt of the burden be shifted to individual households.

The pension problem cannot be solved by shifting the burden of savings from the state towards the private corporate or household sector; ie, by relying on 'funded' private savings. Such a shift merely lightens the state's share of the burden; it does not ensure better pension provision in future. The problem of future pensions can only be dealt with by adopting one or a combination of measures: (a) raising growth and labour productivity; (b) raising collective savings; (c) accepting lower pensions; and/or (d) raising retirement age. The core notion here is that of bringing about an inter-generational redistribution of income.

7.7 The Logic of the Pensions Crisis

Underlying the pensions crisis is a simple exercise in demographics. The logic is explored in the recent parliamentary Reports of the Pensions Commission chaired by Adair Turner.[17]

PAYG pension provision is best understood with the aid of a simplified example first set out by the Nobel laureate, Paul Samuelson. In a world of no population growth and no productivity growth, the ratio of the average worker's contribution to the average retirement income is equal to the ratio of years spent working to years in retirement. Suppose one works for 45 years and retires for 15. This ratio (3:1) is known as the 'support ratio' (SR). If workers' contributions are 10% of average earnings, the pension will be 30% of average earning – or if we want a pension of 90%, workers' contributions must be 30%.[18] The salient point is that for every €1 contribution made during work, you get back €1 in retirement, or a 0% return.

---

[16] See Arrow (1963) and Arrow (1965).
[17] See for example, House of Commons 'Work and Pensions' Third Report, 23 February 2005.
[18] Theoretically, employers' contributions merely feed through to higher prices, thus lowering the real wage. Thus, taxing employers is merely and indirect way of taxing workers.

If we add population and productivity growth to this model, the return on the €1 pension contribution increases. For example, imagine that population grows at 1% per annum over 45 years of working life. If workers' contributions were 20% of the wage, then according to the 3:1 ratio given above a worker would retire on 60% of average earnings. But with 1% population growth the figure is no longer 20% times three, but 20% times three times the compound rate of population growth, which means that the worker can retire on more than 80% of average earnings. This happens because more and more workers fund the retiree's pension contribution. Exactly the same logic applies to growing labour productivity. If we hold population constant and allow productivity to increase by 1% per annum, we get the same result. Where both population and productivity is assumed to grow as above, the retiree does twice as well. PAYG pensions must yield a positive rate of return on investment, and Samuelson showed that this converges towards the long-term growth rate of the economy.

At present, particularly in the United States where the Bush administration has trumpeted its intention to privatise social security, it has become fashionable to dismiss PAYG as a Ponzi[19] scheme; ie, a pyramid investment scheme in which early investors gain at the expense of later investors until, ultimately, the scheme collapses. A Ponzi-type collapse, it is argued, results from the fact that post-war 'baby boomers' are now coming up to retirement age. Instead of new retirees being supported by more workers, today and tomorrow fewer workers will support them. The analogy is quite misleading. Ponzi schemes are fraudulent because they are based on the deceptive premise that they are sustainable; in truth, pyramid schemes must collapse since the exponential growth they require is unsustainable. By contrast, PAYG is sustainable with a steady state population as shown; they will yield a positive return as long as population and/or labour productivity rises. Nevertheless, PAYG is clearly sensitive to changing demographics – notably, a declining support ratio (SR). Two forces are at work undermining the SR: increasing longevity and decreasing fertility.

In all OECD countries – and many middle-income countries as well – life expectancy at 60 has increased very substantially,[20] while the total fertility rate (TFR) has fallen below the replacement rate of 2.0. In the OECD countries, the TFR fell below the replacement rate in the 1970s and will almost certainly continue falling. For a variety of reasons – later marriage, greater workforce

---

[19] Ponzi schemes are named after Charles Ponzi, an American who made a fortune from pyramid schemes in the early 20th Century until his practices were exposed as fraudulent.

[20] Average life expectancy today at age 65 is about +17 years and is predicted to increase by 4–5 years by 2050.

participation, greater access to family planning and so on – women are having fewer children. The trend is somewhat more marked in Europe with a TFR of around 1.4 compared with the United States where it is just below 2. It is even more striking in Japan where the fertility rate is 1.2; even in PR China, the rate is now 1.8. UN forecasts suggest that within the next 15 years fertility rates will fall below replacement in countries as diverse as Brazil, Turkey and Iran.

The bottom line is that the average support ratio in the EU is forecast to decline from their current level of about 4 workers to retiree to only 2:1 by 2050.[21] All else being equal, the average worker will need to save twice as much to fund average retiree. The inevitable conclusion is that pensions must be reformed, unless this decline is mitigated by a reversal in the SR trend.

Such a reversal could take place if, for example, fertility rose. But such a prospect is unlikely. Take the example of Italy, a Catholic country where 'family centred' values are still thought to be dominant. Italy has the lowest fertility rates in the EU (1.24). Unlike Sweden, Italian provision of child allowances and support for working mothers is negligible: crèche facilities are poor while child support only kicks in for the third child. For Italian couples, the cost of having children is high, so they have fewer. By contrast, Sweden provides superb pre-school facilities, maternity and paternity allowances. Until the mid-1990s that policy appeared to be working: Swedish fertility rates were at replacement levels. But since then, the fertility rate has fallen precipitously: from 2.1 to 1.6. Nobody is quite sure why, but it would seem that because Swedes perceive their welfare provisions to be threatened – implying a rise in the cost of having a family – they are producing fewer children.[22] In general, although the TFR decline has been attenuated in a few countries, there is no country in which, having fallen substantially below the replacement rate, it has subsequently risen above it.

Another possibility is to encourage the inflow of immigrants: typically, adding young immigrants to the workforce will increase both the support ratio and fertility; eg, Latin American migrants in the USA have high fertility. But can an influx of new immigrants – even if it were politically feasible – act as more than a temporary palliative? Clearly not since, as they grow older, they in turn will add to the ranks of retirees whose pensions must be supported. (The same is true for increased fertility).

---

[21] The forecast decline in the SR between 2000 and 2050 in the UK is from 3.7 to 2.1; in Italy from 3.4 to 1.4; in the USA from 4.8 to 2.8 – and perhaps most spectacularly in China from 8.8 to 2.4.

[22] See Michael Specter, "Population Implosion Worries a Graying Europe," *The New York Times,* July 10, 1998

Nor is US-style privatisation the answer. While it is true that countries need to set aside funds to support their pension systems, it does not follow that privatising pension provision will achieve this any more efficiently than if it is done in the public sector. Privatising pensions is very expensive. Moreover, shifting decisions about inter-generational transfers from the public to the private domain may increase inequality. This is true in part because of the economies of scale inherent in state provision; most importantly, private individuals command inadequate information and have short time horizons. In particular, the poor typically cannot afford to defer consumption in order to provide for their old age.

7.8 BAD AND LESS-BAD ANSWERS

It will be apparent that there are no simple answers to the pension crisis, nor even any optimistic answers. The above discussion can be characterised as involving a choice in public policy between least-bad outcomes. At the outset, however, some fallacious remedies can be discarded, namely:

- Raising birth rates;
- Encouraging immigration;
- Privatisation and increased voluntary savings.

As should be obvious, while increasing birth rates and/or encouraging migration may help stabilise falling a support ratio, such measures alone do not constitute a solution. It is unlikely that any of the advanced countries will return to the support ratios enjoyed at the end of the twentieth century, figures which were already too low. What then can be done? The alternatives – one, or in combination – suggested by the above discussion are (a) reducing pension benefits; (b) increasing the retirement age; and (c) increasing total savings.

There is a good deal of evidence that, in the EU at least, a reduction in real pension benefits is unacceptable. Europeans generally see their retirement pension as an entitlement, one towards which they have contributed over their working lives. Indexing pensions to inflation rather than average earnings is a relatively painless form of pension reduction. Its perceived cost is low, particularly when average earnings are stagnating; but since real income can be assumed to rise in the long term (ie, the rate of income growth will exceed the rate of inflation), the decoupling of pensions from earnings growth ultimately redistributes income away from pensioners. However, making pensions more portable will help offset such a loss. At the moment, labour mobility within the EU is constrained by the difficulty of carrying one's pension to a new job, particularly if that new job involves crossing borders and changing private top-up pension providers. While we need not dwell on the matter here, suffice it to say that portability and labour mobility has become an increasingly important issue since EMU.

Increasing the retirement age may be part of the answer, although it is certainly not the whole answer. In certain countries (eg, France), attempts to do so have proved highly unpopular; equally, there is good reason to think that this is harder to do in some types of employment than others. Few assembly line workers or even school teachers would wish to work until they are 65 or 70, and in some occupations (eg, airline pilots) employees are forced to retire at a certain age because of stress and age-related deterioration in task-specific skills and faculties. On the other hand, some skilled workers and possibly a majority of professionals might accept working longer, particularly if better opportunities for mid-career retraining, part-time work and other complementary measures were provided. Indeed, given the increase in early retirement visible across the job spectrum, encouraging people to remain in work until official retirement age would be at least as beneficial as raising the retirement bar.

In a similar vein, raising the employment rate is only part of the answer; ie, raising the proportion of the working age population actually in work. As we have seen, this is one of the goals of the Lisbon process, and the EU has made progress in that direction in recent years. Eurostat[23] reports the 2003 employment rate for the EU-15 as 63%; this has risen from 60% in the mid-1990s and the target is to achieve 70% by 2010. Part of the problem has to do with the EU's relatively low participation rate for women. The Nordic countries have been particularly successful in this respect, largely through providing maternity and paternity benefits, pre-school child care, full-day school and so on. By contrast, although the female participation rate appears to have risen greatly in The Netherlands in the past two decades, much of the increase is accounted for by women moving into relatively unskilled, part-time employment, often little more than a few hours per week. Total annual working hours per employed worker in The Netherlands are still amongst the lowest in Europe. The contrast between the Nordic and Dutch cases suggests that raising the participation rate requires long-term investment in facilitating infrastructure.[24]

---

[23] Eurostat Database, Employment, April 12, 2005.

[24] Interestingly, it is often noted that female participation rates are high in the United States largely because traditional 'womens' work at home' is increasingly bought and sold in the market; this is possible because of a large pool of low-wage, unskilled (and often undocumented) labour.

The hard core of raising the employment rate appears to be reducing youth unemployment. Too many young people are spending too long after they finish school before entering the world of work. Doubtless, part of the difference between youth unemployment in the EU and the United States relates to the fact that university students in the US tend to work part-time while their EU counterparts generally receive some form of state support. At the other end of the social spectrum, more than 2mn working age Americans are in prison; the US rate of incarceration is nearly 8 times that of the EU.

While the above may help contain the problem, it is unlikely that existing levels of pensions can be sustained unless action is taken in two further areas; raising savings and raising growth. Higher savings can either be voluntary or involuntary (ie, in the form of higher contributions or higher taxes). To a degree, the private savings route has already been tried and tested in the UK. Many retirees have seen their savings boosted by spectacular gains in house prices.[25] Downsizing in retirement has enabled much of the middle class in Britain to live comfortably, even though British state pensions are amongst the lowest in the EU. However, to achieve a higher (or even comparable) private savings rate in future requires asset prices to continue to rise.

In the UK, the housing boom of the past decade is slowing ominously. Widespread house ownership is in any case a peculiarly British phenomenon. House prices are still rising in France, and while the French bubble is not as large as in the UK, it is likely that this too will soon deflate. Retirees in the rest of the EU depend far more upon their relatively generous state pensions, and are unlikely to accept the wholesale privatisation of pensions and individualisation of savings provision. As the proportion of younger people falls, rates of return on future assets may decline as discussed above.

An increase in savings can take many forms, though. In Britain where top-rate income tax is low by EU standards, an obvious step is to raise it; during the 2005 General Election, the Liberal Democrats suggested raising the marginal rate of tax to 50% on earnings of more than £100,000 a year. More generally, various forms of 'pension levy' have been suggested; eg, the 'pension levy' suggested by Rudolf Meidner in Sweden. Under such a scheme, all public companies employing more than 20 people would be required to fund a new pension reserve fund by issuing new shares specifically earmarked for this task equivalent to ten percent of their annual profit.[26] Clearly, to preserve

---

[25] Over the period 1995–2005, the value of an average house in Britain has approximately trebled. See Charlotte Moore, 'Regional house prices close gap with London' *The Guardian*, July 23, 2005.

[26] See R Blackburn 'The future strikes back: How to address the pension problem' *Renewal*, Vol 13, No 2/3, 2005. The advantage of Meidner's scheme is that it does not reduce a company's cash flow.

generational equity, provision needs to be made today to deal with tomorrow's problem.

The savings argument is closely related to the question of growth and productivity. In much of the EU, it is illogical to argue that greater household savings is the key to future prosperity when it is precisely the absence of buoyant consumption demand which helps explain why the EU core states are growing so slowly. The key notion here is Keynesian. It is growth that generates savings, not the other way around. To achieve growth, at least two things are required. First, existing household savings can be put to far better use than is currently the case, but only if the public sector lays the basis for renewed private investment growth. Household savings do not automatically turn into productive investment unless private entrepreneurs perceive good opportunities to turn cash reserves into bricks and mortar.

Secondly, growth itself will help generate the extra savings needed to finance future pensions. Increasing state funded pensions is far easier when funded out of rising income. This is true whether the extra resources are found by increasing pension contributions, by increasing general taxation or both. Finally, higher growth and higher labour productivity go hand in hand. Increasing labour productivity, as we have seen, directly offsets the squeeze on pensions resulting from a falling support ratio.

In short, while the EU has a pensions problem, there are many ways to tackle the problem, some more effective than others. Privatisation is not the answer; it may reduce the financial pressure on the state but, ultimately, it merely shifts the burden somewhere else rather than resolving it. Increasing the support ratio (SR) by raising the birth rate is probably not feasible, nor is large-scale immigration more than a palliative. A higher SR is more likely to result from increasing employment opportunities; notably, for the over 55s, for women and for youth.

Ultimately, though, if existing levels of pension provision are to be maintained for a higher proportion of long-living retirees, savings must be raised. This cannot be achieved by relying on a rise in voluntary household savings; the key to this increase is a rise in forced savings. Some of this extra savings can come out of achieving a more equitable distribution of income; ie, by reversing some of the trends towards inequity which have developed in the past three decades. But much of the new savings must come out of growth, or to put it another way, out of higher labour productivity driven by high investment. The state has a crucial role to play in undertaking the sort of infrastructure investment which will 'crowd in' private investment. Every euro which goes into new hospitals, more schools or better transport will involve generating more contracts for private sector firms, in turn enabling more employment, higher demand and more investment. Dealing with the pensions crisis is feasible under conditions of growing prosperity; it is not if Europe pursues macroeconomic policies resulting in another decade of stagnation.

CHAPTER 8

The EU Budget, the CAP and Enlargement

The main limits on stabilisation policy derive from the fact that adjustment mechanisms in a Monetary Union should be linked to a federal budget able to cope with either a general shock hitting the whole Union or a country-specific shock with asymmetric effects on different Member States. This is the predominant view in the literature on stabilisation policy. It accordingly seems reasonable to endow the {EU's} budget with a built-in insurance mechanism to deal with asymmetric shocks. (A. Majocchi, 2003, section 5)

8.1 THE EU BUDGET

The EU may be an emerging economic power, but its central budget is miniscule in comparison with the Federal Budget of the United States – about a quarter of Gross National Product (GNP) – or even with that of EU member states where the share of state expenditure is typically some 40–50 percent of GNP. (The minor differences between GNI and GNP or GDP need not detain the reader.) The EU central budget is capped at 1.24 percent of combined EU GNI[1], while actual spending in 2003 was less than one percent, or roughly €100b. As Ian Begg has remarked,[2] the squabble between member states about budgetary contributions and rebates is out of all proportion to the budget's size. Whatever legitimate criticisms may be made of the Brussels bureaucracy, it is nonetheless remarkable that the European Commission costs less to run than the Mayor's Office in London. The entire cost of running EU institutions

[1] The Maastricht Treaty capped the budget. Strictly speaking, the 1.24 percent cap refers to combined Gross National Income (GNI) of the member states; it was originally capped at 1.27 percent, but a revision of National Accounting conventions has resulted in the current figure. For present purposes, it matters little whether one takes GNI or GDP.

[2] See Begg (2004); also Begg (2000).

including the Commission, the European Parliament, Eurostat and so on is less than the €6bn spent annually to administer the city of Paris. In short, citizens of the EU pay very little for central government; they can hardly complain if it sometimes fails to live up to their expectations.

How Brussels raises and spends it money forms part of the EU's embryonic fiscal policy. In theory, fiscal policy – whether at local, national or supra-national level – plays a key role in three areas. First, it can be used to promote efficiency. It is generally recognised that because of imperfect information, externalities and the existence of public goods, government needs to act where markets are inefficient; for example, by providing common services like law and order, common health and safety provisions, legislating against environmental pollution and so on. Secondly, fiscal policy can be used to promote equity; most Europeans would agree that taxation should be broadly progressive (ie, graduated with respect to income and wealth), or that Europe's richer regions should contribute towards the development of poorer ones. Finally, fiscal policy plays an important role in macroeconomic policy: notably, in dampening the amplitude of periodic fluctuations in economic activity known as the 'business cycle'. Improving EU fiscal policy raises two issues; that of the requisite degree of fiscal harmonisation between member states, and that of the optimal size of the EU's budget.

Although Brussels provides few common services (little other than a court, an embryonic EU defence capability, a statistical office – and of course the CAP and structural funds), it does initiate legislation and harmonise member-state legislation on health and safety standards, environmental pollution and the like. It also plays a small redistributive role in providing infrastructure and social support to poorer regions. Otherwise, the principle of 'subsidiarity' reigns supreme; ie, supplying public goods remains the prerogative of member-states. There is little in the budget for EU-level direct expenditure in areas such as health, education, welfare provision and environmental policy. The EU regulates trade, competition policy and several other matters, but the only area in which it spends a significant amount of EU money is agriculture – and to a lesser degree for infrastructure in poorer regions.

Nor does the budget play a role in the area of macro-economic policy; as we have seen, the EU budget is constrained to balance annually thus excluding *a priori* a stabilising role in macroeconomic management, while the Maastricht Treaty and the SGP seriously constrain counter-cyclical spending at member-state level. Nor can federal Europe borrow money abroad, in contrast to (say) the US Treasury. It would be illegal, for example, for the EU to run a budget deficit in order to stimulate economic activity. This was not always the case. In 1977, when Europe was formed of only the six 'core' members, the

Commission asked a group of experts under the chairmanship of a British civil servant, Sir Donald MacDougall, to examine the role of public finance in European integration, counter-cyclical policy and redistribution. The report concluded that, minimally, the budget would need to amount to 7% of combined GDP if Brussels were to have any macroeconomic impact, and that budgetary contributions should be based on progressive taxation.

The report also considered an intermediate phase in which Brussels would assume responsibility for foreign aid, some unemployment benefits and some vocational training as well as providing grants for poorer regions; MacDougall thought that 2–2.5 percent would be a sensible figure. One would expect that as the integration process proceeds, Brussels's budget would grow; ie, that the size of the budget is a barometer of integration. Contrary to expectations, one of the key effects of expanding the size of the Union and achieving EMU seems to have been the abandonment of even a minimal aspiration to federal government.

8.2   RECEIPTS AND EXPENDITURE

The EU's budget comes from customs receipts and levies gathered from the Common external tariff (known as 'original own resources'), a small slice of each member-state's VAT and, finally, member-states' contributions (the 'fourth resource'). Today, member-state contributions account for about 60 percent of the EU's revenue. This fourth own resource is in effect an inter-governmental grant. Its size is negotiated on a 'willingness to pay' basis which, although roughly proportional to GNP, bears no clear relationship to the country's per capita income level or to the net benefit derived from EU membership.[3] The EU has no power to raise money above and beyond what the member-states agree to. While the Commission would like to see a rise in the proportion of funds allocated automatically to Brussels, national Finance Ministers have consistently opposed this view and wish to remain firmly in control of the purse strings.

Prior to 1988, budgeting was an annual process; this came under strain because of growing annual disagreement between the European Parliament and the Council of Ministers. Since then a medium-term budgeting framework has been adopted called the 'financial perspective'. At present, member-states are busy negotiating a framework for the period 2007–2013 to which they must eventually agree unanimously. The process of negotiation has been going on for several years, and the current mood is one of tight-fisted cost cutting.

---

[3]   Spain proposed redesigning the inter-governmental contribution along the lines of a progressive income several years ago, but no progress has been made on this principle.

Initially, it was proposed that spending rise slowly to reach a level of about 1.15 percent of combined GDP, well short of the Maastricht limit. Although enlargement and making Europe 'more competitive' should ideally be accompanied by a growing budget, in December 2003 six of the richest member states (including Britain) requested that a *de facto* cap of 1 percent of combined GNI be imposed for the perspective period. In June 2005, an attempt to reach agreement on the 2007–2013 financial perspectives was effectively blocked by Britain, which refused to give up its 'rebate' negotiated under Margaret Thatcher. It is unlikely that there will be any increase in total funds available for running the EU-25; each member-state continues to be concerned with receiving its own fair share rather than acting in the interest of the EU as a whole.

Figure 8–1 shows the Commission's proposed budget ceiling[4] for the medium term starting in 2007, when total spending envisaged would be about €115b (at constant 2000 prices), or 1.15 percent of combined GNI. Some new labels have appeared: the 'structural funds' and the 'internal policies' have been merged under the heading 'sustainable growth'. Agricultural subsidies paid by the CAP come under the label 'sustainable management and protection of natural resources'. New budget items include 'growth and employment' which brings together monies for research, energy and communications, the Trans-European Network (TENs) and 'citizenship, security etc' which includes justice, home affairs and EU cultural identity. As Begg (2004) has noted, the labels are largely window dressing. Taken together, the structural funds and the CAP – on which more below – will continue to account for nearly three-quarters of spending; room for manoeuvre is restricted to the remaining quarter of the pie where policies to promote growth and competitiveness are more prominent. Aid for accession members would be financed from the extra 0.15 percent of GNI, although this rise is still within the 1.24 percent limit.

The Commission's budget contrasts with a recommendation made by an expert group chaired during 2002 by Professor André Sapir, which in essence would have ditched the CAP and the structural fund, allocating about half the budget to growth, a third to convergence (particularly for the 10 new states) and the remainder to restructuring (including the phasing out of CAP).[5] But implementing Sapir's proposals was ruled out in practice by the Franco-German deal over the CAP in October 2002.

At present, the main issues of discord over the Commission's proposal are the budget's composition, its total size and who pays for it. The strong skew

---

[4]   The proposal was published in February 2003; the figures are represent 'ceilings' rather than targets.
[5]   See Sapir (2003).

Policy Heading	2007	2008	2009	2010	2011	2012	2013
1a Competitiveness	9.1	10.4	11.7	12.9	14.1	15.3	16.3
1b Cohesion	35.6	34.9	34.3	33.6	32.9	32.5	32.2
2a Agriculture	32.6	31.4	30.3	29.3	28.4	27.6	26.7
2b Other 'sustain-able development'	10.2	10.3	10.3	10.2	10.1	9.9	9.8
3 Citizenship, security ctc	1.2	1.5	1.6	1.8	2.0	2.1	2.3
4. EU as a global partner	8.5	8.8	9.0	9.4	9.7	9.8	9.9
5. Administration	2.8	2.8	2.8	2.8	2.8	2.8	2.8
Total	100	101	100	100	100	100	100

Source: Begg (2004, 5)

Figure 8–1: Total Expenditure Shares in Commission's 2007–2013 Financial Perspectives

towards agricultural subsidies remains, although somewhat mollified by the agriculture's falling share (only about a quarter in 2013), the shift towards direct payment and more environmentally friendly policies as discussed below. Accession countries are unhappy that the Commission has failed to raise significantly the availability of structural funds to the 10 new members. As for the size of the budget, the large countries have already complained about the figure of 1.15 percent of GNI; six Finance Ministers including Germany's Hans Eichel and his British counterpart, Gordon Brown, have deemed any rise unacceptable. And of course, there is the near-permanent row about net gainers and losers.

8.3 NET GAINERS AND LOSERS: THE UK REBATE

How the bill is to be divided has always been a contentious issue. In theory, net payment might be based on the richer states paying most. In practice, there is no clear guiding principle. Some states are net contributors (Germany) while others are net recipients (Ireland) – since 1984, Britain has received a special rebate – worth about €5b per annum at present – and so lies in fourth place amongst the ten largest countries. The net contributors to the budget (before the British rebate) in order are The Netherlands, Sweden, Germany, Britain and Austria; France is about neutral while the net beneficiaries are Italy, Spain, Greece and Ireland [6]

[6] See *The Economist* 'The battle of the budget' London, March 3 2005.

During the UK presidency of the EU in 2005, disagreement over this issue could derail the passage of the EU budget. The UK rebate, originally agreed because Britain's payment was out of proportion to its per capita income level while its benefit from CAP was minimal, has become increasingly contentious over the years. It amounts at present to some £3b (€5b) per annum, roughly two-thirds the size of Britain's net budget contribution. Some rich countries have seen themselves as larger net losers than Britain and, in effect, paying for Britain's rebate. In 1999, some net contributors towards the UK rebate negotiated a better deal for themselves with the result that some of the poorer members had to pay more of Britain's rebate. This has resulted in a proposal by the Commission to replace the rebate with a 'generalised corrective mechanism', which would also produce rebates for Germany, The Netherlands and Sweden, but this mechanism would also increase Britain's contribution.[7]

While Britain continues to veto any change in the rebate, its case is far weaker than it was a generation ago. Compared to 1984, Britain *per capita* income is now higher than that of The Netherlands, France or Germany, the other three net losers. All three pay more per head than does Britain. Moreover, although Britain is now the fourth largest net contributor after the rebate, by 2013 it will fall to ninth place. Moreover, by refusing to cede ground on this matter, Britain antagonises the new accession states who already have accepted lower benefits from the budget than were envisaged at the outset. Yet it is likely that Britain will only compromise if there is a major revision in the Common Agricultural Policy (CAP). By insisting on this point, Britain sees itself as setting the agenda on European 'modernisation'. Britain's critics would argue, first, that much has already been accomplished in reforming the CAP; most importantly, they would point out that by insisting on its rebate 'come what may', Britain is exhausting its already depleted fund of EU goodwill.

8.4 THE ORIGINS OF THE CAP

The Common Agricultural Policy (CAP) is the subject of endless controversy, partly because it is the largest single item of EU budgetary expenditure and partly because consumers pay the non-budgetary cost. European farmers receive 40 percent of their total revenue from CAP, an annual cost of roughly €100b to consumers and taxpayers. The CAP is neither efficient nor equitable. Although Europe is not alone in subsidising agriculture – so too does the USA, Canada and Japan – pressure for reform has been building for many years.

---

[7] See *The Economist loc cit.*

Disputes in the World Trade Organisation (WTO) plus the recent accession of ten countries considerably poorer and more rural than the EU-15 norm, have added to this pressure.

Following the signing of the Treaty of Rome (1957), the CAP was created both as a means of supporting farm prices and of modernising the structure of agriculture; in practice, the latter was largely ignored so that the CAP became synonymous with price support. The support mechanism was indirect: it guaranteed minimum prices for farmers' produce rather than directing aid to poorer farmers. Moreover, it was financed indirectly: by passing the higher cost of products to consumers rather than through taxation. In contrast to the system of 'deficiency payments' financed from general taxation once used in the UK, the CAP placed the burden of support directly on consumers, who paid higher prices for selected agricultural commodities than they otherwise would. When commodity prices fell below a pre-determined support level, the EU budget kicked in to make up the difference. Although gradual reform has resulted in the proportion of the EU budget allocated to CAP support falling to about 45 percent at present, in the 1980s the figure peaked at nearly 75 percent. Moreover, CAP expenditure by Brussels, high as it has been, is only a fraction of total CAP support, most of which was paid for by food purchasers and member-states.

Over the years, the inequitable nature of CAP support has become increasingly apparent. Agriculture accounts for only 2 percent of EU-15 GNP and 4.3 percent of employment, but the annual cost to taxpayers and shoppers of artificially high food prices is estimated to be over €250 for each EU citizen. Like any flat-rate tax, the 'tax' on food is regressive. Poorer Europeans pay relatively more than the rich simply because food expenditure is a larger proportion of their expenditure.[8] The intensification of agriculture has in some cases led to environmental degradation. Subsidies have led to serious overproduction and spiralling costs. Moreover, it is not merely Europeans who pay but farmers in the world's poorer regions; EU surpluses of such commodities as sugar and food grains are dumped on international markets forcing down world prices. This matter has been highlighted by the Cairns group of countries in the current (Doha) round of negotiations at the WTO.

Nor are the benefits of food subsidies divided equitably amongst European farmers. CAP payments are based upon production, not household income; consequently, the larger the farm, the greater the total subsidy. It is estimated that the largest 40 percent of farms received 90 percent of all direct subsidies, while nearly 25 percent of direct subsidies go to the largest two percent of farms. Agribusinesses, not small farmers, are the main beneficiaries of the CAP.

---

[8] See Thurston (2002: 17).

It is often said that it is the French who do best out of the EU; in fact, the 'net benefit' per head of membership (costs minus revenue) is nearly neutral. What is true is that, in absolute terms, France receives about €10b in CAP subsidies annually, 80% of which goes to agribusiness. (Britain receives only about €4b annually.) But the bulk of French peasants are poor – French farmers account for just over 4% of the population of which some 40% earn an annual income below the minimum wage. Without CAP payments, many French peasants would be forced off the land. This helps explain why the CAP is such a politically contentious issue in France.

Figure 8–2: French Farmers and CAP

Nevertheless, because a large number of relatively inefficient small farmers would be the first to suffer from a cut in CAP subsidies, they are amongst its most vocal supporters. This is particularly true in France where there are many small farmers and the majority belong to a trade union.

For all its lack of efficiency and equity, it would be wrong to dismiss CAP as a monster created by bureaucrats in Brussels and their French backers, a caricature which finds wide resonance in the British press. Historically, the agricultural sector has provided the resources for industrialisation; once industry is dominant, it is hard to argue that agriculture should receive nothing in return. The CAP has contributed to food self-sufficiency, rapid technological change and the falling share of agricultural in total employment, which characterised European agriculture in the 1970s and 1980s. It has helped harmonise the diversity of national laws regarding production or trade; for example, the use of preservatives, colouring agents, hormones and disease control. Moreover, various studies have shown that the largest net beneficiary of the CAP has not been France – The Netherlands, Ireland, Denmark and the Mediterranean countries have all done better.[9] In short, although the CAP is not a monster, as a means of helping EU farmers it has been woefully inadequate, poorly targeted and expensive to consumers, taxpayers and third parties. At present, the EU has far more urgent tasks on which to spend collective resources.

Doubtless a UK-style system of deficiency payments would have been more equitable and less costly in total, but it could not have been replicated at European level in the late 1960s for two reasons. Deficiency payment, or any form of 'direct payment' (DP), represents a direct budgetary claim and is expensive to administer. While DP worked in the UK, where only a small fraction of the workforce remained in agriculture, a DP-based system in the 1960s would have been nearly impossible to administer in other European countries where farmers were more numerous. Equally important, DP then

---

[9] See Lintner and Maizey (1991), Chapter 7.

would have shifted the entire burden of subsidy payment to the EU budget and/or to that of member-states. Even allowing for the far lower cost of a fully DP-based system, its budgetary cost would have been politically intolerable.

8.5 REFORMING CAP

Since the 1980s, the CAP has been reformed in various respects. Reform measures can be grouped under various headings, notably:

- quota limits and price cuts;
- surplus reduction;
- direct payments;
- 'second pillar' reforms.

Until the 1980s, the CAP operated through a combination of tariff and quota barriers on agricultural imports from outside the EU, subsidies to exporters and the fixing of prices above world prices. Despite successive rounds of reform starting in 1984, change has proved exceedingly difficult. Member states that were net gainers have not wanted to change the system – although by the late 1990s some countries that had previously been net gainers saw their position reversed (eg, The Netherlands). In terms of budgetary transfers in 1998, Ireland, Greece, Spain, France, Portugal, Denmark and Finland gained while Belgium, Germany, Britain, The Netherlands and Sweden lost.[10] But budgetary transfers are far from the whole story. Farmers form powerful pressure groups in most EU countries. The farming vote is important and can sometimes be decisive, particularly in France, Spain, Italy, Ireland and Greece. Apart from the farming vote, government of member-states have been subject to increasingly well-organised pressure from the agribusiness and small-farmer lobbies, although counter-lobbying from consumer and environmental groups has also grown. The veto system in the Agricultural Council of Ministers has made it relatively easy to block reform, a problem exacerbated by the fact that Ministers generally place short-term national interests ahead of long-term interests of the EU as a whole.

Despite these pressures, the CAP has gradually been reformed. The first round of reform was agreed at Fontainebleau in 1984 when, in the midst of an EU budgetary crisis, Mrs Thatcher demanded a rebate and CAP reform as the *quid pro quo* for Britain's continued budgetary contribution. The implementation of the Fontainebleau Accord between 1985 and 1989 resulted

---

[10] See Thurston (2002: 35).

in cuts in production quotas, memorably the milk quota, in taking some land out of production (set-aside) and in a 10 percent average reduction in support prices for a wide range of produce. Moreover, specific policies were introduced to address surplus production – the 'butter mountains and wine lakes' of the 1970s – which by the late 1980s had largely disappeared.

The next round of change came after 1992 with the implementation of the MacSharry Reforms, named after the then Commissioner for Agriculture. The reforms were a response to both the continuing problem of food surpluses and to pressure on the EU to agree in the Uruguay Round of GATT negotiations, the key to which proved to be the Blair House Accords. What emerged from the MacSharry period was less radical than what the Commissioner had originally proposed. Although support prices for grain and beef were reduced and quota limits placed on oilseeds (the Blair House Accords), attempts to effect similar reductions in case of milk, wine, fruit and vegetables failed. Nevertheless, the reforms marked the first real move away from a price-support system towards direct payment (DP).

Taking the example of one EU member-state, in the Republic of Ireland the proportion of average family farm income derived from the market (as opposed to direct payments) decreased from 73 percent in 1993 to 37 per cent in 1997. At the same time the corresponding proportions for DP increased from 27 per cent to 63 per cent. Equally important, 'analysis of the distribution of family farm income by deciles (based on FFI) and for all farms indicates a more equitable distribution of income between 1993 and 1997. This improvement in equity is attributed to the effects of direct payments on farm incomes.'[11] Direct Payments have made the burden of European farm subsidies more transparent, thus helping to signal the need for further change.

In early 1999, the UK, Sweden, Denmark and Italy joined forces in the 'Agenda 2000' negotiations, an agreement driven by the eastward enlargement of the EU and a new round of WTO negotiations. France and the southern countries opposed the proposals; Germany, the largest net loser from CAP, initially sat on the fence although it tended to favour handing back agricultural policies to member-states (or 'repatriation'). The outcome was a compromise reached at the Berlin Summit in July 1999, widely perceived at the time as a deal between the French President and German Chancellor delaying necessary reform.[12]

---

[11] Frawley, J and M Keeney (2000: 1) 'The Impact of Direct Payments on Farm Income Distribution' Project No. 4656, Irish Agriculture and Food Development Authority, Dublin.

[12] As a historical footnote, Tony Blair's main contribution to the Summit was not to oppose the cuts in provision for the new accession states but rather to call stridently for keeping Britain's rebate.

The deal was occasioned in part because, although the reform would reduce the total cost of CAP, increased DPs would shift more of the burden from consumers to national budgets—and budgets were particularly tight in France and Germany. Nevertheless, Agenda 2000 reduced subsidies, and it gave renewed impetus to structural spending, the so-called 'second pillar' reform aimed at promoting environmental management and sustainable rural development representing some 10–15% of Brussels's CAP budget.

- *The CAP costs the average family in Europe €20 per week in higher food prices*
- *Each European cow costs taxpayers $2.20 a day while half the worlds' population lives on less than $2 a day;*
- *The 224 largest cereal producers get €70m per year between them, more than the UK spends on aid to Ethiopia*
- *Sugar giant Tate and Lyle received more than €170m in CAP subsidies last year*
- *Prince Charles received £300,000 in subsidies for his Cornwall estate.*

Source: Heather Stewart 'Scrap the CAP' *The Observer* 19 June 2005.

Figure 8–3: Dunce's CAP

Finally, for the first time, a mid-term review process was set up to monitor progress and extend reform. It has been estimated that once fully implemented in 2008, the Agenda 2000 reform will result in annual net benefits to EU citizens of €7.5b.[13]

To this must be added the mid-term review reforms proposed by the EU Commissioner, Franz Fischler, and accepted by the 2003 European Council. In essence, the Fischler proposals reduce payments to farmers by a further 20 percent over seven years. In the words of one commentator:

> The European Commission's proposals for the 2002/03 Mid-Term Review have the potential to be the most radical in CAP history. The proposed reforms could reduce food prices for shoppers, make it easier for farmers to read market signals, remove incentives for farmers to overproduce and make the countryside a better place to live and work … Farmers would no longer enjoy artificially inflated prices and farm support payments would be made conditional upon observing good farm practice.[14]

---

[13] See Thurston (2000: 15).
[14] See Thurston (2002: 2).

To date, the reform record has undoubtedly been positive. What was once a hugely expensive system of subsidies paid for by consumers has now become less costly, more transparent and its cost has been largely shifted to national budgets through the direct payment system. 'Modulation' – which signifies capping subsidies and providing for their automatic annual reduction – has reduced the inequitable division of the spoils favouring agribusiness at the expense of small farmers. CAP expenditure has fallen to around 45% of the EU budget, and part of remaining expenditure has switched from subsidies (Pillar I) to environmentally friendly 'Pillar II' support. Member states have had to co-finance a growing share of 'Pillar I' subsidies. Farm support in the ten new accession states is considerably less than would have been the case in the absence of reform, and the accession states have incurred co-financing responsibility immediately upon joining.[15] Given the reduced agricultural subsidy to accession states and the fact that co-financing will prove expensive, it is possible that the new members themselves will demand further cost-cutting measures.[16] At the same time, critics of the CAP point out that the shift towards Direct Payments is really sleight-of-hand and that most farmers receive nearly as much today as they received under the old production-based system of subsidies.

8.6 CANCÚN AND THE DOHA ROUND

It is particularly in the international arena that the CAP has been highly contentious. Farm subsidy reduction has proved insufficient for the EU's main negotiating partners in the WTO. The WTO has set certain broad goals for CAP reform, distinctively summarized by the 'three box' system shown in Figure 8–4. Trade and production distorting measures, about 20 percent of the CAP spending, fall into what is called the 'amber box' (left) and are outlawed. Production linked subsidies for livestock and arable land, or 'blue box' (centre) measures accounting for 70 percent of CAP spending are temporarily allowed while 'production neutral' pro-environment and other measures (a further 10 percent) are encouraged, as shown in the 'green box' on the right. On this basis, the MacSharry reforms moved spending from amber to blue, while Agenda 2000 and subsequent reforms emphasized green spending (or Pillar II) at the expense of blue. Still, the main issue at Doha concerned the 80 percent of spending in the amber and blue boxes.

In 2003, the Cancun Meeting – part of the Doha Round of trade talks –

[15] Farm support for the ten new members starts at about one-quarter of what it was to the original members.
[16] See Knorr (2004).

failed even though the European Council (the heads of all the EU's member states) had unanimously approved the Fischler proposals in January 2003. This proposal envisaged the reduction of import tariffs by 36 percent, a reduction of export subsidies by 45 percent and a 55 percent reduction in internal agricultural support. Nor was agreement reached on the compromise solution put forward by the WTO mediator, Stuart Harbinson: notably, a 60 percent reduction in agricultural tariffs and the total abolition of export subsidies within 10 years. The EU found the compromise too radical, for USA the Cairns group it did not go far enough. If the Doha round is to end as scheduled in 2007, further negotiations will be needed.

20% CAP Budget	70% CAP Budget	10% CAP Budget
Trade & Production Distorting • Intervention Buying • Refunds to Export • Import Duties Charged	**Production Linked** • Arable Area Payments, • Livestock Headage Payments	**Production Neutral** • Rural Development Regulation, incl. • Agri-environmental schemes and Hill Farm Allowance
TO BE OUTLAWED	**TEMP. ALLOWED**	**ALLOWED**

Figure 8–4: The 'three boxes'

In general, the question of what to do with the CAP boils down to two key points. The first is that despite past reform – much of it quite successful – CAP needs to be reformed further, particularly in light of the need to reach Agreement at the WTO. The second is that farmers in the EU no longer need subsidies and that CAP should be phased out. Given increased competition for EU budgetary resources, the growing dissatisfaction of countries that are net contributors and that of EU consumers, it is difficult to see the CAP surviving beyond the 2007–2013 perspective budgeting period.

8.7   THE CHALLENGE OF ENLARGEMENT

The current round of budgetary perspective negotiation is linked not merely to the CAP, but to the vital question of making current enlargement work. Will enlargement bring new dynamism to Europe's economies or, *per contra*, will the rightward-leaning 'new' Europeans retard the process of integration? Will the ten new members 'catch up' like Spain and Portugal or will the income gap between the rich and poor countries grow? Should the new countries join the euro immediately, or should they be asked to adhere to an extended timetable of convergence? And what of the prospective members who are queuing to join?

The 2004 round of accession was quite unlike those of 1995 (Austria, Finland, Sweden) and 1986 (Portugal, Spain). Broadly, the recent accession means that the EU's population has grown by 20% but it's combined GDP by only 9%. The accession countries are poorer – their per capita GDP is only half that of the EU-15. The new round will double Europe's farm population; if the Commission's modest budgetary perspective proposals are accepted, by 2013 Brussels will need to find an extra €5bn per annum to subsidise agriculture in the new states.

Although extra spending is foreseen on accession countries' infrastructure in the Commission's financial perspectives, it falls far short of what is needed to achieve rapid modernisation. According to the rosiest forecasts prepared by The Economist Intelligence Unit in London, Polish living standards will take nearly 60 years to catch up to the average of the EU-15.[17] How long will it take the Baltic States to catch up – where living standards are only one-third of the EU-15 average?

Eight of the ten accession states are from the former Eastern Bloc, the so-called 'new' Europeans identified by Donald Rumsfeld. Although there is much enthusiasm for joining, there is also much legitimate concern. After all, these countries were promised a glorious future upon abandoning 'socialism' 15 years ago. Instead, the transition to the market economy proved traumatic; in most of Eastern Europe in the early 1990s, *per capita* income fell precipitously and unemployment surged. Since 1995, the trend has in most countries has sharply

---

[17] See The Economist 'A Club in need of a new vision' April 29, 2004.

reversed. But it is only today that Poland, Hungary and the Czech Republic – the largest accession economies – are at last returning to their 1989 level of *per capita* income.

Understandably, these countries do not want to be placed once more under stringent IMF-style tutelage. Nevertheless, that is what the Maastricht rules require. To join the Eurozone – as all new entrants must – strict targets must be met with respect to each country's budget deficit, level of indebtedness, level of inflation, exchange-rate regime and so on. Most recently, both Hungary and Poland have experienced serious pain in attempting to tighten their belts. Although the new countries generally have low levels of public debt, their budget deficits and inflation rates are mainly above the Maastricht limit. Moreover, upon joining the euro, inflation may become more pronounced as was the case with Portugal and Spain.[18] This has led some economists, most prominently France's Charles Wyplosz, to call for a change in the Maastricht rules lest the central and eastern European countries be forced into a new recession.[19]

8.8 SHOULD NEW MEMBERS RUSH TO JOIN THE EUROZONE?

Within a few days of accession, Cyprus, Estonia, Lithuania and Slovenia announced plans to join the euro by late 2007. Brussels is not keen, arguing that only by spending many years within the new Exchange Rate Mechanism (ERM 2) will countries converge sufficiently with the Eurozone to qualify for membership. Is this a sensible argument? According to Professor Barry Eichengreen of the University of California at Berkeley, it is not.[20] Prolonged membership of the ERM only increases the probability of a currency suffering a speculative attack, of the sort Britain experienced in 1992. Eichengreen's alternative is called the 'Nike strategy': ie, if you want to join the euro, just do it! Hungary, for example, has experienced several serious and destabilising currency fluctuations since 2001. The best way to avoid speculative attack is, as with sunburn, to minimise exposure.

While some smaller accession countries may adopt the euro in 2007 (and thus join ERM 2 in 2005), the larger ones will probably wait until the end of the decade. It is possible that Slovenia, Cyprus and the Baltic states will adopt the euro in January 2007. Hungary, Poland, the Czech Republic and Slovakia

---

[18] The tendency under fixed exchange rates for high productivity-growth 'catching-up' states to have higher than average inflation than is referred to by economists as the Belassa-Samuelson effect.
[19] See Wyplosz (2003).
[20] See Eichengreen (2000).

are unlikely to be full Eurozone members much before 2010. Nor are any of the accession states members of the Schengen area of passport-free travel, and membership is unlikely before 2007. Perhaps most important, the accession states do not enjoy automatic freedom to work throughout the EU; only Britain, Ireland and Sweden opened their labour markets at the outset, although it is probable that the remaining EU-15 will do so soon.

A further contentious area is that of taxation. An increasing number of former eastern-bloc members are adopting flat-rate taxation; ie, a single rate of tax for everything from VAT to corporate and personal income tax.[21] It all started in 1994 when Estonia became the first country in Europe to introduce a 'flat tax' at a single uniform rate of 26%. The flat tax principle has since spread. By 2005 it had been adopted in eight countries: Estonia, Lithuania, Latvia, Russia, Serbia, Ukraine, Slovakia, Georgia and Romania. The flat rate in these countries ranged between 13 percent in Russia to 33 percent in Lithuania. The new system has the advantage of being simple to administer – there are no schedule of rates, no allowances, no deductions – all of which appeals to countries lacking both western-style progressive tax systems and the required administrative capability to collect taxes. There are several dangers however. Because rich and poor alike pay the same rate, such a system is highly regressive. Moreover, a flat tax eliminates the stabilisers built in to a progressive system and designed to protect against business cycle fluctuations. In countries like France and Germany, the adoption of a flat system in former Eastern Europe will be seen by many as a form of 'social dumping'. This strengthens the position of enlargement sceptics who argue that too many jobs are already being lost to the new, low-wage member-states; equally, it would make fiscal harmonisation – generally supported in the Eurozone but opposed by Britain – nearly impossible. Most important, unless a flat tax is set at quite a high rate, its fiscal yield is far lower than that of a progressive system. The goal of those backing the flat tax principle is clear: to achieve a dramatic reduction in the size of state spending on social provision.

Economists assumed that new countries would experience much higher growth rates than the average for the EU-15 as a consequence of the 'catching-up' effect. But the effect may not be as pronounced, and there is no guarantee that the accession states will find membership of the EU a magic potion to remedy all economic ills. Indeed, the opposite seems equally likely. According to the projections of the *Centre Economique de l'Université de Paris Nord*[22], while adhesion may prove a blessing for the more advanced countries enabling them to achieve Spanish-style transformation, others may fall even further behind

---

[21] See The Economist , 'The flat tax revolution' London, May 4, 2005.
[22] See Dupuch, S, Jennequin, H and El Mouhoub Mouhoud (2004).

the EU-15. Unless measures are taken to reduce vulnerability to speculative attack, a prolonged transition to the euro could prove more painful than staying out altogether.

True, part of these problems might be avoided were the core members of the Eurozone more understanding and more generous. But overly tight fiscal and monetary policies have nearly paralysed the economies of Germany, France and Italy. Under current conditions of economic stagnation EU generosity is in short supply, as illustrated by the fate of the Sapir (2003) proposals to ditch CAP and concentrate on improved social and economic infrastructure in the adhesion countries.

8.9   THE FUTURE OF ENLARGEMENT

If the future of the 2004 enlargement round is uncertain, the prospect of adding another half-dozen states is even more so. With core states facing slow growth and cutting back on welfare in order to balance government budgets, it is hardly surprising that many Europeans worry that further enlargement will turn 'their' Europe into an entity which is uncontrollable and unrecognisable. Prospective members are Bulgaria, Romania, Croatia and Turkey. Further down the road lies the prospect of membership for Albania, Belarus, Bosnia, Georgia, Moldova, Macedonia, Serbia and the Ukraine. Even with Qualified Majority Voting and a limited number of Commissioners, a Europe of 38 member states clearly could not possibly function along its present lines. For one thing, almost all the prospective new members are even poorer than the ten who joined in 2005. For another, there is considerable resistance already to membership of a country like Turkey – not merely because of its size and poverty, but because some Europeans argue that Turkey is neither geographically nor culturally part of Europe. If one adds the former Soviet Republics to the list, the problems multiply.

Several things are pretty obvious. For one thing, Europe's absorption of ten new states has made the running of the EU more difficult; indeed, it is arguable that there is a major trade-off between 'widening' and 'deepening', and that if any further advance is to be made in achieving 'ever closer union', the process of widening must stop—or at least be placed on hold for some considerable time. For another, a growing current of political opinion in the richer states is opposed to widening. Britain may favour further rounds of accession – most candidate countries are seen as strongly pro-market and Atlanticist – but Britons, just like Frenchmen and Germans, are likely to be unhappy about taking on board more foreigners, particularly poor ones from distant lands.

The failure of France's referendum has brought this point home very clearly.

One of the fears of ordinary French citizens is that the EU has grown into a huge free-trade area, far surpassing the size and nature of the Europe envisaged 20 years ago. True, a referendum is often treated as a plebiscite; ie, as a costless opportunity to vote against the national government rather than on the issue at hand. The policies of the now-defunct Balladur Government, and more generally of President Chirac, have not been popular. In France – just as in Germany , Sweden and other member-states – the notion of a prosperous 'social' Europe lies at the heart of people's vision of what the European project is about, and it is precisely the erosion of this vision which is at the root of popular dissatisfaction. It is the promise of secure employment, universal social services, education and decent pensions which speaks to people, not the promise of expanding markets. It is hard to see the European project moving forward again without a reaffirmation of these principles, together with the adoption of new and concrete measures to bridge the democratic deficit separating Brussels from its citizens.

CHAPTER 9

Alternative Growth Strategies

One message yet to get across to those people who espouse conventional wisdom in the Eurozone is that, when private saving is so high and consumer spending so restrained, budget deficits are not the problem: they are an essential part of the answer. It is only when – if and when – a more expansionary policy in the Eurozone restores the confidence of consumers and boosts their spending that policymakers should become concerned about the budget deficit. (William Keegan, 2005)[1]

9.1 SUPPLY-SIDE AND DEMAND-LED VIEWS

There are many alternative views of what Europe might be. Some see a future Europe much like the United States where the role of the state is minimal, structural obstacles to reform such as trade unions are largely dismantled and the market is given free rein. Others want a more 'social' Europe, but disagree about whether the right climate for growth is best fostered by balanced budgets and greater competitiveness or, alternatively, by throwing fiscal caution to the wind and concentrating on a strong programme of investment in economic and social infrastructure. Still others believe that growth itself is a bad thing since it pollutes the environment and uses up non-replenishable resources. The permutations and combinations are seemingly endless.

One cannot hope to do justice to the many variants by reducing them to schematic alternatives. In what follows, therefore, the reader is asked to accept a certain amount of simplification in order to better focus on how Eurozone growth might be rekindled. At the end of the day, all will agree that what happens economically in the medium- and long-term determines the fundamental shape of the political and social choices available to the Europe's citizens.

---

[1] See William Keegan 'Kinnock could have given King a tip' *The Observer*, 19 June 2005.

This chapter draws heavily on two documents, both of which are critical of current EU policies but offer quite different alternatives. The first is the Sapir Report of 2003. It is adopted as a benchmark here largely because it purports to address itself directly to the problem of growth and suggests a number of radical new departures, most cogently ditching the Common Agricultural Policy and channelling spending towards economic and social infrastructure, particularly in the accession countries, while at the same time stressing sustainable development. With respect to the Eurozone's macroeconomic policies and institutions, however, the Sapir Report does not challenge the orthodox theories underlying the Brussels Consensus.

The alternative benchmark chosen is based on the EPOC[2] Report, a document prepared by a group of European economists of a more Keynesian persuasion who wish to reform the ECB, scrap the SGP, and greatly enlarge the EU budget. Their emphasis is on the construction of a distinctive European Social Model (ESM) as distinct from what they feel is the US-influenced economic model currently on offer.

The Sapir Report recognises that EU-15 growth performance has been poor and contains many sensible recommendations for reform: ending the CAP; improving the functioning of the single market; paying more attention to income disparities between states rather than between regions; addressing the needs of the 10 new accession states; addressing inter-generation disparities implied by poor pension provision; increasing investment in the knowledge economy and so on. But the report addresses growth issues almost exclusively in terms of improved micro-economic efficiency.

The report, published in mid-2003, was drawn up by the Belgian economist André Sapir and his colleagues and was commissioned by Romano Prodi, at that time President of the European Commission. Its terms of reference were widely defined, although limited to the Eurozone countries – Britain is hardly mentioned, as is increasingly the case in debates on the structure and efficiency of the EU. The timing of its publication was perhaps unfortunate as it coincided with that on the draft Constitution; in consequence, Sapir has not received the sort of attention given to the subsequent Kok Report, although in many respects it is far more comprehensive.

On the general problem of European growth, Sapir accepts the near universal view that the core Eurozone economies have grown too slowly, not merely relative to the United States but relative to their potential. And the report is equally correct in signalling that faster growth is paramount for the

---

[2]   EPOC stands for 'Improvement of Economic Policy Co-ordination for Full-Employment and Social Cohesion in Europe'.

sustainability of the European social model, particularly where technological and demographic change are increasing the cost of social protection. Financing social cohesion is far easier under conditions of prosperity than under stagnation. Under zero-growth, the capacity to deliver reforms shrinks while political conflict over competing welfare claims intensifies.

Nor can the problem of growth be resolved uniquely at the EU level of policy and governance; the member states must play a more active role. It is true that greater policy co-ordination is required, but such co-ordination will not be achieved solely on the basis of the Broad Economic Policy Guidelines (BEPGs), which are hardly ever discussed in national Parliaments. Nor is it sensible, Sapir argues, to add to the 'carousel' of Council meetings at which leaders pledge themselves to yet another set of distant goals; eg, Cologne, Cardiff, Luxembourg and Lisbon. Sapir's group finds homilies about the 'open method of co-ordination' particularly irritating.

The Report attaches much importance to 'catch-up' growth; ie, the sort of rapid growth that needs to take place in the ten or more new member states. It cannot be assumed that such growths will happen automatically. In the words of one commentator, 'the main determinants of such catch-up growth are found in the proper functioning of the deep internal market, a solid macroeconomic framework sensitive to some characteristics of these countries, especially in the first decade of their membership ... There is no place anymore for 'them' and 'us' distinctions in national EU politics; their growth must also be our priority'.[3] It is precisely this matter on which Sapir's proposals for reform of the EU budget are compelling; the Report urges Brussels to phase out agricultural subsidies and support to poorer regions, concentrating resources instead on modernising the social and economic infrastructure of the adhesion countries.

Sapir's recommendations are grouped together under six headings: making the single market more dynamic; boosting investment in knowledge; improving EMU's macroeconomic policy framework; convergence and restructuring in an enlarged EU; effective governance; and mobilising the EU budget. In broad terms, the report gives overall priority to microeconomic reform and to enhancing the 'shared sense of ownership' of reform amongst the EU's members. Below, I skip Sapir's discussion of governance while consolidating these headings further.

---

[3] See Pelkmans and Casey (2004: 3).

9.2   DYNAMIZING THE SINGLE MARKET

Sapir argues that while substantial progress has been made in integrating the EU market for goods, not enough has happened in other areas; eg, transport infrastructure; the internal market for services; the liberalisation of network industries (telecoms); the market for patents, and the promotion of venture capital.

Here, some – though not all – of the Report's recommendations deserve full backing. In principle, the TENs (trans-European network) is a competence shared between the EU and its member-states, although in practice the principle of 'subsidiarity' has played havoc with motorway and train networks, or even air-traffic control. Sapir can be criticised for not following up this matter. Because of the over-riding interests of member-states, there is still no equivalent in the EU to the US 'inter-state' highway system, and high-speed TGV-style rail links have developed unevenly (and in some places not at all). Although EU air-traffic control (ATC) is now far more centralised, the hugely expensive ATC computer systems at Le Bourget and Swanwick use incompatible protocols and cannot communicate with each other directly. Common economic and social infrastructure is as much a part of an EU growth strategy as are common rules about product labelling or indebtedness limits. A sensible subsidiary principle would recognise this as an EU-level competence, rather than relegating the matter to bilateral co-operation.

In much the same way, the slow pace of liberalisation of national telecoms is criticised as is the lack of an EU-wide patent law, despite years of discussion. The Sapir Report also backs the Risk Capital Action Plan (RCAP), which has eliminated a variety of obstacles in the cross-border venture capital market. Perhaps most important, it argues for an end to the non-transferability of acquired health, pension and other rights across national borders; non-transferability is increasingly recognised as a major obstacle to an EU-wide labour market.

But when it comes to cross-border services, Sapir's universal vision is curiously simplistic. Whilst it is true that the services sector accounts for nearly two-thirds of EU GNP and that the country-of-origin principle is widely applied in other areas, it would have made far more political sense for Sapir's supporters to restrict service liberalisation to the EU-15 states, with a provision that these principles gradually be extended to the accession states once their legal infrastructure and levels of social protection are more clearly in line with the EU-15 average. The veto of the Bolkenstein services directive was a setback that might have been prevented had the Commission recognised at the outset the awkwardness of applying the country-of-origin principle to cross border services.

It has become commonplace to say that Europe invests too little in education and to call for greater university mobility as well as more high-level research. Sapir adds a few new twists here, notably in calling for an independent European Agency for Science and Research as well as tax-credits to boost incentives for private research. Where Sapir has been rightly criticised is in failing to make any recommendations on how to promote co-ordination in R&D.[4]

9.3 ENLARGEMENT, CONVERGENCE AND THE EU BUDGET

The area of promoting faster integration of new member-states and of mobilising the EU budget in support of this goal is perhaps the Report's most important contribution; not surprisingly, the EU Commissioner for Agriculture was one of the first to strongly criticise Sapir. A major proposal is the overhaul of the EU budget's 'structural' funds, which would be replaced by a 'convergence fund' and a 'restructuring fund'. The convergence fund would be used to aid low-income countries, not low-income regions. Sapir's argument here is that such an approach eliminated payments to poorer regions in rich countries; more generally, it strikes at the *juste retour* principle according to which each member-state is in principle entitled to receive a national benefit from the EU level in return for its budgetary contribution.[5] It is estimated that in the EU-15, paying money to countries rather than regions would avoid some 40 percent of transfers.[6] The restructuring fund would be very similar to today's Social Fund; monies would be channelled towards worker retraining and industrial relocation. But the most contentious proposal is to replace CAP with a Growth Fund, which would aim at providing an enhanced R&D capability and new infrastructure. In effect, the entire EU budget in future would be channelled to Convergence, Restructuring and Growth.

---

[4]   As Pelkmans and Casey (2004) rightly note, national R&D is sacrosanct and it seems to be taboo to propose an EU-level capability in this area.

[5]   A good example of the inefficiency of the *juste retour* principle is to be found in the defence industry. In the past, the first aim of collaborative programmes between EU member-states has been to reduce procurement costs for the participating countries and to promote the development of their technological and industrial capacities. In consequence, each country wants to reap the benefits of orders placed with its own industry and expects a return - both financial and technological - on its investments. This has worked against the consolidation of the industry at EU level, making it difficult to compete with giant US defence contractors.

[6]   See Pelkmans and Casey (2004: 16).

The idea is radical. Even though the CAP has shifted increasingly away from generalised subsidies and towards supporting poorer farmers, the argument advanced by Sapir is that if the EU has a redistributive competence, it should not be restricted to agriculture. Moreover, any extension of the CAP to East and Central Europe will tend to become institutionalised, subsidising inefficient agricultural enterprises and holding back catch-up growth. As an extra twist, Sapir adds a new source of revenue to the EU budget. 'Own resources', he suggests, should be augmented by revenue from *seigniorage*[7] on the issue of euro banknotes – worth nearly half of total EU budget revenues – and possibly an EU-level capital gains tax.

There is obviously much to chew over in the Report. If its proposals for the EU budget have been brushed aside in the present round, this is more a reflection on the deep inertia in Brussels and the powerful vested interests groups at work in the lobbies. Before moving to what I regard as the weakest link in the report, it must be stressed that the Report is rich in new ideas and directions: it is required reading, particularly because the problem of growth is placed centre-stage. Some of the best ideas – notably redrafting the EU budget – may have been bushed aside by Brussels, but their day will surely come.

9.4   A MACROECONOMIC POLICY FRAMEWORK?

Where the Sapir Report disappoints is in failing to address macroeconomic policy issues at EU level. It recommends a 'more effective and flexible implementation of the Stability and Growth Pact, while sticking to the 3% ceiling'.[8] While Sapir hints that countries with lower levels of public indebtedness might be given more leeway to breech the 3% threshold, there is no mention of scrapping the SGP and adopting a system for monitoring member-states indebtedness – such as the 'Sustainability Council' discussed in a previous chapter. Instead, the report suggests that there should be increased incentives for countries to secure surpluses in good times, thus giving more space for fiscal stimuli to work in bad times. In short, the report does not challenge current macroeconomic orthodoxy.

Chapter 4 of the report focuses on the EU's economic performance. About half the chapter is devoted to looking at the EU's performance in comparison with the USA, where the usual points are made about the EU's faltering productivity growth, higher unemployment, lower employment and worsening

---

[7]   'Seigniorage' is the difference between the printing cost and the face value of a banknote accruing to a central bank as profit; in olden times this profit was minimal since gold coins were literally 'worth their weight in gold'.

[8]   See Sapir (2003: 5).

demographic trends. US growth is treated as technologically driven: there is no mention of the uncertain foundations sustaining US growth, namely, the huge twin deficits and the declining dollar. The low figures for average EU-15 growth, the report notes correctly, hide wide discrepancies in performance amongst member-states; nonetheless, it is the core states – Germany, Italy and France – which have done poorly. Depressed levels of final demand in these countries are ignored (as is the cost of German unification); instead, the focus is on technological innovation and the erosion of Europe's competitive advantage after the 1970s.

Sapir is quite right to look at innovation and at how the institutional basis of innovation might be improved. Equally, Sapir is right to point to the widely divergent shares of GDP spent on R&D in northern and southern Europe. But as I have argued about the Lisbon process, the notion that Europe is technologically backward and must become the world's most competitive economy has its roots in the 'new economy' discourse trumpeted in the United States. Doubtless Europe could benefit from more research and faster innovation, but the stagnation story is about far more than 'mere' technology; it is above all about promoting new investment.

The same is true of Sapir's passing reference to the link between education and inequality.[9] The report argues that because of the structural shift towards more highly educated workers in advanced economies, those with lower educational attainment have lost out in the distribution of income. Once again, this is the conventional textbook model in which growing inequality is conveniently ascribed to a mismatch of supply and demand at one end of the labour market, eschewing the Reagan-Thatcher distributional agenda, the meteoric rise of salaries in the financial sector, tax breaks for CEO stock option schemes and so on.

Much is made in the report of the success of post-Maastricht fiscal consolidation and the establishment of a low-inflation climate as a pre-condition to long-term growth. Sapir praises the ECB for its anti-inflationary record. The authors of the report do not think monetary policy has been too tight, although they do recognise that where inflation differs significantly between member states, a one-size-fits-all interest rate can be pro-cyclical; eg, the real interest rate has been too low for Ireland with its higher-than-average growth and inflation, and too high for Germany. But, Sapir adds, other policy instruments can offset this bias. What Sapir implies is that a more expansionary fiscal stance is appropriate for Germany. But in the same breath the report condemns Germany for having been fiscally too lax.

---

[9] See Sapir (2003: 32).

In the public finance area, budgetary policies have not reverted to those of the pre-Maastricht era, but several countries (notably the largest members of the euro area) failed to create the necessary room for manoeuvre under the 3% of GDP deficit ceiling during favourable growth conditions. As a result, they found their fiscal policy increasingly constrained in a situation of protracted economic sluggishness.[10]

This is simply a restatement of budgetary orthodoxy. Nor is the report consistent about the Stability Pact rules. It does not want them changed, but it does want the Commission to take total indebtedness into account when dealing with the structural budget deficit limit; ie, for countries having a public stock of debt less than 40% of GDP, a 1.5% structural budget deficit (ie, the average deficit over the cycle) would be allowed.

On the positive side, Sapir revives the idea of a 'rainy day fund'; a facility controlled by the Commission and subject to Council approval, which could be used to 'finance' deficits exceeding 3% in the downturn. Most importantly, Sapir recognises that the new accession states will need special treatment. Because most of these have low levels of indebtedness and need to invest in new infrastructure if they are to catch up, Sapir argues that the Commission should be flexible about their running 'temporarily higher deficits'.

In the words of Charles Wyplosz, a leading critic of the rigidity of the Maastricht and SGP rules:

> There is a serious gap between the principles stated at the outset [of the Report] and the policy proposals. While the Report expresses the intention of working through incentives, it accepts without justification the imposition of rules. While it argues in favour of national ownership, it seeks to reinforce the powers of the Commission. While it implicitly recognizes problems with numerical targets (3%, 60%) by proposing various ways of moving away from them, it still insists on placing them at the heart of their proposals. While it notes that long-term sustainability is at the heart of the SGP, they [the authors] fail to recognise that this implies that the pact should be defined in terms of the long run evolution of public debts, not annual budget deficits.[11]

More generally, Sapir characterises the differing macroeconomic philosophies on each side of the Atlantic in the following terms:

---

[10] See Sapir (2003: 54)

[11] See Charles Wyplosz (2004) 'The Sapir Report: Proposals for Fiscal Discipline within the Euro Zone' Graduate Institute of International Economics and CEPR, April.

The macroeconomic framework has consistently improved on both sides of the Atlantic, although macroeconomic "philosophies" continue to differ: the commitment to rules-based policies is stronger in Europe than in the US where monetary and fiscal discretion appears to be stronger. A clear anti-inflationary commitment by the central banks has helped anchor inflationary expectations, thus contributing to lower and more stable inflation. As to fiscal policy, over the 1990s and until very recently, enhanced budgetary discipline both in Europe and the US has contributed to macroeconomic stability On a more specific basis, the effectiveness of automatic stabilisers appears to be stronger in Europe than in the US, given its more extended tax and welfare system. As to discretionary policy, there is evidence that it may have become more counter cyclical in OECD countries, but its effectiveness may have decreased over time[12]

What this says is that low inflation is due to the increased prudence of central banks, and that Europe's rules-based fiscal tightening together with its superior stabilisers have set the right low-volatility environment for growth. As has been noted several times in this book, the US is seen as 'more discretionary' in its use of macroeconomic tools; the budgetary prudence of the Clinton administration has been replaced by fiscal laxity under George W Bush. The lesson drawn by the report is not that Bush's expansionary tax cuts are insanely inequitable, or that they benefit military spending while penalising the environment. The lesson is that Americans are more Keynesian than Europeans. Alas, Sapir seems to think that is bad news.

9.5   THE RADICAL VIEW

The second document examined here is that prepared by the EPOC group,[13] an EU wide network of economists concerned at the erosion of 'social Europe' by a combination of inappropriate macro-economic rules and the excessive free-market zeal. In its most recent 2005 draft Report, EPOC notes that five years after the Lisbon summit, growth in the EU is only half the rate needed to meet the Lisbon objectives. Nor is it possible with such low growth for Europe to pursue the 'European Social Model' agenda envisaged at Barcelona

---

[12] See Sapir (2003: 46).

[13] The author has had access to the EPOC Report before its publication in 2005. The group comprises social scientists from most EU countries formed into the thematic network called 'Economic Policy Coordination for Full-employment and Social Cohesion in Europe' (EPOC); see www.epoc.uni-bremen.de.

in 2002, or even to mobilise the financial resources necessary if the ten new accession states are to catch up with the rest of Europe within a reasonable time span.

The EPOC authors are well aware that it is inappropriate to speak of a 'single' European Social Model (ESM); in reality there are wide discrepancies between welfare models to be found in the Nordic countries, in Germany and France or even between those of southern Europe. Nevertheless, they argue, a broad characterisation of an ESM would stress common features such as the universal provision of education and health care as concomitants to democracy, a commitment to social solidarity and poverty eradication and the need to complement the 'free market' by the twin notions of sustainable growth and a strong and efficient public sector. In a globalised world, they argue, the ESM is bound to be contested since the pressures of international competition push governments to deregulate markets, privatise public services and shed social expenditure. However, EPOC stresses that the weakening of social Europe is not an inevitable consequence of globalisation. Rather, it is argued that Europe has been weakened by the adoption of a neo-liberal agenda and that this weakening of 'social' Europe is, in turn, leading to a growing anti-European backlash.

It is not just the Brussels Consensus that is to blame. A decade of stagnation, privatisation and welfare cuts is creating a political crisis in Europe, one that threatens the political legitimacy of a unified Europe – the so-called 'democratic deficit'. Thus, the EPOC Group addresses broad issues of political economy and purports to set out guidelines for re-launching 'social' Europe on more solid economic and political foundations. For ease of exposition, I concentrate below on the economic and political-institutional changes such a re-launch would involve.

9.6   BREAKING WITH THE BRUSSELS CONSENSUS

The conservative nature of the Brussels Consensus, in the view of the EPOC's economists, can only be understood in the context of the post war economic alliance between France and Germany which, as already discussed, started with the creation of the Coal and Steel Communities in 1951. The project of Economic and Monetary Union (EMU) dates back to a report prepared by Pierre Werner, the Prime Minister of Luxembourg, for the European Commission – the Werner Report (1970) – when the OECD countries still lived under a fixed exchange rate regime. The collapse of the Bretton Woods system of fixed exchange rates in 1971–73 disjointed the Werner timetable and led to the formation of the 'monetary snake', later to become the European

Monetary System, the foundation stone of EMU. The main purpose of these arrangements was to minimise currency fluctuations. Such fluctuations are highly disruptive to economic growth, as proved to be the case in Britain during the post-war years. The 'snake' established an exchange rate anchor that, while flexible, would protect member countries from inflation.

While the 'snake' was sorely challenged by repeated economic shocks in the 1970s, ultimately it survived because of French fears of devaluation and the *Bundesbank*'s commitment to defending the Deutschmark, the *de facto* currency anchor.[14] By the early 1990s, as the Maastricht Treaty was being negotiated, France accepted the largely German-inspired EMU project in exchange for having agreed to Germany's political re-unification. Thus, the adoption of the euro on 1 January 1999 marked the end of a convergence process that had lasted for nearly 30 years.

As the EPOC document notes, the theoretical underpinnings of EMU, much influenced by the *Bundesbank*, are orthodox in the extreme. The ECB controls inflation at EU level through the interest rate instrument. (The ECB's 'two-pillar' policy also includes a money supply target for M3, although this has recently been modified.) Inflation is targeted by statute to remain below 2%, a rate considered to be the irreducible 'core rate' of inflation. Equally, the orthodox view assumes that monetary policy has no long-term effect on the real economy. According to this reasoning, monetary policy cannot affect unemployment since this must settle at its 'natural rate', while monetary policy affects growth only indirectly by keeping inflation and thus inflationary expectations under control. Since there is only one goal (low inflation) and one instrument (the interest rate), the ECB cannot have an exchange rate policy; ie, the underlying theory is that once the 'core' interest-rate is attained, the correct exchange rate will automatically be achieved by market forces.[15]

Nevertheless, because of the one-size-fits-all nature of monetary policy in a monetary union, the monetary instrument must be complemented by fiscal policies tailored to meet the needs of member-states. Differences arise between member states because they are of differing size and strength or because their business cycles differ, or else because unpredictable outside shocks affect them in different ways – what economists call *asymmetric* shocks (see Figure 4–3).

---

[14] Economists often use the phrase 'currency anchor' to mean a strong currency which can help defend a country against imported inflation; ie, against rising import prices resulting from currency devaluation.

[15] Not only is such a view untenable theoretically since foreign exchange markets regularly overshoot, it means in practice that the ECB has adopted a policy of 'benign neglect' of the euro, allowing it to appreciate strongly against the US dollar. In this, the ECB accommodates the Bush administration's 'benign neglect' of the dollar, justified on the grounds that the free market can be left to solve the US external account deficit.

But if asymmetric shocks are considered a potential problem, according to bankers' orthodoxy an even greater problem is that of member-states adopting discretionary fiscal policies.

If member states were left entirely free to pursue their own fiscal policy – so the bankers' account goes – they would spend freely, spreading inflation and leaving others to foot the bill; ie, they would become 'free riders'. The centre must impose discipline in the form of a Pact. The SGP requirement that the budget deficit cannot exceed 3% and must balance over the cycle has two aims. In the short-to-medium term, it constrains member-states to extreme fiscal orthodoxy in which there is no room for discretion; ie, macroeconomic balance over the cycle is governed entirely by the action of automatic stabilisers. In the longer-term, the zero budget balance requirement ensures that the size of public debt falls to zero; in other words, that the state – because it can neither borrow nor print money, and is gradually compelled by tax competition to lower taxes – is forced to contract. Equally, this division of labour between the ECB monetary giant and the member-state fiscal dwarfs ensures a unique 'well-behaved' policy environment in which growth can take place.

In the world described above, deficient demand cannot lead to unemployment (ie, Keynes's central hypothesis is wrong). Rather, insofar as the 'natural' rate[16] of unemployment is exceeded, unemployment arises either because inflationary expectations lead to unrealistic wage demands or else because wage markets are 'inflexible'; ie, wage bargains are too strongly influenced by trade union bargaining at national or regional level. Both these problems, in reality opposite sides of the same coin, can be cured by prolonged periods of unemployment, dampening expectations and weakening trade unions. A corollary is that unemployment may also arise because of excessive charges borne by employers leading to a loss of 'international competitiveness'; however, this too is curable since the contraction of the state makes such costs redundant.

If one completes this picture with trade liberalisation (already achieved), services liberalisation (nearly achieved), a competition Commissioner to ensure the liquidation of public monopolies such as power and railways, longer working hours, lower pensions and so on down the list, then in the words of one of the EPOC authors 'the European Union [is] the neo-liberals' ideal world.'[17] But as the EPOC group argues, this world turns out to be one of unemployment and very low growth in the core states, hardly a world designed

---

[16] This 'natural rate' is usually called the Non-Accelerating Inflation Rate of Unemployment' (NAIRU). Orthodox theory posits that although actual unemployment may temporarily differ, in the long term unemployment must settle at NAIRU.

[17] See EPOC (2005) Chap 3, p 17 (prepared by Malcolm Sawyer).

to foster the 'knowledge economy', sustainable growth and social cohesion as envisaged in Lisbon 2000. In short, although creation of the euro may be symbolic of the rise of an alternative model to that of US capitalism, the completion of EMU is unfinished and unbalanced. Unless substantial modification takes place, the economic foundation of Europe cannot sustain the European Social Model.

As the EPOC group and other academics have noted – and as discussed already in Chapter 4 – there is an institutional mismatch between the monetary and fiscal arrangements of the EU; ie, an asymmetry between the single large central monetary authority and many smaller independent national fiscal authorities whose power is constrained by the SGP. Indeed, it is part of the Brussels orthodoxy that limiting member-states' room for fiscal discretion will lead to stability and growth. Per contra, the academic literature on optimal currency areas has generally stressed that where monetary policy is set centrally, national fiscal authorities need more room for manoeuvre, not less, if stability is to be maintained.[18]

In order to deal with this asymmetry, the EPOC Report suggests a number of fundamental reforms. These concern the European Central Bank, the EU budget, the Stability and Growth Pact and various other areas; for simplicity, the discussion concentrates on these four.

9.7 Monetary Policy

The ECB is open to a variety of criticisms as has been shown. The first is that its anti-inflationary remit is too narrow. If the sole objective of the ECB is low inflation then, as the EPOC report observes, this means the sole objective of EU-wide macroeconomic policy is inflation targeting. The objectives of monetary policy should surely be derived from wider considerations. A fundamental change would be to require the ECB to balance the goals of growth, full employment and low inflation – as does the US Federal Reserve Bank. This can be done either by statute, or by changing the composition of the ECB's policy-making Board. For example, the Bank of England's Monetary Policy Committee (MPC) includes various independent advisors – including notable academics – and membership rotates at regular intervals. Although the MPC does not have as wide a remit as its US equivalent, it clearly does take wider policy goals into account.

---

[18] The seminal publication on fiscal federalism is Musgrave (1959). More recently, see Kenen (1995) and Arestis and Sawyer (2002). In particular, a recent paper by Tamborini (2003) sets out econometric evidence challenging the consensus view that EU member-states can take it for granted that existing arrangements will deliver stability and growth.

The pursuit of multiple objectives by the ECB logically implies multiplying the policy instruments at its disposal. Thus, fiscal and exchange rate policies are required; since the ECB policy instruments are limited, it should logically co-ordinate its policies with member-states to achieve some balanced set of macro policies. Constitutionally, however, the ECB is required to operate in complete independence from member-states, or even from ECOFIN.

A closely related matter is the ECB's lack of accountability. Unlike the Fed or the Bank of England, the ECB Governing Council does not publish its minutes nor is any record available of members' voting record. This means that while the European Parliament can debate monetary matters, it has no means of establishing how and why the ECB reaches its conclusions. To a degree, this is mitigated by the fact that the ECB President now addresses the European Parliament and gives monthly press conferences. But the secretive nature of the ECB does little to reinforce its authority; rather the perceived lack of democratic accountability detracts from its legitimacy. Equally, as EPOC notes, in the absence of an EU level fiscal authority to act as a counterbalance, the ECB is more autonomous than the US Fed or even the *Bundesbank* before EMU.

The constitutional requirement that national governments must not influence the ECB both reinforces the view that the ECB lacks democratic accountability, and makes it nearly impossible to co-ordinate EU-level monetary policy with state-level fiscal policy. At the same time, there is evidence that the Central Bank governors sitting on the Governing Council do vote according to the interests of the member-states they represent rather than determining EU-wide interest.[19] If the evidence is correct, then the political justification collapses for maintaining a Chinese wall between the ECB, member-states and Parliament. As argued, there is no economic justification for this wall other than in a world of highly orthodox theory. In the words of the EPOC authors:

> ... it is possible to enhance the responsibility of the ECB to the European Parliament and to the Council and to broaden and intensify the dialogue with national political authorities. The ECB would maintain an operational independence in day-to-day activities but with a much broader set of objectives with democratic accountability, and the obligation to co-ordinate policy decisions with other EU institutions and national governments.[20]

---

[19] The evidence from a study by Meade and Sheet (2001) is quoted in Arestis and Sawyer (2002).
[20] See EPOC (2005), Chap 3, p 4.

In addition to the reform agenda implicit in the above, EPOC's main recommendation is the setting up of a Monetary Policy Committee (MPC), to include representatives of the European Parliament, ECOFIN and the 'social partners'.[21] Although I agree with EPOC's analysis of the weaknesses of EU monetary policy, the recommended composition of the suggested MPC seems something of an afterthought.

9.8 FISCAL POLICY

The EPOC Report – in contrast to the Sapir Report or the Kok report – calls for repeal of the SGP and major surgery to institutional arrangements guiding macro-policy. This is hardly surprising given the theoretical perspectives set out above. The view of EPOC is that national fiscal policies should be designed as far as possible to achieve the economic objectives of national governments rather than set artificial limits on national deficits. In the words of the authors, this 'by no means preclude[s] some co-ordination of national fiscal policies as such co-ordination should enhance, rather than detract from, the use of national fiscal policies.'[22] Nor, as explained below, does it preclude the counter-cyclical use of an expanded EU budget. What it does ensure is that national fiscal policy could be used more effectively to address problems not addressed by a unitary monetary policy.

Although the EPOC Report makes no mention of replacing the SGP with an alternative arrangement for monitoring member-states' indebtedness such as a 'Sustainability Council', it does see the Commission as promoting fiscal co-ordination between member-states in five main areas. These are:

- stabilisation, growth and employment;
- economic infrastructure;
- ecological sustainability;
- social welfare and cohesion;
- other.

In the area of stabilisation and growth, the Report calls for the setting up of a European Stabilisation Fund (ESF) which, broadly speaking, would resemble an IMF facility. The fund would be financed by soft loans from the European Investment Bank and be disbursed in the event of a serious economic downturn

---

[21] 'Social partners' in this context are presumably employers' and trade-union organisations.
[22] See EPOC (2005) Chap 3, p 4 (prepared by Malcolm Sawyer).

(whether in one or several member-states). Each state would be required to draw up a contingency plan for its use in recession, and equally to draw up a plan to offset overheating; these would allow rapid reaction to excessive expansion or contraction by an amount equivalent to up to 2% of the member-state's GDP. In principle, the ESF would supplement (and substantially strengthen) the operation of automatic stabilisers at national level. The activation of the ESF would be subject to the approval of ECOFIN.

EPOC sees the accelerated development of common – or at least compatible – structures in such areas as telecommunications, air, sea and rail transport and research as a vital part of Europe. The argument here is that privatisation of transport and telecommunications prove expensive in the long run and may fail to provide compatible standards. This argument is not entirely convincing since compatibility of privately funded projects can be assured by means of a regulatory authority. At the same time, it is probably true that the privatisation of utilities has been driven by a combination of neo-liberal economics and growing budgetary constraints, in some cases leading to Private Financial Initiatives (PFIs) or Public Private Partnerships (PPPs) – see Figure 5–2 – under which current capital costs are taken off-budget only to reappear as expensive handouts to industry in future. However viewed, few would quarrel with the underlying principle of undertaking compatible EU-wide infrastructure investment. The EPOC report might have added that the European Investment Bank was meant to serve precisely this function.

Nobody will quarrel with the Report's call for the use of public money to promote ecologically sustainable development, whether in the form of renewable energy generation, environmental clean-up or the restructuring of transport systems. Sustainable development – and the supporting research required – features as an agenda item in almost every European summit, and EPOC recognises that there has been much progress in this field.

Somewhat more contentious is EPOC's call for common standards of social welfare and cohesion policies in defence of the European Social Model. While recognising the 'welfare' heterogeneity of the EU, it suggests that certain minimum levels of welfare achievement should be preserved and extended – for instance, in the areas of social security, workers' protection, education and health – and that agreement might be reached between member states on spending a certain proportion of GDP on welfare. While various qualifiers are added about the difficulty (or even undesirability) of setting benchmarks for all member-states, the Report does suggest that common targets might be set in such areas as literacy, doctors per 1000 inhabitants and other 'human development' indicators. In the words of the author of a recent Fabian pamphlet:

There can be no objection in principle to a framework of minimum social standards at EU level (which largely exists already as a result of the Social Chapter) ... Similarly in the field of tax, social democrats should adopt a pragmatic approach. VAT rules are already harmonised ... and there are some other obvious examples of where action on tax may be desirable at European level.[23]

The heading 'other' is a residual box housing equally interesting if controversial ideas. For example, the report argues that 'the co-ordination of national tax policies is indispensable to recover the room for manoeuvre within national expenditure policies which many member states have lost during the last two decades due to increasing pressure on taxes and to tax competition amongst member states.'[24] At the same time, it is noted that 'co-ordination' does not mean the same as full tax harmonisation; the latter goal is unrealistic. Amongst the suggestions are moving to a common centralised system for the calculation of VAT based on national accounts; a pan-EU system of dividend withholding tax for non-EU residents[25]; the harmonisation or corporation tax throughout the EU – though not of personal taxation; and the co-ordinated introduction of energy taxes (particularly on carbon dioxide emissions).

9.9 THE EU BUDGET

Probably the most radical item in the EPOC Report is the call for a relatively large federal EU budget.[26] The MacDougall report's original target was of the order of 7% of combined EU GDP, large enough to be used as an instrument of counter cyclical fiscal policy but small in comparison to the US Federal Budget. An EU Federal Budget, it is argued, would redress the asymmetry between centralised monetary and decentralised fiscal policy described above, while mobilising the resources necessary to strengthen the European Social Model and intensify activity in the areas of security and development aid. EPOC recommends aiming at a target figure of 5% of combined GDP, to be achieved by making member-states' contributions a progressive percentage of their GDP and incrementing contributions in stages of 0.5% per annum between the present and 2012.

---

[23] See Liddle (2005: 68).
[24] EPOC (2005), Chap 16, p 6.
[25] Such a system already exists in the USA and has recently been adopted by the EU.
[26] See MacDougall (1977).

The main expenditure items in the 2012 enlarged 5% budget would be comprised as follows. The Stabilisation Fund would received 0.5% of combined GDP; a somewhat modified Common Agricultural Policy would receive 0.8%; structural funds – largely directed towards adhesion countries – would command four times their current share, or 1.6%; spending on social policy would help setting minimum standards of provision throughout the union and would amount to 1.0% of EU GDP; all other public goods (including research, TENs for transport, energy and communications, and environmental policy) would claim a further 1.1%.

Obviously, funding this level of expenditure will require radical changes on the revenue side. The current system comprises the original or 'first own resources' (revenues from the common external tariff plus agricultural levies representing some 10–15% of the budget); the lion's share comes from member-states' VAT-based consumption revenue and their contributions from GDP. At present, VAT-based claims are inter-regionally regressive, placing a greater proportional burden on poorer member-states where consumption accounts for a larger share of GDP than in richer states. GDP-based claims (ie, the 'fourth resource') account for just under half of total revenue and are neither regressive nor progressive.

The EPOC Report proposes replacing existing arrangements with a unified GDP-based revenue raising system based on a progressive tax schedule, a variant of the 'modulation coefficients' based GDP contribution proposed by Spain in 1998. In order to raise revenue equivalent to 5% of combined EU GDP, EPOC calculates that country-specific progressive tax rates (proportional to per capita GDP) would range between 1% of GDP for Latvia to 5.3% for Italy and 11.4% for Luxembourg.[27] In addition to changing current revenue arrangements, EPOC recommends that the EU, like the US Federal Government, be allowed to borrow. This would entail the abrogation of Articles 268 and 269 of the Maastricht Treaty requiring the annual EU budget to balance and to be financed entirely from 'own resources'. EU-level deficit financing would be justified in two cases; first, where long-maturation investment was required in research or infrastructure on an EU-wide basis whose beneficiaries would be future generations; and secondly, where such finance was required for EU-wide stabilisation; ie, for the European Stabilisation Fund described above.

EPOC recognises that these recommendations will be seen as radical; as the authors admit:

---

[27] See EPOC Report (2005), chap 16, Table 18.1.

This is of course a perspective which is far from realistic under present circumstances … But then the current course of tax competition and austerity policy in the EU is obviously not only unsuccessful; it has for some time been the subject of growing theoretical criticism and social opposition. In this situation, … a thoroughly different proposal … may be helpful in the sense that it encourages people to engage in activities to change the political constellation.[28]

CONCLUSIONS

Despite their quite different ideological orientations, there are some similarities between the Sapir Report and the EPOC Report. Both find that low EU growth is a threat to economic (and political) cohesion. Both would like to see greater co-ordination of fiscal policies between member states going beyond the 'open method of co-ordination' and the carousel of council declarations. Both recommend making major changes to the EU budget; in particular, making more resources available to facilitate catch-up growth in the new adhesion states and making some provision for EU-wide shocks in the form of a 'rainy day' (stabilisation) fund.

In one sense, Sapir goes further than the EPOC Group, in calling for the complete phasing out of agricultural handouts in the form of the Common Agricultural Policy. However, the Sapir Report – like the later Kok Report – ignores demand management and suggests that most of the EU's ills can be remedied by supply-side policies. The EPOC Group, by contrast, places Keynesian policies of active demand management at the top of the agenda. Sapir is comfortable with the ECB's focus on inflation targeting, while leaving fiscal policy to be driven solely by automatic stabilisers at member-state level within the confines of the SGP fiscal rules. The EPOC Report recommends a serious restructuring of the ECB to give it broader targets and greater accountability, and it wants to scrap the SGP. In its place, looser country-level fiscal policy would be complemented by a much larger Union-level budget used, inter alia, for counter-cyclical demand management. Such a budget, EPOC admits, would move Europe decisively in the direction of a Federal State, and far wider powers would need to be granted to the European Parliament, starting with the power to initiate legislation. But what is perhaps most significant is the warning by the EPOC group that unless the EU changes direction and adopts the explicitly political goal of enhancing the European

[28] EPOC (2005), chap 16, p 20.

Social Model – together with economic policies designed to attain this goal – it risks facing a major political crisis. In this regard, the EPOC report is prescient.

CHAPTER 10

Unfinished Business for Britain

In the 1980s, Europe ... was seen as the progenitor of a more successful, and for Social Democrats, more socially just form of capitalism than the raw crudities of Anglo-Saxon Thatcherism. ... But in the last decade, pro-Europeans have, catastrophically, allowed this argument to be completely turned around. Eurosceptics have secured widespread acceptance of two key propositions, first, that Britain is significantly outperforming the rest of Europe and second, that this success is to a considerable extent due to the Angle-Saxon flexibility that is now seen to characterise the British economy. . In retrospect, supporters of early Euro entry had lost the argument before one word of the Treasury's voluminous economic assessment was written. (Roger Liddle, 2004, p 24)

10.1 UNFINISHED BUSINESS

Sooner or later, Britain must make up its mind on Europe. The failure of Giscard's Treaty does not preclude the need for adopting a constitution; in the meantime, the EU will soldier on under present arrangements until a suitable new (and hopefully shorter) document is drafted. A referendum will be required, and Britain will need to vote. Nevertheless, unless there is reform of Eurozone's economic structure that produces faster growth and lower unemployment in the core countries, it is likely that the UK will remain semi-detached from the Eurozone or, in the extreme case, line up with the United States.

Nor can decisions on these matters be postponed indefinitely. Because of its growing external account deficit, the US exports deflation; ie, Europe, including Britain, must absorb part of the adjustment process in the form of an appreciation in the euro and in sterling which undermines competitiveness. Britain, mainly by virtue of its huge financial services sector, seems unconcerned that industry is declining and that UK industrial exports are increasingly difficult to sell abroad. Here too, there is a limit as to how long British prosperity can continue in light of these developments, particularly as consumer demand follows the declining fortunes of the housing market. Whoever succeeds Gordon Brown as Chancellor is unlikely to ride the wave of buoyant demand that made it possible to pay for much needed social investment while maintaining an unblemished reputation for fiscal prudence.

More important, a new recession in the United States could have serious consequences for the world economy – leaving the Eurozone as the only player big enough to provide an effective counterweight. To many, whether Britain joins the euro seems yesterday's politics. In reality, however, it is more vital today than at any time in the past. New Labour – under new leadership – potentially has a vital role to play in reversing Europe's economic fortunes.

10.2 BRITAIN AND THE EURO

On 9 June 2003, Gordon Brown announced that Britain had once again failed four of the five 'economic tests' for euro-entry. While New Labour scrambled to paper over the cracks, the spluttering debate over joining the euro became emblematic of Britain's increasingly uneasy relationship with the EU, a relationship strained by years of indecision about economic and political integration, damaged by Britain's alliance with the US during the Iraq war and, more recently, poisoned by the tabloid press campaign against the draft Constitution. Prior to mid-2005, the prospect of a debate and referendum on the EU Constitution had pushed the single currency well down the agenda. Now that the Constitutional debate has been put on hold, the euro debate has disappeared altogether from our radar screens. But if economic crisis grips the US and the world economy contracts, trade and currency markets will become unstable. Britain – particularly if the economy has slowed and a looming public sector deficit makes sterling look vulnerable – will need to take refuge in a strong currency zone, or else run the risk of its currency being squeezed between the colliding tectonic plates of the euro and the dollar. In 1997, the newly elected Labour Government appeared to be the very antithesis of the Euro-phobic wing of the Tory party. But Labour, while remaining rhetorically pro-European, has shifted steadily rightward; today, its European pronouncements recall the flag-waving chauvinism of the Thatcher-Major years.

Indeed, a significant segment of the British labour movement is Eurosceptic. The spectrum includes unreconstructed Bennites, a new generation of militant trade unionists and some disillusioned Blairites whose allegiance is shifting to Gordon Brown. The implications of drifting away from Europe are worrying. Whatever the pros and cons of British euro-membership, the underlying question is about the geo-politics of Europe and America. Britain cannot stand still; it must either move forward within Europe or drift further into the mid-Atlantic, ultimately into the neo-liberal grasp of the Unites States. Starkly put, the choice for Britain is between European social democracy and US-style neo-liberal capitalism.[1]

As Roger Liddle[2] has written, Black Wednesday in 1992 was a defining moment for Britain's relationship with Europe, enabling the Eurosceptic wing of the Conservative Party to argue that Britain's interest could never be successfully reconciled with Europe. Equally, Black Wednesday wrong-footed Labour's Shadow Cabinet. Neil Kinnock, John Smith (shadow Chancellor) and Gordon Brown (then shadow Industry Secretary) had all backed the Exchange Rate Mechanism as part of a 'modern' economic strategy devised to reassure the City and Middle England that the party was prudent and wedded to an anti-inflationary stance.

> Black Wednesday left Labour's modernisers without a clear economic framework of their own, unable to resurrect the ERM and hesitant about the even bigger commitment implied by the single currency. (Liddle, 2005: 23).

Furthermore, Britain's economic performance was strong during the 1990s, in part spurred by the 1992 devaluation. By the time Gordon Brown's evaluation of the euro took place in 2003, Britain had consistently outperformed the core Eurozone economies in terms of growth and employment. A traditionally euro-sceptic electorate could not be convinced to buy further into the euro and Europe as long as Britain was seen to be doing better than its continental neighbours. The case for joining the euro needs to be refashioned not just with greater emphasis on the 'political', but as part of a broader argument for transforming the economic governance of Europe. It is precisely this point I consider to be central. The Eurozone cannot fulfil its potential unless and until it acquires more of the attributes of a federal government with a viable economic structure. Britain has a potentially vital role to play in reshaping Europe as a modern federation, capable of delivering long-term prosperity to its members. But few at present would lay odds on Britain playing this role anytime soon.

The debate has moved on since Gordon Brown's verdict on the euro-tests in 2003. Heads of government may have reluctantly accepted Blair's

---

[1] Some will argue that this states the argument too simply. However, it is an argument put eloquently by a range of political commentator; see for example Hugo Young (1998); Will Hutton (2002); and George Monbiot 'The bottom dollar' *The Guardian*, April 22, 2003.
[2] See Liddle (2005).

constitutional 'red lines' in 2004, but the Brussels summit in June 2005 broke up in acrimony. New Labour's attempt to position itself as a chief European 'moderniser' over CAP might have been more successful has it not been for the use of the British rebate as a bargaining chip. In consequence, little progress on the EU budget is likely to be made during the British presidency. New Labour's poor track record in Europe betrays a fundamental lack of strategic thinking. Had Blair genuinely wanted to place Britain at the heart of Europe, it would have been sensible to set out a vision of a modern and economically competitive European federation rather than indulge in displays of national arrogance while disparaging the co-operative efforts of others.

10.3 THE EURO-TESTS

Even if the euro-tests are ancient history, any future attempt to enter the euro will almost certainly see them resuscitated – thus, it is worthwhile reviewing them. As everyone knows, the 'five tests' were hastily concocted at the Treasury in October 1997 shortly after Labour came to power, and have since served basically as smokescreen for not joining. Few non-specialists were clear what these tests were then, and hardly anybody recalls them today. In the event, one test – whether the euro would be good for Britain's financial services sector – was passed in 1997 and again in 2003. What has changed, though, is that the City has continued to prosper despite Britain's retention of the pound. Opinion is divided between those who think the euro is now largely irrelevant to Britain's financial sector, and those who argue that just as New York could not act as America's financial centre were it not part of the dollar-zone, so London cannot be Europe's financial centre wile remaining outside the Eurozone.

With regard to the other criteria, the Chancellor in his Mansion House speech of 18 July 2003 conflated them into two:

- *Convergence*: it must be shown that Britain's interest rate is sufficiently close to that of the Eurozone, and its exchange rate sufficiently competitive such that entry will not harm the UK economy. More generally, Britain's business cycle cannot be too far out of line with that of the main Eurozone countries if Eurozone interest and exchange rates are to remain appropriate.
- *Flexibility*: this translates as 'labour market flexibility'. Joining the euro means that Britain can no longer devalue and that the weight of adjusting to any loss of competitiveness vis-à-vis the Eurozone would fall exclusively on wages. Unless productivity rises, UK wages must be flexible enough to bear the burden.

The conventional argument on *convergence* has been that the UK business cycle is more closely aligned with that of the US than Germany and France. In 1997 the pound was too high relative to the (then) DM – indeed it had appreciated after 1992 – and Britain's interest rate was still several percentage points higher than that of its continental counterparts. The Treasury view in 2003 was that closer symmetry existed between the UK and Eurozone economies, that interest rates were converging and that the pound was nearly aligned competitively with the euro. Nevertheless, the Chancellor remained unwilling to specify what degree of convergence was required for entry. Indeed, he introduced a new argument: because UK mortgages are variable and linked to short-term interest rates, house price swings are greater in the UK than in other EU countries. He therefore proposed to move to the system of fixed rate mortgages based on long-term interest rates. Long-term rates in Britain and the Eurozone were broadly in line, but this changeover would take time.

Since 2003, Britain has probably increased its degree of divergence with the Eurozone in that the UK economy has grown faster. And while the Eurozone interest rate has remained unchanged at 2%, Britain's rate is 4.5% at the time of writing. This is not because Britain's inflation is higher; inflation has remained broadly in line with the main Eurozone countries (and Britain now measures inflation in the same way as do Eurozone countries).[3] Rather, the interest rate is higher because of the Bank of England's concern to slow the inflation of house prices, one of the key factors explaining buoyant consumer demand. House prices clearly peaked in 2005, and this fact in combination with a slowdown in public spending means that Britain's growth rate is falling towards the average Eurozone level and interest rates are being relaxed.

The *flexibility* test is a curious one. If Britain were to join the euro, a fixed exchange rate (within the Eurozone) would prevail, leaving adjustment to any external shock dependent on flexible wage rates and labour productivity growth. While Britain claims to have Europe's most flexible labour markets, low productivity growth and the overvaluation of the pound since the late 1990s has been such that UK manufacturing has declined more sharply than at any time since the Thatcher years.[4] But the Treasury, instead of asking whether wages in Britain are flexible enough, is asking instead whether the rest of Europe – notably Germany – is flexible enough? Clearly Gordon Brown

---

[3] In December 2003, the RIPX index was replaced by the Eurozone's HICP (Harmonised Index of Consumer Prices), lowering apparent inflation by about half a point.

[4] In May 2000, the GBP peaked at DEM 3.46, nearly 20% above the value at which it was forced to leave the ERM in1992. Huhne estimates that between 1998 and 2000 when the pound peaked, British manufacturing lost 350,000 jobs. See Huhne in Forder, J and C Huhne (2001), p 14.

and his advisors think not. They argue that the EU needs to reform its labour market along UK lines; ie, employers' indirect labour costs should be lower, they should be able to shed labour more easily and the jobless should be encouraged, in Norman Tebbitt's infamous phrase, to 'get on their bikes and find work'. The implicit assumption is that, were Britain to join, it might catch the German unemployment disease, a clear *non sequitur*.

As for the exchange rate, it has remained in the range €1.40–1.45 for some years while more recently, sterling has – like the euro – appreciated against the US dollar. Some economists suspect that sterling may be tracking the euro within (say) a 2% band; if true, this would make sense since well over half of Britain's trade is with the Eurozone. At the same time, it should be noted that €1.45 is very close to the 1992 rate against the DM that resulted in Britain's ejection from the European Exchange Rate Mechanism. The Treasury cannot have it both ways: it cannot be argued that Britain's trade with the Eurozone has prospered at the current exchange rate while suggesting that Britain could only join the euro at a significantly lower rate. Either the current rate is deemed acceptable, or else a lower rate more suitable for manufacturing should be targeted.

10.4 FOR AND AGAINST?

Looking at the wider debate, there are two main questions that Labour's Eurosceptics need to address. First, does abandoning the pound matter? Second, does remaining in mid-Atlantic carry a significant opportunity cost?

To readers of the Sun or the Daily Mail, having the sovereign's head on our banknotes clearly does matter. Indeed, for some diehard euro-sceptics, no possible evidence can be adduced which would tilt the balance in favour of the euro. Metaphysical debate is quite pointless. The concerned reader will presumably want to know the balance of costs and benefits; eg, whether the loss of control over our exchange and interest rates in favour of 'one size fits all' is not a genuine cost, whether the costs of conversion to the euro will be outweighed by transaction costs saved, whether the economy will be less prone to exchange-rate shocks and so on.

If Britain abandons the pound, it loses control over its exchange rate and, by logical extension, over its interest rate.[5] Much has been made of this point by the anti-euro camp; by contrast, many pro-euro economists argue that interest rate and exchange rate autonomy in the UK has, over the long term,

---

[5]   Note that Britain does not lose full control since, as a major EU economy, Britain's economic performance influences that of the eurozone and Britain gains a voice

been a bad thing. Looking at the 30-year period 1966–96, the pound fell from DEM 11 to DEM 2.3 – a relative fall of 5% per annum – while in terms of labour productivity and GDP growth, Britain remained well behind Germany.[6] To appreciate this argument fully, one must look more closely at Britain's vulnerability to exchange rate movements and the relative weakness of interest-rate policy.

Until the price of gold was freed in 1971 and fixed exchanged rates collapsed in 1973, exchange rates were not set by the market and nor was monetary policy the main instrument of macroeconomic policy. The Thatcher-Reagan years – combined with the internationalisation of capital markets – changed all that. Today's conventional wisdom says that the exchange rate is set by the international market and government uses the interest rate[7] to steer the economy through the business cycle and offset the effect of unanticipated external shocks (eg, a sudden rise in oil prices).

The problem is that in a world of speculative capital flows, exchange rates are unstable and tend to over- or undershoot their equilibrium level.[8] Nor can Central Banks always intervene successfully to keep the exchange rate at the desired level, as 'Black Wednesday' in 1992 showed.[9] In the intervening years, massive capital flows have produced contagious financial crises in Latin America and Southeast Asia. Most recently, after years of defying gravity, the overvalued dollar threatens to fall dangerously low. Because over 50% of Britain's visible trade is with the EU – versus 17% with the USA – large exchange rate fluctuations between sterling and the euro are undesirable. As long as the UK holds on to sterling, UK investment in the Eurozone will carry exchange rate risk and a higher rate of return on such investment will be sought. Exchange rate fluctuations against the currency of our major trading partners carry a real cost in terms of risk, even if particular types of exchange rate risk can be minimised through forward contracts. If sterling's value is left to the mercy of

---

[6] See Currie quoted in Huhne's section of Forder, J and C Huhne (2001), p 71.

[7] By 'interest rate' is meant the short-term interest rate on monetary instruments, itself closely aligned with the rate at which the Central Bank will lend to the commercial banking sector.

[8] The 'equilibrium level' is best thought of as that exchange rate at which domestic prices would be closely aligned with world prices such that purchasing power parity (PPP) would be achieved; ie, a hamburger would cost the same in New York, London and Buenos Aires. For the pound the 'equilibrium' is thought to be in the region of 1.35–1.40 euros.

[9] After Nigel Lawson began shadowing the DEM in 1987, the new Chancellor, John Major, took the pound into the ERM in 1990 at DEM 2.95, a rate that most analysts considered too high. The 1991 recession convinced international markets that the rate was unsustainable and by late 1992, the position became untenable. The *Bundesbank* had suggested Britain might renegotiate before Black Wednesday but this warning went unheeded by the Treasury; after the event, such was the embarrassment that the Treasury remained firmly opposed to the ERM and its successor, the single currency.

an increasingly volatile capital market, the magnitude of exchange rate fluctuations will almost certainly rise in future.

The 'one-size-fits-all' objection to adhering a Eurozone interest rate can be equally problematic. Opponents of the euro often conflate two arguments. The first concerns how far lowering the interest rate can stimulate investment. Keynes called this problem the 'liquidity trap'; namely, the fact that when an economy is in recession, lowering the nominal interest rate to near zero may not work. The example of Japan has been cited above. The same misleading belief in the power of interest rates informs the argument of those who proclaim that Germany's poor performance is due entirely to the excessively monetary stringency of the *Bundesbank* after reunification in 1990 and, more recently, the 'conservative' monetary stance of the ECB and its lack of transparency. While Germany may have a supply side problem of a high reservation wage and an over-regulated service sector, its main problem – as argued in an earlier chapter – is too low a level of aggregate demand.[10] Growth depends essentially on rising productivity, and productivity cannot rise while growth prospects look bleak and investment remains stagnant.

A further argument concerns regional policy. There is as much variation in performance between rich and poor regions in Britain (hence the demographic drift to the southeast) as there is within the Eurozone, yet nobody suggests that Britain should abandon currency union – indeed, few are aware that Britain is a currency union. The answer to regional variation in Britain lies in adopting sensible regional policies. The same logic applies to the Eurozone, where linguistic and cultural barriers make labour less mobile than in the UK. But as discussed above, the small size and rigid structure of the EU budget precludes automatic regional transfers.

The most serious argument against joining is that the Eurozone suffers from an in-built 'deflationary bias'. I fully accept the 'deflationary bias' argument, as indeed do many supporters of the euro[11] – most notably the previous President of the Commission, Romano Prodi, and his Trade Commissioner, Pascal Lamy. The danger today is not inflation but rather its opposite, deflation. Even the ex-President of the *Bundesbank*, Karl-Otto Pohl, said at a conference in late 2002 that in the EU 'the main problems are stagnation or even a recession'.[12] As Germany and Italy stagnate, French unemployment remains

[10] See Bibow (2004).
[11] See Will Hutton 'Now can we join the euro' *The Observer*, Sept. 22, 2002. There a various papers on how to reform the ECB of which two are: Fitoussi, J-P and J Creel (2002); Begg, D, Blanchard O et al (2003).
[12] See William Keegan 'How many angels can dance on the head of a pin' *The Observer*, November 24, 2002.

high, the Bush 'stimulus package' redistributes income in the wrong direction and the dollar falls, a veritable chorus of academic and business economists has been urging the EU to abandon pre-Keynesian orthodoxy and adopt actively expansionary monetary *and* fiscal policy.[13]

At national level, fiscal reform is required if the 'social market economy' is to have any meaning. While much current discussion is devoted to cutting 'unaffordable' expenditure on pensions[14], unemployment benefit, medical services and so on, few political parties (even on the left) have called for the higher tax levels required to finance an 'affordable' level of public spending compatible with maintaining a social market economy under conditions of increasing demographic strain. The tax burden differs greatly between the different member states: from about 50% in France to 33% in the Irish Republic (slightly lower than the UK), and this is precisely what lies at the heart of the 'tax harmonisation' debate. If the inclusive nature of social benefits is not to be eroded, 'tax competition' must be minimised and the tax-burden question must be treated as an EU-wide issue, and not merely left to national competence.[15]

10.5 THE COSTS OF ABANDONING EUROPE?

The UK has not joined the euro and appears unlikely to do so any time soon. As David Begg *et al* noted in 2003, the Treasury's 'no' to entry could at that stage be interpreted in different ways. Either it meant 'not yet but the tests would be re-examined soon' in which case Britain's 'pre-in' status might be retained for a time; or it meant 'no and probably not any time soon' in which case the UK would become a 'probable out'. Although the 2003 verdict was interpreted as 'not yet' rather than 'never', the number of tests deemed 'passed' was one of five – no better than in 1997. What is certain is that the longer

---

[13] See William Buiter (2003) 'Deflation: causes, prevention and cure' LSE Centre for Economic Performance, London, 19 May 2003; Paul Krugman (2000); John Greave Smith (2001); Wynne Godley, 'The new interest-rate orthodoxy is as flawed as the old one' *The Guardian*, November 11, 2002; Larry Elliot 'Brown can relax the reins this year, *The Guardian*, April 7, 2003;

[14] Although the Chancellor boasts that 'Britain's pension liability' is one of the lowest in the EU, far better than that in Germany and France, see Will Hutton 'The Great Pensions Lie' *The Observer*, February 16, 2003. As for the argument that joining the euro would entail Britain assuming responsibility for the 'unfunded pension deficit' of other countries, that assertion is simply untrue.

[15] To suggest that evidence from different US states – eg, high taxes in Vermont and none in Florida – shows otherwise is to miss the point that state taxes are minor compared to the federal taxes paid by all US residents. For a revealing article on how the UK is becoming an EU 'tax haven' see 'Fluchtpunkt London', *Der Spiegel*, Nr 19, 5–5–03.

Britain waits to join, the less likely are other trading partners to believe Britain will join. It must by now be clear that most countries have taken the Treasury verdict to mean Britain is an 'out'. Since July 2003, Britain's share of inward investment has fallen dramatically. What remains unclear is the effect on British trade with the Eurozone and, ultimately, on trade growth?

One of the oldest pro-euro points is that by joining, Britain avoids the costs of exchange rate conversion. As the story goes, back in the 1990s if one started out from London with £100 and changed the entire amount into local currency each time one crossed the border into another EU country, one would return to London with only £50. The transactions cost argument is correct, but relatively trivial since such costs account for only a fraction of one percent of UK GDP.

The most important argument in favour is that membership of a large single currency area like the Eurozone gives companies the chance to trade in a single market and enjoy the scale and technological economies so long available to industry in the USA. Moreover, there is quite compelling evidence that given the option of trading within the currency area (intra-trade) and outside it, intra-trade will generally win. Several studies have examined the case of Canadian provinces trading with each other compared to trading with US states across the border; the results suggest that a Canadian province is twenty times more likely to do business with another province than with an equidistant US state.[16]

The evidence on intra-EU trade is that Britain has already lost out. If one considers British, German and French trade with other EU countries in 1998 and 2001 (ie, before and after the launch of the euro), Germany and France both raised their share of trade in GDP – from 27 to 32% and 28 to 32% respectively – while Britain's trade share fell from 23 to 22 %. Over the same period. Britain's share of FDI (foreign direct investment) into the EU also fell: from an average of 39% over the period 1990–98 to 24% for 1999–2001. In 2002–2003 as Britain retreated from joining the euro, its share of EU foreign direct investment fell precipitously to less than 7%, although it recovered somewhat in 2004. If one considers labour productivity – output per hour worked – Britain has lost out even more sharply; its productivity level in 2004 was 20% lower than the average of Germany and France[17] The

[16] See McCallum, J (1995) 'National borders matter: Canada-US regional trade patterns' *American Economic Review*; Helliwell, J (1998) 'How much do National Borders Matter?' Washington DC: Brookings Institution.

[17] The early figures are from R. Layard, 'The case for joining the euro' LSE *Centre for Economic Performance* Public Debate, 28 April 2003. Trade here means trade in goods (sum of imports and exports). Productivity figures are from 'The UK's productivity gap: the latest evidence from economic research', *Centre for Economic Performance*, London School of Economics, 30 Sep 2004.

loss of FDI is serious since FDI is a crucial provider of new technology, the technology needed to manufacture high-tech goods and create high-skill jobs.

A further benefit of EMU (economic and monetary union) is that it creates greater market integration within member states. The argument in Britain about *convergence* has tended to ask: is Britain's economy sufficiently like the rest of the EU to make entry advisable? Here, the empirical evidence has been mixed: Britain's cycle has not fully converged with the core countries, but it is certainly more similar to the EU average than that of some of the peripheral countries (eg, Spain, Ireland). Moreover, it would appear that membership of a monetary union accelerates convergence; ie, if Britain were to join, it could expect its business cycle to move more closely with the core countries. On the other hand, if Britain remains outside the Eurozone, the EU-12's economies will converge more with each other than with Britain.

It is worth quoting from Begg *et al* (2003) on the crucial question of the opportunity costs of remaining outside the Eurozone.

> The Sixth Test should be whether the further gains of waiting outweigh the further costs of waiting. Those who argue that the UK can afford to wait until the convergence tests are met 'beyond reasonable doubt' have ignored the first lesson of economics. Optimal behaviour equates the marginal costs and the marginal benefit. Driving the marginal benefit of waiting to zero means waiting too long. [Begg et al, p 13]

10.6 CONCLUSION

This book is deeply critical of economic policy in the Eurozone. The main argument has been that the economics of Maastricht is based on a doctrine of 'sound money' quite irrelevant to the current needs of the EU; in its place, the EU needs to fundamentally rethink the architecture of economic governance. Against this background, I have argued that the 'costs' of failing to join the euro outweigh the 'benefits' of staying out. As David Begg, Willem Buiter, Richard Layard, Robin Marris and many others have argued, if this is true today, then the longer Britain waits, the greater the opportunity costs incurred. Moreover, only once it is committed to joining can Britain push for growth-orientated change in Eurozone monetary and fiscal policy. The argument becomes all the more compelling if the prospect of a slowdown in US growth is considered. Britain cannot act as locomotive of the world economy. But a newly dynamic EU could serve this function.

Why then has Britain not joined? The answer is clearly political – more precisely, it is about political weakness.[18] When the Labour Government came to power in 1997, the tabloid press was against the euro and public opinion was divided. Gordon Brown at the Treasury was already sceptical, and Tony Blair was unconvinced that a referendum could be won. The 'doctrine of unripe time' was borne – we would only join when it could be shown to be unambiguously in the country's interests to do so. The pro-euro Britain-In-Europe (BiE) campaign was put on hold; debate could not begin until the Treasury had ruled, and unless Brown backed euro-entry, the debate could not be won. Blair – whether by design or by default – handed the Treasury and its allies at the Bank of England a veto. Central Banks are generally reluctant to abolish themselves, and no Ministry of Finance wants its powers constrained by treaty obligations, particularly those of Maastricht.

As the late Hugo Young pointed out bitterly, with the decision effectively placed in the hands of the Treasury, no effort has been made to steer economic policy in a manner that would return a positive verdict. Politically, New Labour has made no attempt to campaign in favour of a social democratic model for Europe, preferring to extol the virtues of US-style 'flexibility'.[19] Even after the resounding Labour victory in 2001 the Government was unable to decide on a referendum. By the time of the 2004 General Election, New Labour was preoccupied with having to face a possible Constitutional referendum, and the euro was put on the back burner. With the loss of the referendum vote in France and The Netherlands, the Government quietly pulled the plug on Britain-in-Europe. Following the Iraq invasion and most recently the London bombings, Britain's alliance with the US in the 'war on terror' has again become the most prominent aspect of foreign policy. In the words of a former Blair adviser:

> On Europe, Blair has taken a Eurosceptic lurch that has led him to call on our partners to abandon the very social ideals that once made integration attractive to Labour. In fact, it has become increasingly hard to see how Blair's European policy differs from the one pursued by John Major.[20]

A progressive British government could still advance a programme for modernising the EU. A vision of a European federation mounted on solid economic foundations is available. Such a federation would eschew a budget focussed on agricultural subsidies and the principle of the national *juste retour* in favour of greater flexibility for member-states and a truly federal budget –

---

[18] See David Clark 'The Weakest Link' *The Guardian*, April 23, 2003.

[19] See Hugo Young, "A tight Treasury fist still grips our European future' *The Guardian*, June 10, 2002.

[20] See David Clark 'Labour's new divide' *The Guardian*, August 15 2005.

growing perhaps to 5% of combined GDP over a decade. The EU budget would be funded by a combination of progressive taxation of member-states' international borrowing. It would be used to fund both current expenditure – including an element of basic social provision needed to bring the EU closer to its citizens – and the long-term investment needed to ensure core-growth and accelerated growth of the poorest states. Assuming EU investment raised average EU growth by a mere 0.5% per annum, budget growth would be self-financing. Moreover, assuming the EU budget were required to balance over the cycle, the balanced budget multiplier of a budget equivalent to 5% of combined GDP would be very much greater than that of the present 1% budget. Most important, Britain would command genuine political support amongst other member-states in advancing a genuinely 'modernising' project for Europe rather than forever proclaiming its parochial Anglo-Saxon superiority. It is not inconceivable that a Government committed to a new European vision – one placing Britain centre-stage in promoting the development of the world's largest economic market and strengthening the democratic institutions of our 'common European home' – could win the support of an electorate weary of participating in US-led military adventures and now facing an economic downturn.

Or again, perhaps the time has past and Britain will never join the euro, preferring instead to form a free-trade area with America; this is the preferred solution of Murdoch, Black and right-wing economists like Patrick Minford[21]. Perhaps as Robin Marris has argued:

> ... there will soon be only three significant currencies in the world—the dollar, the euro and an Asian currency based on the yen. ... If sterling stayed out, our currency would become the repository of large amounts of short-term funds, unwanted at any particular time in the other three... our society and economy would be seriously damaged."[22]

Or perhaps even more pessimistically, as John Gray has argued: 'So long as it serves the Blairite agenda, Britain's deeper integration into the EU spells the end of any European project worthy of the name ... not only in foreign and defence matters but also in economic and social policy, Britain's goal will be to "modernise" Europe on an Anglo-American model.'[23]

Whatever position the reader may hold on Europe, he or she can be certain that Britain's current popular mood of semi-detached indifference toward the

[21] See Patrick Minford 'Should Britain join the euro – the Chancellor's five tests examined' *IEA Occasional Paper* 126, Sept. 2002.
[22] Robin Marris 'Five steps to nowhere' *The Guardian*, February 1, 2000.
[23] John Gray 'For Europe's sake, keep Britain out' *New Statesman*, Monday 19 May 2003.

EU will pass. In this book I have argued that the referendum crisis is forcing Europeans to rethink how to combine the goals of economic prosperity, social justice and inclusiveness. The European Union is already a major economic power and, over the next generation, its political power will grow and its institutions of governance will adapt to meet new challenges. Europe's cultural diversity, its educational traditions rooted in the Enlightenment, its folk memories of the terrible cost of internecine conflict and its post-war social settlement, far from being a source of weakness, give it great strength.

The United Kingdom is itself a union of England, Scotland, and Wales; its history over the ages is one of Saxon, Nordic and Norman invasion, assimilation and cultural enrichment. In terms of its geography, history, and culture, Britain has always been an integral part of Europe. Despite the legacy of Thatcherism, Britain's post-war social settlement still finds popular expression in the value the great majority of citizens place upon improved state health care, educational provision and social insurance. In this sense, being European is not an abstract ideal for British men and women. It is quite simply part of our everyday reality.

References

Ackerloff G, Dickens W and G Perry (1996) 'Low Inflation or No Inflation: Should the Federal Reserve Pursue Complete Price Stability?' *Brookings Papers on Economic Activity 1996:1*; Washington DC: The Brookings Institution

Adams, T (2004) 'Give Me Some Credit', London: *The Observer*, 18 April 2004.

Alesina, A, Blanchard, O, Gali J, Giavazzi, F and H Uhlig (2001) 'Defining a Macroeconomic Framework for the Euro Area', London: *Centre for Economic Policy Research* (CEPR).

Andersen, J G, Clasen, J van Oorshot, W and K Halvorsen [eds] (2002) *Europe's New State of Welfare: Unemployment, employment policies and citizenship*, Bristol, UK: The Policy Press.

Anderson, P (2002) 'Force and Consent', *New Left Review* 17, Sept-Oct.

Arestis, P and M Sawyer (2002) 'The euro, public expenditure and taxation' *Working Paper No 357*, The Levy Economics Institute: Annandale-on-Hudson, NY

Arestis, P and M Sawyer (2003) Macroeconomic Policies of the Economic Monetary Union: Theoretical Underpinnings and Challenges', *Working Paper No 385*, The Levy Economics Institute: Annandale-on-Hudson, NY

Arrow, K J (1964). 'The role of securities in the optimal allocation of risk bearing' *Review of Economic Studies*, 31(2):91–96.

Arrow. K (1963) *Social Choice and Individual Values*, London: Chapman and Hall.

Atkinson, A B (2003) 'Income Inequality in OECD Countries: Data and Explanations', *CESifo* (Centre for Economic Studies, University of Munich) *Working Paper No 881*, February.

Baker, D, Glyn, A, Howell, D and J Schmitt, (2004) 'Labour Market Institutions and Unemployment: A Critical Assessment of the Cross-Country Evidence', in Howell, D [ed] (2004), *Unemployment and the Welfare State*, Oxford: OUP.

Balls, E (2004) 'Stability, Growth and UK Fiscal Policy' Lecture given at the University of York, 23 January 2004.

Beckett, F and D Hencke (2004) *The Blairs and Their Court*, London: Aurum Press

Begg, D. Blanchard, O. *et al* (2003) 'The Consequences of saying no' London: Britain in Europe.

Begg, I (2005) 'Funding the European Union Budget', *Federal Trust Report on the European Union's Budget* London: Federal Trust.

Begg, I (2004) 'EU Budget: Common Future or Stuck in the Past?', London: *Centre for European reform, Briefing Note,* 19 February 2004.

Begg, I [ed] (2002) *Europe: Government and Money: Running EMU, the Challenges of Policy Co-ordination,* London: Federal Trust.

Begg, I (2000) 'How to pay for Europe' *European Essay No 5*, London: Federal Trust.

Bergstrom, F and R Gidehag (2004) *EU versus USA*, Stockholm: Timbro.

Bibow, J (2004) 'Assessing the ECB's Performance since the Global Slowdown: A Structural Policy Bias Coming Home to Roost?', *Working Paper 409*, July, The Levy Institute of Bard College, New York.

Blackburn, R (2005) 'Capital and Social Europe' *New Left Review* 34, July/August

Blackburn, R (2003) *Banking on Death or Investing in Life; the History and Future of Pensions*, London: Verso.

Blommestein, H (2001) 'Ageing, Pension Reform and Financial Market Implications in the OECD Area' Moncalieri, Italy: *Center for Research on Pensions* (CerP) Working Paper 9/01.

Boltho, A (2003) 'What's wrong with Europe', *New Left Review* 22, Jul-Aug.

Brunila, A, Buti, M and D Franco [eds] (2001) *The Stability and Growth Pact: the Architecture of Fiscal Policy in Emu* London: Palgrave Macmillan

Buiter, W (2004) 'The return of Deflation: what can central Banks do?' in Stephenson, H [ed] (2004) *Challenges for Europe*, London: Palgrave

Buiter, W, Corsetti G and N. Roubini (1993) 'Excessive Deficits: Sense and Nonsense in the Treaty of Maastricht' *Economic Policy*, 1993

Burgoon, B and P Baxandall (2004) 'Three Worlds of Working Time: The Partisan and Welfare Politics of Work-Hours in Industrialized Countries' Politics and Society, Vol. 32, No. 4, 439–473.

Buti, M and D Franco (2005) *Fiscal Policy in Economic and Monetary Union: Theory, Evidence and Institutions* London: Edward Elgar

Buti, M, Franco, D and H Ongena (1997) *Budgetary Policies during Recessions: Retrospective Application of the 'Stability and Growth Pact' to the Post-War Period,* Brussels: European Commission.

CEPR (2003) 'Stability and Growth in Europe: Towards a Better Pact' Monitoring *European Integration 13*: London: *Centre for Economic Policy Research*, 4 December 2003.

Collignon, S (2004) 'The End of the Stability and Growth Pact?' *International Economics and Economic Policy*, 1 (1), January.

Collignon, S (2003) *The European Republic: reflections on the political economy of a future constitution* London: Federal Trust and Bertelsman Foundation.

Connelly, B (1995) *The Rotten Heart of Europe; Dirty war for Europe's Money*, London: Faber and Faber.

De Grauwe, P (2003) 'The SGP in need of Reform' Dept. of Economics, University of Louvain.

De Grauwe (1992) *The Economics of Monetary Integration*, New York: OUP.

Dinan, D (2004) *Europe Recast: a History of the European Union*, London: Palgrave Macmillan.

DIW Economic Bulletin (2003) 'Demand too Weak for an Upturn - A Cyclical Comparison' *Deutsches Institut fürWirtschaftsforschung* June 2003

Dore, Ronald (1994) 'Incurable unemployment: a progressive disease of modern societies?' London School of Economics: *Centre for Economic Performance, Occasional Paper No. 6*, August.

Dupuch, S, Jennequin, H and El Mouhoub Mouhoud (2004) 'EU Enlargement: what does it change for European Economic Geography?" *Centre d'Economie de l'Université de Paris Nord*, March ; paper delivered to the Conference 'A New All-European Development Model in an Enlarged EU ; Social and Economic Aspects' University of Poznan, 7–9 May 2004.

EC (2003) Commission of the European Communities, *Green Paper on Services of General Interest*, Brussels COM(2003) 270 final.

Eichengreen, B (2000) 'When to dollarise' Paper presented at the Conference on 'Dollarisation', *Federal Reserve Bank of Dallas*, 6–7 March.

EPOC Report (2005) 'Economic Policy Coordination for Full-employment and Social Cohesion in Europe'; forthcoming; see <www.epoc.ini-bremen.de>

Esping-Andersen, Gøsta *et al* (2002) *Why we need a New Welfare State* Oxford: Oxford University

Esping-Andersen, Gøsta (1999) *The Social Foundations of Post-industrial Economies*. Oxford: Oxford University Press.

Esping-Andersen, Gøsta. (1990) *Three Worlds of Welfare Capitalism*. Princeton, NJ: Princeton University Press.

Euro-Memorandum Group (2003) 'Full employment, Welfare and a Strong Public Sector: Democratic Challenges in a Wider Union' *European Economists for an Alternative Economic Policy in Europe* (Professor J Huffschmitt, Department of Economics, University of Bremen).

European Commission (1989), 'Report on economic and monetary union in the European Community' April 17, 1989 (commonly called the Delors Report) by *Committee for the Study of Economic and Monetary Union*.

European Commission (1993) 'Growth Competitiveness and Employment' (Delors White Paper). Luxembourg: OOPEC

Eurostat (2005) 'Euro-Indicators', 7 January 2005.

Fatas, A and A Milhov (2003) 'The Case for Restricting Fiscal Policy Discretion' *Quarterly Journal of Economics,* 4, 1419–1448.

Feldstein, M (1999) 'Reducing Poverty, Not Inequality' *The Public Interest*, Fall.

Fitoussi, J-P and F Saraceno (2004) 'The Brussels-Frankfurt-Washington Consensus Old and New Tradeoffs in Economics' Paris: (OFCE) *Observatoire Français des Conjonctures Economiques* N° 2004–02, February.

Fitoussi, J-P and J Creel (2002) 'How to reform the European Central Bank' London: *Centre for European Reform*.

Freeman, R (1999), *The New Inequality; creating solutions for poor America*, Boston: Beacon Press.

Freeman, R (2004) 'Are European labour markets as awful as all that? London School of Economics, *Centre for Economic Policy Discussion Paper* No. 644, August.

Freeman, R and W Rodgers (2004) 'Jobless recovery; whatever happened to the great American jobs machine?' *CentrePiece* , Autumn 2004, London School of Economics: *Centre for Economic Performance*.

Ginsborg, P (2001) *Italy and its Discontents* London: Penguin Books.

Glyn, A (2005) 'Global Imbalances' *New Left Review* 34, July/Aug.

Godley, W and A Izurieta (2004) 'Balances, Imbalances and Fiscal Targets: a new Cambridge View' *Cambridge Endowment for Research and Finance (CERF);* Judge Institute, Cambridge.

Godley, W and A Izurieta (2005) 'Balance and Imbalances in the US. The Missing Link' Cambridge: CERF Strategic Analysis Series, forthcoming)

Gordon, D and P Townsend [eds] (2000) *Breadline Europe: The Measurement of Poverty* Bristol: The Policy Press.

Gowan, P and P Anderson [eds] (1997) *The Question of Europe*, London: Verso.

Gray, A (2004) *Unsocial Europe; Social Protection or Flexploitation?* London: Pluto Press.

Grieve Smith, J (2001) *There is a Better Way: a New Economic Agenda*, London: Anthem Press.

Gros, D et al (2003) 'Adjusting to Leaner Times', 5th Annual Report of the CEPS Macroeconomic Policy Group, *Centre for European Policy Study* (CEPS, Brussels).

Haseler, S (2004) *Super-State: The New Europe and its Challenge to America*, London: Tauris.

Hobsbawm, E (1995) *Age of Extremes: the Short Twentieth Century 1914–1991*, London: Abacus.

Holland, S (2006) *Europe in Question – and what to do about it*, London: (forthcoming).

Huhne, C and J Forder (2001) *Both Sides of the Coin*, London: Profile Books.

Hutton, W (2002) *The World we're In*, London: Little Brown

IMF (2003) 'Deflation: determinants, risks and policy option', IMF, Washington DC, 30 June 2003.

Irvin, G (2005) 'The Implosion of the Brussels Consensus' *Working Paper No. 11/05*, International Centre for European Research (ICER): Turin.

Irvin, G (2004) 'Eurozone economics, enlargement and the Maastricht rules' *Soundings 28,* Winter, London: Lawrence & Wishart .

Irvin, G (2003) "The Euro: snatching defeat from the jaws of victory" *Soundings 24*, Autumn, London: Lawrence & Wishart

Jencks, C (2002) 'Does inequality matter?' *Daedelus* 131 (1) pp 49–65.

Kagan, R (2003) *Of Paradise and Power; America and Europe in the New World Order*, New York: Alfred Knopf .

Kaletsky, A (2005) 'Apolitical Economy' *Prospect*, May.

Keegan, W (2004) *The Prudence of Mr Gordon Brown*, London: Wiley.

Kenen, P B (1995) *Economic and Monetary Union in Europe: Moving beyond Maastricht,* Cambridge: Cambridge University Press.

Knorr, A (2004) 'Will Eastern Enlargement Force the EU to Fundamentally Reform its Common Agricultural Policy (CAP)?' IWIM - *Institut für Weltwirtschaft und Internationales Management*, Universität Bremen.

Kok, W (2004) 'Facing the challenge; the Lisbon strategy for growth and employment' *Report from High Level Group chaired by Wim Kok*. European Commission.

Krugman, P (1994) *Peddling Prosperity*, New York: Norton.

Krugman, P (1999) *Pop Internationalism*, London: MIT Press.

Krugman, P (2000) *The Return of Depression Economics*, London: Penguin Books.

Krugman, P (2001) *Fuzzy Math: An Essential Guide to the Bush Tax Plan*, New York: W W Norton

Lakin, C (2003) 'The effects of taxes and benefits on household income, 2001–02' London: Office of National Statistics.

Leaman, J (2001) *The Bundesbank Myth: Towards a Critique of Central Bank Independence* London: Palgrave.

Liddle, R (2005) 'The New Case for Europe; The crisis in British pro-Europeanism – and how to overcome it' *Fabian Ideas* 615, London: The Fabian Society.

Lintner, V and S Mazey (1991) *The European Community: Economic and Political Aspects*, London: McGraw Hill.

Lombard, M (1995) 'A re-examination of the reasons for the failure of Keynesian expansionary policies in France 1981–83' *Cambridge Journal of Economics*, 19(2), pp. 359-72.

MacDougall Report (1977) *Report of the Study Group on the Role of Public Finance in European Integration*, Brussels: European Commission, April 1977.

Majocchi, A (2003) 'Fiscal Policy Co-ordination in the European Union and the Financing of the Community Budget' University of Trento (Italy), School of International Studies, *Working Paper 01/2003*.

March, R J (2003) 'Germany and the Challenge of Global Aging' Washington, DC: *Center for Strategic and International Studies*.

Martinez-Mongay, C and K Sekkat (2004) 'The Trade-off between efficiency and macro-economic stabilisation in Europe' Working Paper No 05.04RS, *DULBAE*, Université Libre de Bruxelles.

Mishel, L, J Bernstein and J Schmitt (2001) *The State of Working America*, Ithica: Cornell Univ Press.

Morley, J, Ward T and A Watt (2004) *The State of Working Europe*, Brussels: European Trade Union Institute.

Musgrave, R.A. (1959), *The Theory of Public Finance*, New York, McGraw-Hill

O'Connor, J (1973) *The Fiscal Crisis of the State*, New York: St Martin's Press.

O'Mahoney, M and W de Boer (2002) 'Britain's Relative Productivity Performance: Updates to 1999' *NIESR*, March.

OECD (1994) *Jobs Study*, Paris: Organisation for Economic Cooperation and Development.

Papatheodorou, C and Pavlopoulos, D (2003) 'Accounting for Inequality in the EU: Income disparities between and within member states and overall income inequality' *CHER Working Paper* 9, CEPS/INSTEAD, Differdange, Luxembourg.

Pearce, N and M Dixon (2005) 'New Model Welfare' *Prospect*, May.

Pelkmans, J and J-P Casey (2004) 'Can Europe deliver growth? the Sapir report and beyond' *Centre for European Policy Study* (CEPS, Brussels), Policy Brief no. 45; January.

Pinder, J (2005) 'The Federal Idea and Europe in the World' London: Federal Trust.

Pisani-Ferry, J (2005) 'Only teamwork can put the eurozone on a steady course', *Financial Times*, 31 August 2005

Reid, T R (2004) *The United States of Europe: the new superpower and the end of American supremacy*, New York: Penguin.

Rifkin, J (2004) *The European Dream*: Cambridge UK: Polity Press.

Sapir, A et al (2003) *An Agenda for a growing Europe: making the EU economic system deliver* London: Oxford University Press.

Schmitt, J and J. Wandsworth (2002) 'Is the OECD Jobs Strategy Behind US and British Employment and Unemployment Success in the 1990s?' Paper prepared for Conference 'Liberalisation and Employment Performance in the OECD' New School University, May 18–19, 2001 (revised July 2002).

Sen, A K (1973) *On Economic Inequality*, Oxford: OUP.

Smeeding, T M (2002) 'Globalisation, Inequality and the Rich Countries of the G-20; evidence from the Luxemburg Income Studies (LIS)' Paper prepared for the G-20 Meeting: *Globalisation, Living Standards and Inequality; Recent Progress and Continuing Challenges*; Sydney, Australia, May 26–28.

Soares, F B (2005) 'An alternative scheme to compute the Common Agricultural Policy direct payments to farmers' (first draft working paper) *International Centre for European Research (ICER)*, Turin.

Soukiazis, E and V Castro (2004) 'How the Maastricht Criteria and the Stability and Growth Pact affected the convergence process in the European Union. A panel data analysis' Discussion Paper no 24. Centro de Estudos da Uniao Europeia. Faculty of Economics: Coimbra.

Standing, G (2004) 'Evolution of the Washington Consensus: Economic Insecurity as Discontent' Geneva: International Labour Office.

Stiglitz, J (1969) 'Distribution of income and wealth among individuals' *Econometrica*, vol 37: 382–397.

Stiglitz, J (2003) *The Roaring Nineties* London: Penguin Books.

Tamborini R. (2004) 'The "Brussels consensus" on macroeconomic stabilization policies in the EMU. A critical assessment', in Torres F., Verdun A., Zilioli C. and H. Zimmermann [eds.] *Governing EMU: Political, Economic, Historical and Legal Aspects*, Proceedings of the 1st EUI Alumni Conference, European University Institute, Florence, October 2003; European University Press, Florence, 2004, pp.157–176.

Taylor, R (2005) 'Sweden's new social-democratic model: proof that a better world is possible' London: Compass.

Taylor-Gooby, P (2004) *Making a European Welfare State* Oxford: Blackwell.

Toynbee, P and D Walker (2005) *Better or Worse? Has Labour Delivered?* London: Bloomsbury Publishing.

The Economist (2004), 'A Club in need of a new vision' April 29.

Thurston, J (2002) 'How to Reform the Common Agricultural Policy' *European Rural Communities Paper 1*, The Foreign Policy Centre, London.

Turner, A (2000) 'Growth, productivity and employment' London School of Economics, *Centre for Economic Performance*, December 2000.

Turner, A (2001) *Just Capital: The Liberal Economy*, London: Macmillan

Watkins, S (2005) 'Continental Tremors', *New Left Review* 33, May/June.

Werner Report (1970), Report to the Council and the Commission on the realisation by stages of Economic and Monetary Union in the Community, *Bulletin of the European Communities*, Supplement 11/1970.

Wilkinson, R G (1996) *Unhealthy Societies: the afflictions of inequality.* Routledge: London

Wyplosz, C (2001) 'Do we know how low inflation should be?' *CEPR Discussion Paper* No. 272, London.

Wyplosz, C (2002) 'The Stability Pact Meets its Fate' Paper prepared for the 'Euro Group 50' Meeting, Paris, 27 November 2002.

Wyplosz, C (2003) 'Do not impose a currency crisis on Europe' *Financial Times*, June 16, 2003.

Young, H (1998) *This Blessed Plot: Britain and Europe from Churchill to Blair*, London: Macmillan.

Index